ULTIMATE

Campsites

AUSTRALIA

PENNY WATSON

Hardie Grant

EXPLORE

Introduction

My childhood camping memories are of tents taking way too long to put up, sleeping bags not fitting into covers and air mattresses going down overnight. But somewhere in the effort it took my parents to get us into the fresh air, next to a log-fire and under the star-strewn night sky, a love for sleeping – comfortable sleeping – in the great outdoors took hold.

I've since camped in many countries around the globe and the experience has created travel memories that stick. In Italy, my sister and I spent lazy days camped on the grassy edge of Lake Garda and cool nights in the Dolomite mountains, surrounded by Triassic rock formations and peaked-roof *Heidi* houses. On a road trip through France and Spain, my partner and I pitched tents on ocean cliffs near Biarritz, under the stars in the rural countryside of Andalucía and, randomly, when our linguistic skills failed us, on a soccer field on the outskirts of Seville. In the USA, I took myself to Yosemite National Park and shared its magnificence camped out with a bunch of strangers. In more recent years, as an expat in Hong Kong, I joined friends on remote Tai Long Wan beach where we slept in polyester tents and spent three humid days playing cards and eating fried noodles.

When I returned to Australia after a decade living abroad, the idea of exploring Australia's great camping locales, beyond the Murray riverside spots of my childhood, took hold. I've since become a little obsessed about finding the most magnificent and natural camping surrounds imaginable. Ever pitched a tent within a stone's throw of a waterfall? Ever woken in a sleeping bag to the sound of crashing waves? Ever seen the sun go down from a swag in the desert or fallen asleep in an ancient rainforest? Well, now is the time.

In this book, I've mapped out 75 of the country's most wild and wondrous nature-immersed campgrounds, from those on the turquoise water and white sandy beaches of Queensland to pristine alpine parks in Victoria. From the unspoiled wilderness areas of Tasmania to the surf-washed coastlines of South and Western Australia. In these pages, you'll find campgrounds on remote islands, campgrounds on mountaintops, campgrounds on the route of great walks and campgrounds within heady proximity to Australia's most important Indigenous sites.

There are some quirky ones too. I've snuck in a winery campground in South Australia, a campground next to a pub on Victoria's Upper Murray River and a cute urban campground in a coastal NSW town run by the local surf club. One of my favourite finds is a campground in an outback sculpture park on the outskirts of Broken Hill. Surfers, dog-lovers, birdwatchers, snorkellers and 4WD-ers, I'm hoping you'll find your favourite campground somewhere in these pages, too.

I've slept far and wide, in tents, swags, campervans and tent-topped vehicles, with a mix of friends, my beautiful family, colleagues and strangers. Finding 75 'ultimates' is a tricky job – not because they're hard to find, but because once you start exploring Australia's vast land you tend to 'discover' them as a matter of course. What I did try to do was balance popularity and accessibility with natural beauty and immersion.

For ease of navigation, this guidebook is organised into Australia's states and territories. Each chapter contains detailed maps and what, when, why, where and who information about each campground, alongside tips and anecdotes about the surrounding region, its Indigenous stories, the local wildlife and tidbits about the food, culture and vibe.

Ultimate Campsites Australia is the kind of guidebook that will get plenty of wear and tear on the coffee table while you're planning your next adventure. But where it really works best is as an essential addition to your glovebox, be it in your car or camper-trailer. Then you can rest assured that a log-fire, a starry night and a sleepover in Australia's great outdoors are always at your fingertips.

Penny Watson

Opposite Contemplative views from Gunlom swimming hole over the savannah wetlands and eponymous campground in Kakadu National Park, NT

Helpful information

ACKNOWLEDGEMENT OF COUNTRIES

I'd like to acknowledge the Traditional Owners of the various countries I visited during research, and pay respect to Elders past, present and emerging. I thank all Traditional Owners for sharing your stories, sacred land and culture on country with me.

In this book, I have made a special effort to note the Traditional Owners. It has been my intention to emphasise the Indigenous connection to the land, given that the natural world that Australia's First People share with us is at the very heart of what I love about camping.

PUBLIC AND SCHOOL HOLIDAY PERIODS

Australians love camping and there are some big weekends throughout the year when camping is the done thing – and has been for generations. The month of January is the summer holiday period (including the 26 Jan weekend), and Easter weekend, Labour Day weekend (March) and Melbourne Cup weekend (Nov) stand out in particular. Some of the campgrounds mentioned in this book, especially those close to major cities, are booked up to a year in advance and will be full to tipping point during these peak times. In order to really make the most of these destinations and get a deeper sense of their natural beauty, I'd advise avoiding peak times where possible. Aiming for off-peak times, mid-week stays or shoulder seasons can mean the difference between having a campground to yourself, and not. If you're willing to drive a little further to somewhere more remote and perhaps with fewer facilities, you'll be rewarded with less crowds.

BUSHFIRES

Australia's devastating 2019/2020 bushfire season broke out at the end of my research period for this book. It devastated whole communities – many whose lives depended on the tourist dollar, and also derailed the summer holiday plans for campers throughout Victoria, NSW and South Australia. Sadly, some of the campgrounds lovingly researched for this book were too decimated for inclusion. Rocky River on Kangaroo Island is one of them. Others, such as Wingan Inlet in Croajingolong National Park (*see* p. 71), and Banksia Bluff at Cape Conran (*see* p. 75), both in Victoria, remain closed. But I have retained them to support local communities in the hope that their rehabilitation is imminent. Campgrounds such as Woody Head in NSW (*see* p. 3) have already re-opened and there is still beauty to be found in the rejuvenation of the post-fire landscape surrounding them. I have introduced a bushfire symbol to denote which campgrounds have been affected by or are recovering from bushfires so that campers can ring ahead for updated information.

NATIONAL PARK ENTRY FEES

Most national parks throughout Australia require visitors to pay an entrance fee and camping fees are usually on top of these fees. In my view, it's money well spent. The funds raised go directly towards the maintenance and upgrade of the parks and reserves, and cover visitor centres, facilities, walking tracks and other services. When you come across a sparkling clean national park loo, well-stocked with toilet paper, you'll know what I mean.

Depending on how many parks you are visiting and how long you are in the region, it's worth checking individual states and territories to see whether options such as annual passes or holiday passes will save you money. It's also worthwhile buying your passes online before heading to your destination, as there's usually no mobile coverage or internet in the more remote places (but the park rangers are about and will come and check whether you've paid).

Also, keep an eye out for the expert guided tours and activities run by park rangers at many of the bigger parks. You'll often pay a bit extra, but the local knowledge and immersive qualities – especially from Indigenous guides, is always excellent.

How to be pitch perfect

Camping in some of the wildest, most scenic and remote places on the continent comes with a wildlife warrior urge to protect and care for the natural diversity and scenery. Here are some pointers:

INDIGENOUS CULTURE

Australia's Indigenous culture and heritage, both tangible and intangible, is breathtaking. Rock art, shell middens, scarred trees and other important sites in national parks, forests and landscapes country-wide connect Traditional Owners, Indigenous people and new Australians with thousands of years of culture. These sites are irreplaceable. Treat them with care so that our children's children's children can enjoy them too. I've included some excellent Indigenous experiences in this book and also a First Peoples Know-how section in many of the chapters to talk about the Traditional Owners and significant sites.

WILDLIFE

In many of the campgrounds in this book, Australia's unique native animals are a delightful part of the experience, whether they're hopping through the nearby underbrush or waddling down a dirt trail. I've included a Wildlife Watch section in many of the campgrounds so you know what you're looking for. That said, it's important to love the plants and animals by leaving them alone. They are protected in national parks and reserves, and should be respected in all natural environs. Watch your step when hiking and walking, and erect your tent only at designated campsites. Please do not feed the animals - human food is harmful to wildlife and it disrupts their natural feeding habits. It can also cause some animals, particularly mothers protecting their young, to become aggressive. If you see people feeding animals (and I so often do), educate them.

LEAVE ONLY FOOTPRINTS

Consider taking your rubbish with you even when rubbish bins are provided - many campsites are remote and don't have regular rubbish pick-ups and it's more likely to be recycled properly at home. Consider taking your soft plastic to the nearest supermarket instead of binning it. Definitely don't bury or burn it. Perhaps take a bag of extra rubbish with you when you leave a campground, especially bottle tops, bits of plastic, Band-Aids/plasters (my pet hate) and cigarette butts that tend to be overlooked in a clean-up. Always clean those fab free Aussie gas barbecues after you've used one. It's barbecue etiquette, but it also helps keep native wildlife and pests at bay. Turning the heat on, then pouring cold water on the hot plate should lift most of the muck fairly easily.

BUSH LOO

Use toilets. If they are not available, dig a big deep hole (at least 20cm so that animals can't dig it up!) and bury all faecal matter and (only sustainable) toilet paper. The hole should be well away from campsites, walking tracks and waterways (100m minimum). Take nappies and sanitary products home with you and don't ever leave tell-tale scraps of toilet paper scattered through the bush - it's disgusting and dangerous to habitats.

FIRES

After the catastrophic 2019/2020 bushfire season, we've all seen how destructive a stray ember can be. Preferably use a fuel stove for cooking. Use only fire-pits and fireplaces provided by campgrounds for sitting around and toasting marshmallows, but ensure you have first checked with the campground management about fire restrictions. Put the fire out with water when you finish. BYO firewood rather than collect it (so to protect small animal habitats and ecosystems), especially in national parks. It's also a thing now to buy firewood from rangers and campground managers, if available. When camping, especially during summer, be alert, download the appropriate fire apps, and have a contingency plan in response to a bushfire. Make sure you know the fire danger rating each day. Take the fire restrictions seriously, as the relevant authorities do.

KEEP IT CLEAN

Help pristine waterways and environments stay that way by cleaning boots, clothes and camping gear - particularly shovels and tent pegs, as well as the bottoms of boats and kayaks, before leaving home. Similarly, brush soil and leaves off tents, tarpaulins, floor coverings and shoes before leaving a campground. Soaps, shampoos, detergents and toothpaste pollute water. Don't wash yourself, your clothes or your dishes near waterways (about 100m away is the guideline). Sunscreen is one of the biggest polluters of our natural waterways, and seeing slicks of it floating on otherwise pristine water always saddens me. Consider rash vests and stinger suit-style swimwear as an alternative to sunscreen. Insect repellent is a similar issue. Put it on after your swim.

Different styles of camping

TENT

I set out to research this book as a devoted tent camper. Having just a flimsy piece of canvas between myself and the fresh air, the squawk of the cockatoos and the fading embers of a log-fire, puts me as close to the great outdoors as possible without actually being outside. Naturally, there's a bit of organisation and set-up involved (forgetting your tent pegs can put a dampener on the whole experience), but the challenge and achievement makes it, I think, worth the effort. That said, during my research I was fortunate enough to trial different modes of camping, and, along the way, talk to fellow campers about their varied experiences. It turns out pitching a tent is just one way to get out amongst nature.

CAMPERVAN

Who doesn't envy a Kombi or a pimped-up van that cleverly converts to a kitchen-cum-bed-cum-hold-all for a camping trip. Campervans can be squishy if you're sleeping inside, but pop-top beds work well for that extra room. The good ones are compact with compartments to store goods away while on the road, and, when stationary, a rear boot that converts into a nifty outdoor kitchen. It's often the case that you'll need to get everything out of the campervan in order to sleep in it (think suitcases and bags), so an awning to protect your gear from foul weather is a good idea.

CAMPER-TRAILER

Camper-trailers are a notch or two above in terms of mobility, convenience and comfort. They're compact when stored and while travelling, but, like a Tardis they fold out to create cool camping spaces complete with built-in kitchens, storage compartments, and ready-made beds that are raised above the (possibly cold/wet/sloping/bumpy) ground. They're easier to tow than a caravan and the more lightweight durable designs are suited to off-road travel (so you can get up to the tip of Cape York Peninsula if it's in your sights). Camper-trailers can be packed and organised slowly and methodically days before you set off (as opposed to trying to slot everything in the car minutes before departure).

CARAVAN

If you're going to tow anything, why not make it a home? Caravans share some of the advantages of the camper-trailer with the addition of being fully set-up so you can pull out a camp chair on arrival and crack open a craft brew. While enviable hipster styles include the smooth-edged 1960s vintage Sunliners, American Airstream 'silver bullets' and boxy 1970s two-tone aluminium Viscounts, those that you'll see on the road are the more conventional and comfortable contemporary designs. They're likely fitted with double beds (and single beds for families), plus a kitchen you could cook a roast in (including stovetop), refrigerators, dining and lounge area, bathroom with toilet and shower, and oodles of storage space. You could conceivably live on the road in a caravan - a very appealing thought.

Remote Chilli Beach on Queensland's Cape York Peninsula is tent and camper-trailer terrain

Checklist

This is my personal camping checklist, although it's not definitive. It has been amended almost every time I go camping, depending on what we've forgotten or what has made its way back to the kitchen. Which is to say, there's no such thing as a truly organised camping trip. Some of these might be helpful depending on how long you're camping for but you'll have your own necessities, too.

- Tent/swag (or caravan/camper-trailer)
- Tarpaulin or two for ground-cover, waterproofing and shade
- Sleeping bags
- Air mattresses
- Pillows (always)
- Fold-up table and camp chairs
- Cooking stove
- All your food
- Drinking water – many campgrounds don't have it
- First-aid kit
- Chopping board
- Sharp knives (emphasis on sharp)
- Plates, bowls, cutlery (or a picnic set)
- Platter & salad bowl
- Dishcloth
- Foldable washing-up bowl or bucket
- Paper towel
- Bin bags
- Scissors
- Batteries
- Billy
- Toast tongs
- Hooks for hanging bin bags and teatowels
- Flask (for cups of tea on the road without having to boil a billy)
- Washing line
- Torch/flashlight
- Overhead light with batteries – if in a tent
- Hammer
- Aeropress coffee maker (essential)
- Keepcups
- Food-storage containers (for leftovers)
- Bottle and can opener
- Tongs
- Baking paper (awesome for lining barbecues with and cooking on – no cleaning needed)
- Towels, including one to use as a tent doormat
- Sustainable toilet paper
- This book

Campsite symbols

 Campgrounds or nearby areas have been affected by the 2019/2020 bushfire season and some facilities may still be unopened or under repair.

Activities

 A boat ramp is within easy access of the campsite.

 Canoeing or paddling is possible. BYO canoe/kayak, unless otherwise mentioned in entry.

 Crocodiles live in waters near the campsite. Observe warnings.

 Cycle trails are nearby, suitable for either normal bikes or mountain bikes.

 Saltwater or freshwater fishing is allowed.

 Hiking trails are nearby (these are more strenuous than walking trails). Recommended for fit adults.

 A horseriding trail is nearby, or horses may be brought by float to the campsite; facilities are available.

 The campsite is in a scenic area, or a scenic lookout is close by.

 There is a walk near the campsite with information or signage about the flora and fauna in the area.

 There is no swimming at, or near, the campsite.

 The sea or reservoir near the campsite is suitable for sailing small boats. It does not mean there is a boat ramp.

 There is a scenic drive within a reasonable distance of the campsite.

 Swimming is allowed at, or near, the campsite.

 A generally flat or gently sloping walking trail is nearby.

Facilities for waterskiing are available at, or near, the campsite.

Facilities

 A 4WD is required to reach the campsite.

 You need to book before staying at this campsite.

 Towed camper trailers can access the campsite.

 There is an undercover camp kitchen area with some equipment.

 A camping fee applies; you may need to pay it in advance or at the campsite.

 Caravans can access the campsite.

 Cold showers are available at the campsite.

 The park, forest or conservation area charges a daily fee, which may be per person or per vehicle.

 The toilets are wheelchair-accessible; showers at this campsite are not necessarily suitable for disabled visitors.

 Some pets are allowed, usually small dogs, and they will need to be on a leash when outside. Always request permission before bringing your pet.

Drinking water is available. It may need to be boiled/treated before drinking; bore water may taste unpalatable, despite being safe to drink, due to high mineral content.

Vehicles of any kind (2WD or 4WD) can only reach the campsite in dry weather.

There is a facility to dump caravan toilet waste.

You don't have to pay a camping fee to stay at this campsite.

No campfires are allowed.

A gas or electric BBQ is at the campsite. It may be coin-operated.

Hot showers are available at the campsite. A fee may be charged for access to the shower block, or coins required to turn on the hot water.

Information about the area is available at, or near, the campsite.

The camping area or caravan park has a kiosk where basic food supplies or prepared food can be bought.

No pets are allowed.

There are no rubbish disposal facilities. Bring rubbish bags with you, and take rubbish away when you leave.

The camping area is not accessible to vehicles. All gear must be carried in; distances are usually indicated in the entry.

There is a sheltered picnic table at the campsite.

There is a picnic area with tables at, or near, the campsite.

The caravan park has sites with electricity, usually 240V.

There is a payphone at the campsite.

A ranger operates in the area. There may not be a permanent ranger station at the campsite, but one will visit regularly, or there will be a ranger station within reach.

This is one of our favourite campsites.

There is a toilet at the campsite. It may be a pit or composting toilet.

The campsite is suitable for a vehicle with a pop-up tent, or for a tent to be erected beside a vehicle.

A wireless internet connection (wi-fi) is available at the campsite or nearby. There may be a charge to access it, or it may be available only in certain parts of the campsite.

When fire bans are not in place, fires can be lit at this campsite, generally in designated fireplaces or BBQs.

BYO firewood.

Map of Australia

MAP LEGEND

BRISBANE ○ State capital city

WOLLONGONG ○ Major city/town

Yamba ○ Town

Cockle Creek ○ Other population centres

🏕 **Campground**

🏕 **Alternative campground**

🍴 **Eat**   ▫ Homestead

● **Attraction**   ▪ Building

🗼 Lighthouse   ● *Gorge, Pass*

▲ *Mountain*   ━ *Waterfall*

∧ Cave   ● *Spring, waterhole*

Kooljaman at
Cape Leveque ●

El Questro ●

BROOME ○

Osprey Bay ●

Yardie Creek ●

WESTERN
AUSTRALIA

Red Bluff
(Quobba Station) ●

Dirk Hartog Island ●

PERTH ○

Conto ●

Lucky
Bay ●

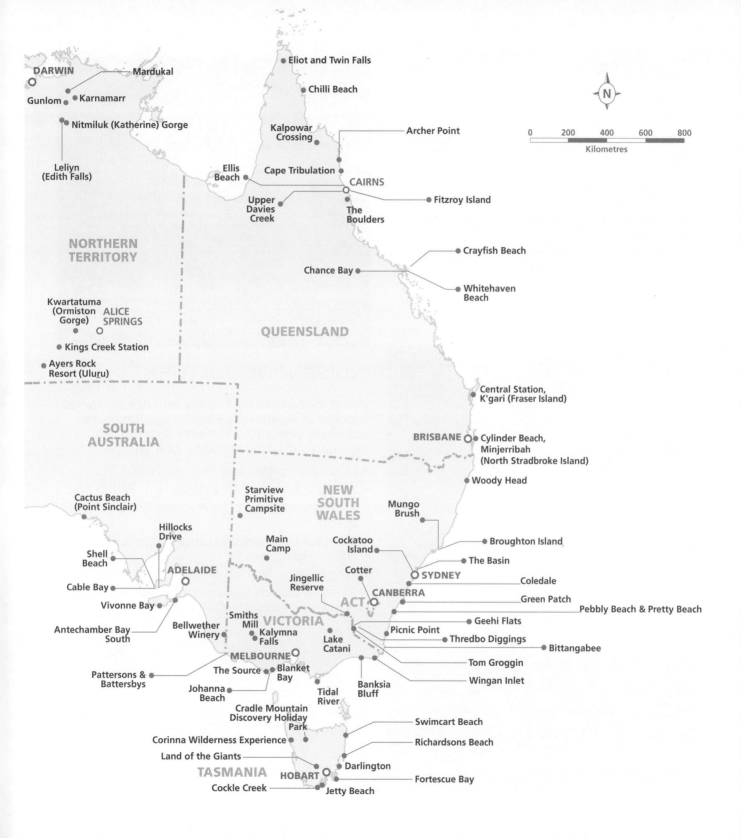

DARWIN
Mardukal
Gunlom
Karnamarr
Nitmiluk (Katherine) Gorge
Leliyn
(Edith Falls)

Eliot and Twin Falls
Chilli Beach
Kalpowar
Crossing
Archer Point
Ellis
Beach
Cape Tribulation
CAIRNS
Fitzroy Island
Upper
Davies
Creek
The
Boulders

Crayfish Beach
Chance Bay
Whitehaven
Beach

NORTHERN
TERRITORY

Kwartatuma
(Ormiston
Gorge)
ALICE
SPRINGS
Kings Creek Station
Ayers Rock
Resort (Uluṟu)

QUEENSLAND

Central Station,
K'gari (Fraser Island)

SOUTH
AUSTRALIA
BRISBANE
Cylinder Beach,
Minjerribah
(North Stradbroke Island)
Woody Head

Cactus Beach
(Point Sinclair)
Starview
Primitive
Campsite
NEW
SOUTH
WALES
Mungo
Brush

Hillocks
Drive
Main
Camp
Cockatoo
Island
Broughton Island

Shell
Beach
Cotter
The Basin

Cable Bay
ADELAIDE
Jingellic
Reserve
SYDNEY
Coledale

Vivonne Bay
VICTORIA
ACT
CANBERRA
Green Patch
Pebbly Beach & Pretty Beach

Smiths
Mill
Geehi Flats

Antechamber Bay
South
Bellwether
Winery
Kalymna
Falls
Lake
Catani
Picnic Point
Thredbo Diggings
Bittangabee

Pattersons &
Battersbys
MELBOURNE
Blanket
Bay
Tom Groggin

The Source
Banksia
Bluff
Wingan Inlet

Johanna
Beach
Tidal
River

Cradle Mountain
Discovery Holiday
Park
Swimcart Beach

Corinna Wilderness Experience
Richardsons Beach

Land of the Giants
TASMANIA
Darlington

HOBART
Fortescue Bay

Cockle Creek
Jetty Beach

N

0   200   400   600   800
Kilometres

Top lists

FREE

What's better than pitching a tent at one of the best campgrounds in the country? Not having to pay for it. These campgrounds do not require parting with your hard-earned cash.

- Kalymna Falls (Gariwerd/Grampians NP), Vic, p. 99
- Archer Point (Cooktown), Qld, p. 201
- The Boulders (Babinda), Qld, p. 221
- Swimcart Beach (Bay of Fires), Tas, p. 245
- Cockle Creek (Southwest NP), Tas, p. 263

INDIGENOUS CULTURE

Invest in the culture, history and natural-world insights of Australia's First People on tours, activities, walks and experiences that will elevate your understanding of Australia.

- Main Camp (Mungo NP), NSW, p. 57
- Conto (Leeuwin-Naturaliste NP), WA, p. 153
- Ayers Rock Resort (Uluṟu-Kata Tjuṯa NP), NT, p. 185
- Nitmiluk (Katherine) Gorge (Nitmiluk NP), NT, p. 173
- Kings Creek Station (Petermann), NT, p. 181
- Cylinder Beach (Minjerribah, North Stradbroke Island), Qld, p. 239

SHOWER POWER

So you love stoking a fire campside, but you're also quite partial to a hot shower, a flushing toilet and a place to plug in your phone. Park your vehicle at one of these campgrounds and you might even find a coffee cart and a restaurant dishing up wood-fired pizza.

- Cotter (Murrumbidgee River Corridor), ACT, p. 27
- Tidal River (Wilson's Promontory NP), Vic, p. 79
- El Questro (Kununurra, the Kimberley), WA, p. 131
- Nitmiluk (Katherine) Gorge (Nitmiluk NP), p. 173
- Ayers Rock Resort (Uluru-Kata Tjuta NP), NT, p. 185
- Kings Creek Station (Petermann), NT, p. 181
- Kwartatuma (Ormiston Gorge, Tjoritja/West MacDonnell NP), NT, p. 177
- Cape Tribulation (Daintree NP), Qld, p. 205
- Ellis Beach (Cairns), Qld, p. 209
- Cylinder Beach (Minjerribah, North Stradbroke Island), Qld, p. 239
- Cradle Mountain Discovery Holiday Park (Cradle Mountain-Lake St Clair National Park), Tas, p. 275

Opposite top Lazy (and free) views over Bay of Fires, Tas
Opposite bottom Uluru rises from the landscape, Uluru-Kata Tjuta National Park NT *Right* The Daintree National Park meets the beaches of the Great Barrier Reef at Cape Tribulation campground in Far North Queensland

ISLAND CAMPING

No man is an island, but he/she sure enjoys camping on one. Put the kayak on your roof-racks, borrow a boat or purchase a ferry pass to tick island camping off your bucket list.

- Broughton Island (Myall Lakes NP), NSW, p. 7
- Cockatoo Island (Sydney Harbour), NSW, p. 17
- Dirk Hartog Island (Dirk Hartog Island NP), WA, p. 149
- Fitzroy Island (Cairns and the Great Barrier Reef), Qld, p. 213
- Crayfish Beach (Whitsunday Islands NP), Qld, p. 225
- Chance Bay (Whitsunday Islands NP), Qld, p. 227
- Whitehaven Beach (Whitsunday Islands NP), Qld, p. 230
- Central Station, K'gari (Fraser Island), Qld, p. 235
- Cylinder Beach (Minjerribah, North Stradbroke Island), Qld, p. 239
- Darlington (Maria Island NP), Tas, p. 253

SURF

If hearing the roar of the waves and the call of the sea is a prerequisite to a camping adventure, strap the board on the roof and bee-line it to these oceanside hang-ten hot spots.

- Coledale Camping Reserve (Coledale), NSW, p. 21
- Johanna Beach (Great Otway NP), Vic, p. 85
- Cable Bay (Innes NP), SA, p. 116
- Conto (Leeuwin-Naturaliste NP), WA, p. 153
- Lucky Bay (Cape Le Grand NP), WA, p. 157
- Red Bluff (Quobba Station, Carnarvon), WA, p. 145

PETS

So your pooch likes snoozing in a sleeping bag just as much as you ... check out these pet-friendly campgrounds for a doggy adventure that doesn't underestimate a hound's love of the great outdoors.

- Johanna Beach (Great Otway NP), Vic, p. 85
- Banksia Bluff (Cape Conran Coastal Park), Vic, p. 75
- Vivonne Bay (Kangaroo Island), SA, p. 119
- Cactus Beach (Point Sinclair) Campground (Eyre Peninsula), SA, p. 107
- El Questro (Kununurra, the Kimberley), WA, p. 131
- Ayers Rock Resort (Uluṟu-Kata Tjuṯa NP), NT, p. 185
- Red Bluff (Quobba Station, Carnarvon), WA, p. 145
- Swimcart Beach (Bay of Fires), Tas, p. 245
- Cockle Creek (Southwest NP), Tas, p. 263

BIRDWATCHING

Don't forget the binoculars. These campgrounds are a paradise for twitchers and a haven for anyone who enjoys waking to birdsong.

- Broughton Island (Myall Lakes NP), NSW, p. 7
- Darlington (Maria Island NP), Tas, p. 253
- Corinna Wilderness Experience (Pieman River State Reserve), Tas, p. 271

Opposite top Enjoying the waves at Lucky Bay, WA
Opposite bottom White sandy beaches of Whitehaven Beach, Qld *Top* A colourful local at Maria Island National Park, Tas
Bottom Bring your whole family along

Camp trails

Got a long weekend? A week? 10 days? A month even? Choose one of the camp trail itineraries below to help map out your own extended camping adventure.

Opposite The striking landscape of Western Australia's west coast, Dirk Hartog Island

Opposite A swim at Gunlom Falls is a must-do if you're spending time in the Top End

New South Wales & ACT

Head to the coast or the Snowies, the inner-city or the Outback, to camp in some of New South Wales's astonishing natural terrain

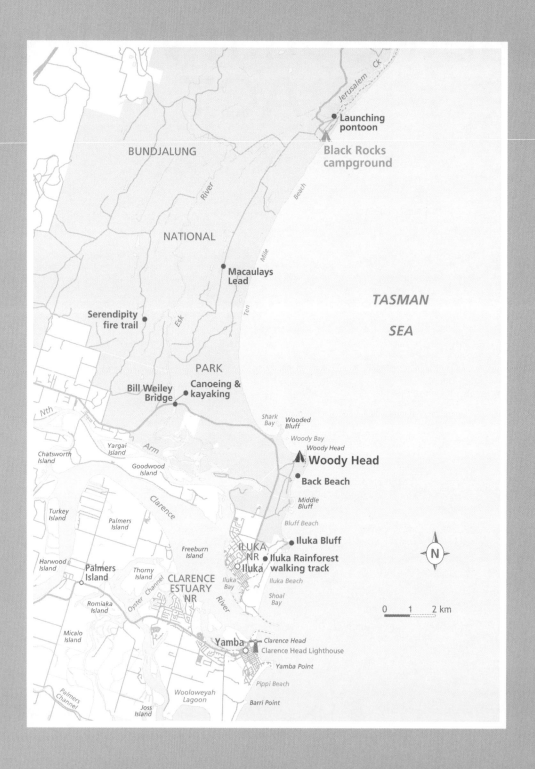

A beautiful beachfront campground with wave-kissing forests and ocean vistas.

Woody Head

Bundjalung National Park, NSW

ACTIVITIES

FACILITIES

Respect to whoever was responsible, in the annals of national park history, for putting a campground at spectacular Woody Head, near the southern tip of beautiful Bundjalung National Park. The campground's expanse of green grass runs right to the water's edge so you can be standing just beyond your tent staring east over rocky platforms to a vast blue ocean, or north to an arch of yellow sand beach and, beyond it, a forest of trees reaching down to the shoreline.

Bundjalung stretches from Iluka, just south of the campground, all the way north to Evans Head. Its beach and forest landscapes ensure beautiful walking terrain, fantastic snorkelling, surfing, rock pooling and beach play. But it also boasts two fresh waterways – Esk River and Jerusalem Creek, where canoers and kayakers have the chance to dip their paddles in a biodiverse wonderland.

The campground is one of the biggest featured in this book, with 94 unpowered sites suited to all types of camping, including a group site that hosts 20 people. There were more swamp wallabies hopping around on my visit mid-year than there were campers, but given it's one of the more popular campgrounds on the north coast, try to avoid summer and long weekends.

The sites are marked and neatly laid-out on rectangular platforms. Sites starting with J and A are closest to the water, and sites G1 to G10 back onto beautiful rainforest. It's well kitted-out and facilities include:

- A boat ramp
- Drinking water
- Two amenities blocks with flushing toilets and hot showers ($1 coin for 4 minutes)
- A public phone
- Picnic tables with killer ocean views are popular at 6pm when families nab them for dinner
- Barbecues and fire-pits, although peak cooking times get busy
- A kiosk with free firewood and other basics such as ice

At the northern end of the campground there's a walking track to Back Beach which has picnic tables. It can be a peaceful alternative to dining at peak times in the campground.

Previous Pristine beach near Mungo Brush, Myall Lakes National Park (*see* p. 9)

CATEGORIES

Young Travellers, Family, Nature, Wi-Fi-Free, No Dogs, Boomers, Nomads

GO DO IT

WHO   NSW National Parks & Wildlife Service (NPWS); 1300 072 757; nationalparks.nsw.gov.au

WHERE   92 Woody Head Road, Woody Head, NSW. It's 676km north of Sydney and 270km south of Brisbane.

ACCESS   From Pacific Hwy, take Iluka Rd turn-off. Drive along Illuka Rd, through Woombah, over the Esk River Bridge for 13km, then follow the signs to Bundjalung National Park and Woody Head campground.

WHAT ELSE?

Tucked between the rainforest and the beach, the campground also has two cabins and five quaint beach shack-style cottages on stilts. They're self-contained with front verandahs perfect for kicking back with a good book.

Go mountain-biking down the Macaulays Lead and Serendipity fire trails, both within the national park.

A sign at the campground tells a story from the 1920s when there were four galleys of sand dunes to traverse before reaching the beach, which was 65 metres away. Today that's hard to believe except for the fact that the sand on Woody Beach is clearly being washed away. In fact, it's one of the fastest-eroding beaches in NSW. According to a sign on Woody Beach (located between the campground and Shark Bay), Woody Beach and the campground will, sadly, be gone by 2050.

Canoes and kayaks can be launched from Bill Weiley Bridge on the Esk River, the longest undisturbed coastal river system on New South Wales's north coast. Glide past old-growth tallowwood, mahogany forests and mangroves – the habitat of pied oystercatchers. It's 15 kilometres one way and takes about four hours return.

You can also launch a boat from the pontoon at Jerusalem Creek, about 65 kilometres north near Black Rocks Campground (see Alternatives). The 4.6 kilometre one-way paddle takes 90 minutes and is similarly wild and wonderful.

Iluka Rainforest walking track (4.5km south to the northern entrance on Bluff Rd) is a 2.6 kilometre one-way stroll through rainforest to Iluka Bluff for a coast view of beaches, the mouth of the river, and the seasonal whale migration. There are picnic facilities here too.

FIRST PEOPLES KNOW-HOW

The Native Title rights of Bundjalung National Park's Bundjalung People have been duly recognised. Visitors can learn more about their culture and traditions on a tour with Aboriginal Cultural Concepts' (aboriginalculturalconcepts.com) host Lois Cook who runs half- and full-day heritage and coastal tours exploring middens, contact sites, fish traps and other areas of interest including Gummigurrah, used as a winter camping ground by the Bundjalung People.

WILDLIFE WATCH

The swamp wallabies have adapted to crowds – expect to see them hopping around the campsite during the day and along the water's edge as the sun sets.

Brush turkeys are actually becoming a bit of an issue. Keep your food out of reach – they'll even attack supermarket bags to get at it.

ALTERNATIVES

Also in Bundjalung National Park, Black Rocks Campground, 65 kilometres north of Woody Head, is tucked in behind the sand dunes of Ten Mile Beach.

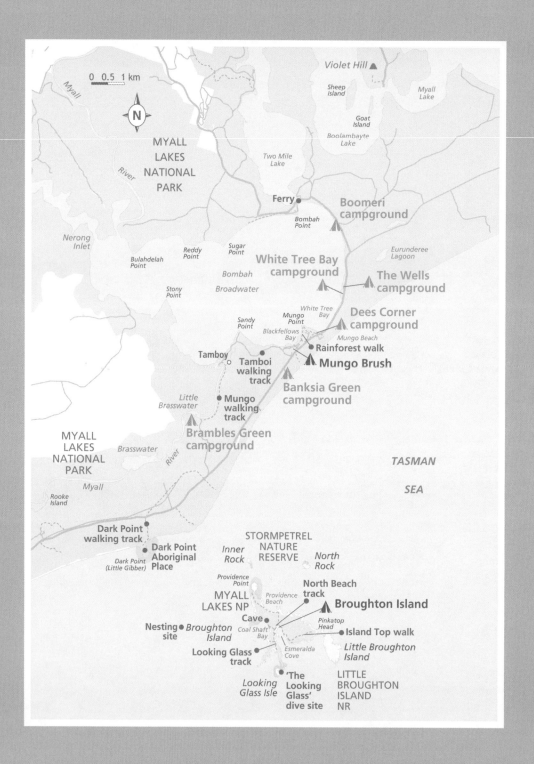

Violet Hill ▲

Sheep
Island

Goat
Island

Myall
Lake

Boolambayte
Lake

Myall

MYALL
LAKES
NATIONAL
PARK

Two Mile
Lake

0 0.5 1 km

N

Ferry ●

Bombah
Point

**Boomeri
campground**

River

Nerong
Inlet

Reddy
Point

Sugar
Point

Eurunderee
Lagoon

Bulahdelah
Point

Bombah
Broadwater

**White Tree Bay
campground**

**The Wells
campground**

Stony
Point

White Tree
Bay

Sandy
Point

Mungo
Point

**Dees Corner
campground**

Blackfellows
Bay

Mungo Beach

Tamboy ○

● **Tamboi
walking
track**

● **Rainforest walk**

▲ **Mungo Brush**

Little
Brasswater

● **Mungo
walking
track**

**Banksia Green
campground**

▲ **Brambles Green
campground**

MYALL
LAKES
NATIONAL
PARK

Brasswater

River

Myall

TASMAN

SEA

Rooke
Island

STORMPETREL
NATURE
RESERVE

Inner
Rock

North
Rock

● **Dark Point
walking track**

Providence
Point

**North Beach
track**

Dark Point ●
(Little Gibber)

**Dark Point
Aboriginal
Place**

MYALL
LAKES NP

Providence
Beach

▲ **Broughton Island**

Cave ●

Pinkatop
Head

Nesting ●
site

*Broughton
Island*

Coal Shaft
Bay

● **Island Top walk**

**Looking Glass
track**

Esmeralda
Cove

*Little Broughton
Island*

*Looking
Glass Isle*

**'The
Looking
Glass'
dive site**

LITTLE
BROUGHTON
ISLAND
NR

Camping that feels like an island paradise on a blue-sky day or a pirates' hideaway when the weather sets in.

Broughton Island

Myall Lakes National Park, NSW

ACTIVITIES

FACILITIES

Broughton Island, off the mid-NSW coast, 14 kilometres north-east of Port Stephens, is the largest of the islands dotting the NSW coast. It covers roughly 114 hectares, and it is shaped like a big paint-splat, an irregular symmetry of rocky headlands, protected coves and hidden sandy beaches. With a maximum of 30 campers allowed on the island at one time, it really will feel like you have the place to yourself.

Broughton is part of Myall Lakes National Park, which runs adjacent along the mainland coastline, but the island has its own unique identity, geography and wildlife. Its sandy heath-covered dunes and rocky outcrops make it the ideal nesting place for seabird colonies, including wedge-tailed shearwaters or muttonbirds. On the island's most northern beach, there's a colony of little penguins (*see* p. 8) that can, unlike other colonies that are set up for tourists, only be spotted commando-style with binoculars. The island's white ghost crabs, with protruding pink eyes, scurry around the sandy beach, making dirt balls in the sand.

Esmeralda Cove, a protected bay on the southern side of the island, is the landing point for visitors. It has a gaggle of eight basic and not especially charismatic beach huts, with green corrugate rooves, solar panels and rainwater tanks. One of them belongs to NSW National Parks and Wildlife Service (NPWS), the others, with names such as Esmeralda, Broughton Hall, Gull's Way and Marlin Hut are weekenders leased to fortunate fisherpersons and local families.

The campground sits north-east of these huts around the cove, past a rocky headland on Little Poverty Beach. It has five unpowered campsites, all suited to tents (or kayakers who sometimes turn up here with just a backpack). Sites 1, 2 and 3 are on lovely wide and spacious timber platforms with small access steps and guard rails. At these sites, you'll need ropes to secure tent flaps. They jut out from the hillside so are slightly elevated for an exceptional view of the bay. Sites 4 and 5 are grassy and sit just below and to the left of site 3. While sites 1 and 2 are more protected by a hill on one side, sites 3, 4 and 5 are closest to the toilet block. You can choose which suits you best when booking. Facilities include:

• A small amenities block with two pit-toilets
• Information board
• Picnic table

You'll need to be self-sufficient for food, water and fuel, and every scrap of rubbish will need to leave with you on departure.

All five sites have spectacular beach views, taking in the heath-covered heads of Esmeralda Bay, its rocky island formation beyond and the boats bobbing around their moorings just shy of the beach huts. With the yellow sand and glassy water a run and jump away, this is an amazing place for swimming, snorkelling, fishing, scuba-diving (if you bring your own equipment, *see* p. 8) and bush walking.

CATEGORIES

Family, Nature, Wi-Fi-Free, No Dogs, Boomers, Nomads

GO DO IT

WHO   NSW National Parks and Wildlife Service
        (NPWS, Nelson Bay office); (02) 4984 8200;
        nationalparks.nsw.gov.au
WHERE   Broughton Island is part of Myall Lakes National
        Park, NSW. It is 14km north-east of Port
        Stephens, and about 250km north of Sydney.
ACCESS The island is boat-access only. Transfers can
        be arranged through tour operators, including
        Let's Go Adventures (letsgoadventures.com.au)
        and Cruiseability (cruiseability.com.au) between
        Nelson Bay Marina and the landing in Esmeralda
        Cove, on the south-eastern side of the island. If
        travelling by kayak or private boat, register your
        movements with Marine Rescue Port Stephens,
        phone: (02) 4981 3585.

WHAT ELSE?

Broughton Island's 'The Looking Glass' dive site is well-known among scubadivers in Nelson's Bay. When the sun is overhead, the narrow rock-cutting with a deep 18-metre-crevasse is lit up and perfect for viewing hundreds of fish (including the rare eastern blue devil fish if you're lucky), stingrays and cuttlefish. It's a nursery for grey nurse sharks so sightings are guaranteed.

The island's short walking tracks are all accessible from the campground. The North Beach track (about 350m) heads north over the heathlands to North Beach. You can also follow it south-west from the campground around the coastline, to make a right-hand-turn to head 200 metres to Coal Shaft Bay, a beautiful beach with steep cliffs, clear water and an Insta-worthy cave. Alternatively, keep walking to where North Beach track joins the Looking Glass track, which leads about 350 metres to Providence Beach and lovely rocky shallows where you can spot marine life from the shore.

Also from the campground, Island Top walk (approximately 1km) leads south around the coast to the island's highest point, Pinkatop Head, which is 90 metres above sea level. It's a great spot for a thermos tea while watching the waves with a sea breeze in your face.

CULTURE VULTURE

The island was used between 1905 and 1907 by a Polish scientist based in France, Jean Danysz who, largely unsuccessfully, was charged with testing biological controls on feral rabbits. These pests overran the island right up until November 2009, when NPWS declared the island free from rabbits and rats, paving the way for a return to the island's natural state.

FIRST PEOPLES KNOW-HOW

According to archaeological finds, the Garrawerrigal group of the Worimi First People, from the eastern Port Stephens and Great Lakes regions of coastal New South Wales, have lived on the main land for tens of thousands of years, and have inhabited the island for at least 2000 years. Their name for the island has never been recorded but Garrawerrigal means 'People of the Sea'.

WILDLIFE WATCH

More than 70,000 pairs of wedge-tailed shearwaters call Broughton Island home when they return each year to the same nests to breed. You can spot the white tail and dark grey wings of these birds of prey as they catch the coastal thermals around the island. You'll also hear their cooing when they touchdown to nest.

Humpback and Southern-right whales can be seen from May to November, and when they've passed through, dolphins can be seen in the warmer months from November to April.

Almost 30 little penguins – not much taller than 30 centimetres – are known to nest on the north of Broughton Island. They are wild, so there is no viewpoint or organised tour to see them. If you're a keen birdwatcher, with the right viewing equipment, talk to NPWS about the best way to approach them in the wild.

AND ANOTHER THING

Before booking your campsite, contact the boat transfer operator (see Access) to check prices and ensure that transport is available.

Take spare food and drinking water in case changing weather and sea conditions delay your departure pick-up when leaving the island.

ALTERNATIVES

There are great campgrounds on the mainland in Myall Lakes National Park, including at Banksia Green, Boomeri, Brambles Green, Dees Corner and Mungo Brush (see p. 9).

Lake-shore camping in a eucalypt forest with a beach across the road and a range of water-based activities.

Mungo Brush

Myall Lakes National Park, NSW

MAP ON PAGE 6

ACTIVITIES

FACILITIES

Myall Lakes National Park, part of the 'Great Lakes' region on the mid-NSW coast, is known and loved for its beautiful coastal lakes systems – a natural-world puzzle of interconnected rivers, lakes, inlets and coast fringed by paperbark forests, swampy wetlands, heath-covered dunes and sandy beaches. The biodiverse habitats encourage a spectrum of birds and wildlife, along with opportunities for water-based activities, including fishing, surfing, swimming and boating.

The beauty of Mungo Brush campground, aside from its setting in a forest of tall sheltering eucalypts, is its accessibility to not one but two of these contrasting water habitats. Campers can pitch a tent on the sheoak-lined shores of Bombah Broadwater, with its still mirror-like surface that reflects the birds above, and spend the day swimming and bodyboarding just across the road on the wonderland of waves and wide dunes at Mungo Beach. The combo is the perfect set-up for groups and families, especially those with both younger kids (who can paddle in the lake) and teens (who can test their mettle in the waves).

The campground is big enough to comfortably host 78 unpowered sites suited to tents, caravans and camper-trailers. It's also spacious with two sections – north and south, diverging either side of the main entry.

Mungo South is a longer space with seven all-vehicle and 40 tent-only sites (with one vehicle per site) running parallel to the lake shoreline. The pick are tent-only sites 68–71, which are closest to the water and set apart from other campers. Access to the lake is via tracks that access two small clearings between protected habitats along the foreshore.

Mungo North is a smaller space with one tent site and 30 all-vehicle/tent sites gathered around the figure-eight road. The campsites here are closer together but they have better access to the lake because the shoreline here is not protected. There's also a designated boat-free swimming area. Sites 1–8 here are the pick of the entire campground because you can be lying in your tent while looking dreamily out across the lake.

Facilities throughout both sections (Mungo South and Mungo North) include:

- Picnic tables
- Sheltered gas barbecue areas
- Fire-pits
- Boat trailer parking
- Boat ramp
- Toilet blocks (no showers) that are spaced along the length of the campground
- Recycling station for rubbish

Such is the diversity here, campers could be walking along an unspoilt beach in the morning, fishing in the lake by lunchtime and kayaking along the river in the afternoon.

CATEGORIES

Family, Nature, Wi-Fi-Free, No Dogs, Boomers, Nomads

GO DO IT

WHO   NSW National Parks and Wildlife Service
(NPWS, Booti Booti office); (02) 6591 0300;
nationalparks.nsw.gov.au

WHERE   Mungo Brush campground is in Myall Lakes
National Park, NSW, 14km north-east of Port
Stephens and about 250km north of Sydney.

ACCESS   From Hawks Nest, take Mungo Brush Rd north
for approximately 20km and follow the signs left
to the campground.
From Pacific Hwy near Bulahdelah, take unsealed
Bombah Point Rd to the Bombah Point vehicle
ferry crossing. Catch the ferry across and continue
along Mungo Brush Rd for about 5km. Follow
signs to the campground on the right-hand side.
The ferry crosses the lake daily every half hour
between 8am to 6pm. It costs $6.50 for cars and
caravans and needs to be paid in cash. Under
some weather conditions the ferry might close.
Check ahead with Booti Booti park office, phone:
(02) 6591 0300.

WHAT ELSE?

There are some chilled nature walks directly from the
campground. From Mungo North, Rainforest walk is a
moderate 1.5 kilometre loop (allow 20 minutes) through a
magical rainforest, with plum pine and brush bloodwood
trees and the unique calls of the golden whistler and regent
bowerbirds. From Mungo South, Tamboi walking (or cycling)
track is a 5.6 kilometre return (allow 2 hours) dirt road
around the edge of Bombah Broadwater through cabbage
palms to a picnic area where you can see across the river to
the historic fishing village of Tamboi (not to be confused with
the nearby town of Tamboy).

Waterside Tea Gardens is a smallish town, known as the
southern gateway to the Lakes Region. It has motels, cafes
and eateries and the 'whistling bridge' which spans the
Myall River.

Across the 'whistling bridge', neighbouring Hawks Nest
is a little seaside town with a supermarket and excellent
Bennetts Beach. There's a good surf and bodyboard spot
at its southern end.

Opposite A group of pelicans preen on Myall Lake *Above* Mungo
Brush Rainforest walk starts at the campgrounds

From Tea Gardens, there's a cute wooden ferry that runs to Nelson Bay, from where you can catch year-round dolphin-spotting cruises and seasonal whale-watching cruises (May to November).

BYO canoe or kayak for a boating adventure straight from the campground along the lower Myall River to Hawks Nest. Alternatively, Lazy Paddles (lazypaddles.com.au) runs a daily Myall River Discovery kayak tour from Tea Gardens. They also have kayaks and stand-up paddleboards for hire.

FIRST PEOPLES KNOW-HOW

Dark Point Aboriginal Place sits on a rocky headland in the south of the national park overlooking Broughton Island. It is close to the hearts of the Worimi people who, for more than 4000 years, used it as a place to gather and feast on seafood. 4WD vehicles can access the beach via Lemon Tree access trail (14km south-west) or via Hawks Nest (16km south-west), but due to the middens and burial sites in the area you'll need to stick to the beach rather than drive over the headland. The Dark Point walking track starts at the carpark on Mungo Brush Road, about 8 kilometres south of the campground. It's a 2 kilometre return walk and takes about an hour.

WILDLIFE WATCH

White-bellied sea eagles catch the thermals along this coast. They have a nesting sanctuary at Broughton Island (*see* p. 7), the island you can see from Mungo Beach. After dark, long-nosed bandicoots join other nocturnal animals, such as possums. Dingos are also seen in the more sandy dune habitats. Dolphins and whales should also be in your binocular sites.

STEP IT UP

Mungo walking track is an easy but lengthy (21km one way) walk that follows the Tamboi walking track (*see* p. 10) road and continues south along historic mining routes and through coastal dunes and grassland vegetation to Hawks Nest. Allow one day, or break it up into smaller sections.

AND ANOTHER THING

There's a pay station and information available from the on-site manager. For everything else, including firewood, you'll need to head to the shop near the ferry (which has a pay phone), Hawks Nest or Tea Gardens.

ALTERNATIVES

There are amazing campgrounds in Myall Lakes National Park. The closest include Boomeri (5km north), The Wells (3km north-east), White Tree Bay (3km north-east), Dees Corner (1km south-east), Banksia Green (1km south-west) and Brambles Green (5km south-west). Incredible Broughton Island (*see* p. 7) is the island you can see from Mungo Beach.

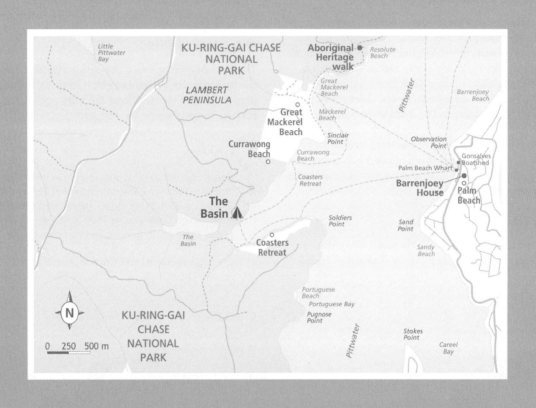

Remote camping accessed by ferry, in the stunning Pittwater surrounds.

The Basin

Ku-ring-gai Chase National Park, NSW

ACTIVITIES

FACILITIES

Distant aeroplanes on a slow line of descent above the wild, native bushland here are a reminder of how close this piece of paradise is to Sydney, but otherwise the proximity is not easy to spot. Endearingly called The Basin Picnic and Campground on a sign on the wharf, this broad expanse of flat and well-maintained grass dotted with picnic tables and shaded by rows of Norfolk Pines is a popular spot for Sydney daytrippers and campers, alike.

Access is via a romantic 20-minute ferry ride (on the rather quaint older ferry if you're bringing camping gear) across Pittwater from the high-end beachy suburb of Palm Beach or via a 2.8 kilometre long walking track from West Head Road carpark. Once here, the surrounding hills of Ku-ring-gai Chase National Park are so densely covered with native red-trunked Sydney gums, kangaroo tails and other native foliage, that it feels like you're miles from anywhere. The view over Pittwater towards Barrenjoey Lighthouse adds to the effect, as does the effort – hauling all your camping gear here from the mainland is no mean feat.

The drawcard Basin, a picturesque lake-like body of water, is so-called because it appears to drain with the coming and going of a tide through a small inlet. Its sandy shallow shores shaded by Moreton Bay figs and sheoak trees make it activity-central in summer. The water's edge becomes a patchwork of picnic blankets, towels and sun tents and the clear water is *the* spot for launching blow-up dinghies and kayaks and hiring stand-up paddleboards. Granddad fishermen hunt for nippers to use as bait and kids stalk hermit crabs. That families have being coming here for generations speaks for itself.

The campground, which is all unpowered sites, is about 200 metres away from The Basin on the Pittwater side.

Unusually for a national park, white posts mark the rectangular boundary of the camping area, but individual campsites are unmarked. Essentially, it's a first-come, first-served free-for-all in terms of which spot you get. When the campground is at capacity – 400 people, expect to fit Tetris-style with other tents. Top spots to pitch depend on your needs. Opt for the central treed area for day-long shade, the Basin end for proximity to toilets, barbecue area and ranger hut (but also the rubbish bins) or choose the Pittwater end for the pretty little beach and sailboat views (but mind the afternoon sea breezes and the long walk to the loo). The campgrounds are well set up and facilities include:

- Flushing toilets
- Cold showers
- Drinking water taps dotted around
- Two barbecue areas (one with tables)
- Vending machines selling coffee, snacks and drinks
- A mobile charging station
- Ice, bait and firewood that can be purchased from the campground manager

A park ranger meets all visitors at the ferry wharf to collect day fees and check that campers are booked in. Emphasising the family friendly nature of the place, rangers do a walk-round at 10pm to ensure music is turned off and noise is kept to a minimum. I camped here during the busiest times of year, between Christmas and New Year, and despite the crowds, was pleasantly surprised by the hush that fell over the campsite come nightfall.

The Basin

CATEGORIES

Young Travellers, Family, Nature, Wi-Fi-Free, No Dogs, Boomers, Nomads

GO DO IT

WHO   NSW National Parks & Wildlife Service (NPWS); 1300 072 757; nationalparks.nsw.gov.au

WHERE   North of Sydney and west of Palm Beach, on the eastern foreshore of Pittwater in Ku-ring-gai Chase National Park, NSW.

ACCESS   Via ferry from Palm Beach Wharf. Or via a steep 2.8km walk/bike ride from the West Head Road carpark (from which you'll need to carry your gear).

WHAT ELSE?

The website ecotreasures.com.au organises pre-pitched camping, rents equipment and leads guided tours. They also have a tent on-site in summer from where you can hire stand-up paddleboards for $25 an hour to explore the far reaches of The Basin, where eucalyptus tree roots tickle the clear waters. Also sign up for a kayak safari to search for the local white-bellied sea eagle population or go on a guided snorkel to find fish and seahorses in the sea grass beds.

Oversized concrete fire-pits are perfect for winter campers, who can buy firewood from the campsite manager and toast marshmallows.

'The Basin shuffle' as described by one of the roaming park volunteers on our visit, is a method used to ward off potentially harmful stingrays. When you enter the water, shuffle your feet so the rising sand sends a warning. Jellyfish are common here, too. Swim clear of them and pack the Stingose or vinegar just in case.

CULTURE VULTURE

Historic Barrenjoey Lighthouse on the other side of Pittwater but still in Ku-ring-gai Chase National Park is a sandstone structure built in 1881. Explore it on a 30-minute guided tour every Sunday between 11am and 3pm (and other times during summer).

EAT IT

Barrenjoey House on Barrenjoey Road across from the Palm Beach Wharf is an eat-treat for weary campers who can manage to step it up a notch. Lobster flat-breads and delicately pan-fried calamari are served with chilled glasses of wine in a beachy-chic setting.

FIRST PEOPLES KNOW-HOW

Ku-ring-gai Chase's Aboriginal Heritage walk, a 4.4-kilometre loop from the Resolute picnic area, pays respect to the Garigal people of West Head who were decimated by smallpox transmitted to them by the First Fleet. See ochre handprints in the Red Ochre Caves and an historic occupation shelter where families would keep the cold at bay. You will also see the West Head Lookout on this walk.

WILDLIFE WATCH

Barrenjoey Head is also an excellent spot for whale-watching during the winter months.

ALTERNATIVES

This is the only camping area in Ku-ring-gai Chase National Park.

About 65 kilometres north, Bouddi National Park, near Gosford on the Central Coast, has similarly beachy campsites, including Little Beach and Putty Beach.

Opposite Plenty of things to keep you busy on land and water at The Basin

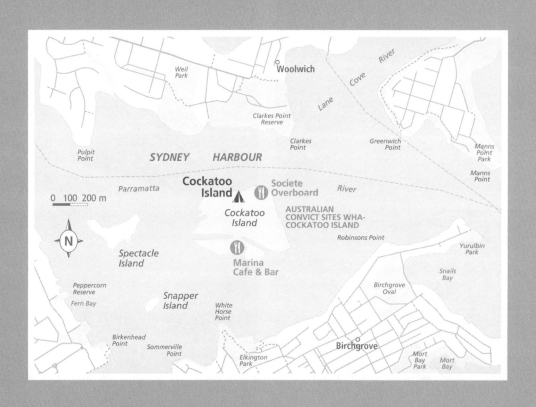

Inner-city camping and glamping on Sydney Harbour.

Cockatoo Island

Sydney Harbour, NSW

ACTIVITIES

FACILITIES

With all the talk of the ghosts of the Biloela reformatory school haunting this place and the 'worst of the worst' convicts once being incarcerated here, Cockatoo Island's colonial-era history could work as the script for a teen horror flick. Rest assured happy campers, today's Cockatoo Island has a somewhat chirpier vibe. From the smiley ranger at the front entry handing out helpful advice, picnic-laden blankets sprawled on the grass and full-sailed yachts gliding by, to the visitors sipping on chilled wine in the cafe, this is camping city-style, with unique appeal. This is the only harbour island where you can stay the night, so enjoy the experience.

Cockatoo Island is the largest in Sydney Harbour, sitting pretty on the Parramatta and Lane Cove rivers. You can take a water taxi or even kayak to get here, but the most popular route is via the lovable Sydney Ferries that depart regularly from Circular Quay. The scenic half-hour ride takes you under the Sydney Harbour Bridge, past the city's mega-money mansions with their own private jetties and within waving distance of boats. With planes flying overhead and the constant thrum of daytrippers, there's no mistaking this for a nature escape, but that's obviously all part of the fun.

There are glamping tents, but not the luxury variety. They're khaki and laid-out in military rows for visitors to drop and flop (and are often taken up with school camps and scout groups). But they're handy, in that they're pre-erected with camping beds, linen and deck chairs. You'll still need to bring your sleeping bag, pillow and torch. For out-of-towners like us the glamping tents were ideal. Alternatively, BYO tents can be pitched on a lawn next door. There's not a tonne of

space – a metre or so between tents, so be prepared to make friends during peak periods.

We BYO-d food (purchased from Sydney fish market that morning, no less) and cooked it on one of those great Aussie barbecues that consist of a hotplate, a button, green light and, importantly, no money slot because they're free. Joy. If you don't want to self-cater, the campground offers pre-order barbecue packs and there are also eateries on the island (*see* p. 19).

For those who don't think camping is camping without a wood fire, there's a communal fire-pit that's lit just as the sun is going down. And for anyone missing screen time, there's a 9pm feature film during the warmer months. Now if that's not inner-city camping, I don't know what is.

Cockatoo Island

CATEGORIES

Young Travellers, Family, Nature, No Dogs, Boomers, Nomads

GO DO IT

WHO   Cockatoo Island; (02) 8969 2100; cockatooisland.gov.au

WHERE   Sydney Harbour, NSW.

ACCESS   Boat access, including the half-hour Sydney Harbour Ferry F8 to Cockatoo Island (transportnsw.info), which departs from Circular Quay via Balmain, Birchgrove, Greenwich and Woolwich.

WHAT ELSE?

Cockatoo Island has an intriguing history that dates back to European settlement. Anecdotes about its Aboriginal history, its convict past, its time as a Naval dockyard and ship repair facility during World War II, along with its UNESCO World Heritage–status can be explored through storyboards dotted around the island and on various tours, including a Haunted History night tour.

In April and May, Cockatoo Island hosts acoustic sunset sessions, featuring home-grown artists – campers get discounted tickets.

Hire a tennis court for a game with Sydney Harbour Bridge views.

Download the Ghosts of Biloela app to your smartphone for a bedtime story with a difference. The geo-locative fictional drama is set on the island and inspired by the Biloela Reformatory and Industrial School for Girls that operated here from 1871 to 1888.

CULTURE VULTURE

Time your run for Sydney's Biennale held from March to June every even year, across a handful of venues – including on Cockatoo Island. Art and artists take over the island with installations, exhibitions, workshops and an outdoor stage on the waterfront with live music and acts. The food and drink offerings will get a leg-up as well with some of Sydney's best food vans popping-up on the island.

EAT IT

Another coup for urban campers – Cockatoo Island has two well-established eating venues aimed at daytrippers: Marina Cafe and Bar for wraps, sandwiches and pizza, or Societe Overboard for Greek-influenced mezze plates and fish and chips.

ALTERNATIVES

This is one of a kind - few campgrounds are this inner-city. For similarly great boat-access camping head out of the city to The Basin at Palm Beach (*see* p. 13).

Opposite Permanent campsites on Cockatoo Island

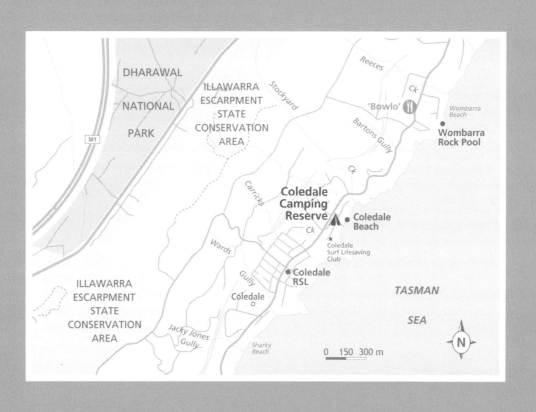

A small charmer of a campground right on the beachfront and run by the local surf club.

Coledale Camping Reserve

Coledale, NSW

ACTIVITIES

FACILITIES

Speedo-clad lifeguards, zinced noses and red-and-yellow swim safety flags are images that conjure the happy-go-lucky Aussie beach lifestyle. A heavenly slice of this scene can be found right here at Coledale Beach Camping Reserve. Coledale is one of a string of adorable little beach suburbs north of the bigger regional city of Wollongong. Despite being only 70 kilometres from Sydney, it is wedged between the wonderfully green Illawarra escarpment and the rolling Pacific Ocean so it hasn't been built out.

This slip of a campground, running along a lush strip of grass metres from the blonde sands of Coledale Beach, is run on behalf of the Coledale Surf Lifesaving Club which sits at the southern end of the beach. The club was founded in 1913 and 'is known as one of the smaller and friendlier clubs in the area', according to its website. The money made from the campground goes towards the club's lifesaver patrols and children's nippers programs and the like. For campers, the surf lifesaver connection and the rolling blue waves offer a snapshot of real Aussie beach life with a few loveable stereotypes thrown in.

If you're standing on Coledale Beach you can look west to see the treetops and sheer red cliff-face of the escarpment, then spin around in the sand to see a view of surfers on nice right- or left-hand breaks, and the big hulk of shipping containers on the horizon. The beach is charmingly small and bookmarked north and south by rocky headlands that offer shelter in storms and strong winds. Rock platforms at the northern end are a hot-spot for local fisherpersons throwing a line in at low tide. Rock-poolers can also be seen looking for crabs and crustaceans among the seaweed. It's a very special place indeed.

The campground feels smaller than its 50 or so sites and it is neat as a pin with tweaks such as manicured grass and small frangipani trees tendered to by the caretakers. Its powered and unpowered campsites, suitable for tents, campervans, caravans, camper-trailers and motorhomes (some sites extend to 15m), run either side of the central campground road adjacent to the beach. The unpowered sites sit on the grassy beachfront expanse, so that you can back your campervan in and flip the boot for uninterrupted views of the ocean. The powered sites, which also have water taps, sit on the other side of the road. Most of these powered sites have views through a majestic stand of century-old Norfolk Pines to the ocean beyond.

When you check-in at the blue-and-white beach hut which serves as the reception, the caretakers will allocate you a designated site. Quieter types will appreciate those tucked away at the northern end of the beach overlooking the rock platforms. Families will appreciate being a bit closer to facilities, which include:

- An amenities block for beachgoers that campers can use (with cold showers)
- Campers-only amenities block (with hot showers before 10am and after 3pm – you'll need to pay a deposit to get a key)
- A camp kitchen with a microwave, television and sinks
- Free electric barbecues on the beachfront under the pines
- Picnic tables
- A beachfront open-air freshwater shower
- Drinking water

Fires aren't allowed here. By night you'll have to make do with the wash of the waves and the starry night skies.

CATEGORIES

Young Travellers, Family, Nature, Wi-Fi-Free, No Dogs, Boomers, Nomads

GO DO IT

WHO   The Coledale Surf Lifesaving Club Inc.;
(02) 4267 4302; coledalebeach.com.au

WHERE 677 Lawrence Hargrave Dr, Coledale, 20km north of Wollongong, and 70km (allow one hour and 15 minutes) south of Sydney, NSW.

ACCESS From Sydney, follow the M1 to the exit onto A1 towards Rockdale/Wollongong for 40km, exit onto Lawrence Hargrave Dr, turn right onto Lawrence Hargrave Dr for 10km (part of the spectacular Grand Pacific Dr over the Sea Cliff Bridge, see below). The campground is on the left.

WHAT ELSE?

Don't miss Wombarra Rock Pool, 1.5 kilometres north of the campground at Wombarra Beach. It is a delightful swimming pool built into the rock platform so that waves swamp anyone doing laps as the tide comes in.

The Sea Cliff Bridge, a winding road that juts over the ocean 5 kilometres north of the campground, is the stuff of luxury car ads. Drive it for fun, then keep going 2 kilometres north to pit-stop at the Scarborough pub. Its grassy beer garden sits on sea cliffs with one of the best ocean views in the country.

Coledale has shops, cafes and eateries, including the RSL (500m south of the campground), which welcomes campers looking for a bistro-style lunch or dinner (Thursday to Sunday) and a draught beer. Scarborough's Wombarra 'Bowlo'

(2.5km north) offers similar vibe and fare. The neighbouring villages of Austinmer (2.5km south), Thirroul (6km south) and Stanwell Park (9km north) have excellent beaches and little town streets with cafes and shops. Wollongong's Kiera and Crown streets are known for their spicy Thai and sizzling Vietnamese eateries.

WILDLIFE WATCH

Pods of dolphins play in the rising waves just beyond the surf at Coledale Beach. This is also a good spot for seeing migrating humpback and Southern-right whales (Apr to Nov). Don't forget the binoculars to keep an eye out for the sooty oystercatcher, an endangered bird species that forages for food on the beach and among the seaweed on the rock platforms.

AND ANOTHER THING

On our visit, mid-week in October, we arrived without a booking and had the place almost to ourselves, but sites do fill up in summer. For the Christmas period, you'll need to book and pay before 1 October.

There's a minimum stay of: two nights on weekends during swim season (Nov to Mar), three or four nights on long weekends, and one week during summer school holidays.

ALTERNATIVES

Wollongong City Council has three big and formally run beachside 'tourist parks' with camping facilities - Windang (33km south), Corrimal Beach (13km south) and Bulli (9km south). Uloola Falls Campground (30km north), is inland at Royal National Park.

A serene campground close to Jervis Bay, with kangaroos, walking trails, hidden coves and stunner beaches.

Green Patch

Booderee National Park, NSW

MAP ON PAGE 24

ACTIVITIES

FACILITIES

There are little travel moments that seem insignificant at the time, but that resonate afterwards – sometimes for many years. I had one of those moments on Murrays Beach in Booderee National Park. I chanced upon it when there was nobody around and had it to myself for an hour, maybe more. I sat there, sank my toes into the yellow sand, watched the waves peel frothy white into turquoise green, listened to the birds causing a ruckus in the fringing eucalypt forest and generally marvelled at the unspoilt beauty of it. I felt like I could have been the only person on the planet.

Wake-up call! There are plenty of people on the planet, and some of them are in Jervis Bay camping at Booderee's Green Patch campground, but fear not – fellow campers don't take away from the experience. The campground might be big, with 70 campsites, and popular, not least of all because it's so close to Sydney, but Booderee is blessed with so many hold-your-breath beautiful beaches that it really is possible for swimmers, snorkellers, surfers, kayakers and meditators to have one of them to yourself for a little while at least.

The campground has 70 unpowered campsites sprawled amid the tall gums and native shrubbery either side of the Telegraph Creek inlet and lagoon, just before it runs into the ocean. Section D on the western side hosts the bulk of campers with both walk-in and drive-in sites in standard and large sizes (sites are allocated according to tent or caravan size and the number of vehicles in the booking). They're spaced around a figure-eight, with two sociable central areas with beautiful bushy trees. Facilities include:

- Barbecues
- Sheltered picnic tables
- Flushing toilets
- Hot showers
- Drinking water
- Shared fire-pits

Section Y, on the eastern side, is my pick. It has 16 drive-in sites on a single loop with similar facilities. The day-visitor area is also on this side of the inlet, and it has its own barbecues, amenities block, and amphitheatre. But the parking for this day-use area is on the other side in Section D, so Section Y remains the more peaceful area.

Weaving around the campground on both sides are lovely trails that lead into the bushland, through trickling water and over little foot bridges to Green Patch Beach and Bristol Point. It's great for kids to explore and there are plenty of kangaroos to meet along the way.

Opposite Coledale Beach is metres away from the campground
Above A picnic spot overlooking Murrays Beach

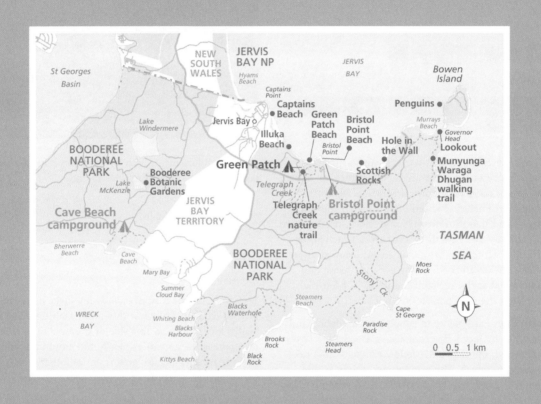

CATEGORIES

Free, Family, Nature, Wi-Fi-Free, Boomers, Nomads

GO DO IT

WHO   Parks Australia; (02) 4443 0977;
         parksaustralia.gov.au
WHERE   Booderee National Park is in Jervis Bay on the
         east coast of NSW. It's 190km south of Sydney
         and 200km east of Canberra.
ACCESS   Heading south along the Princes Hwy, turn left
         into Jervis Bay Rd for about 20km, left onto
         Green Patch Rd for 80m, and slight left on
         Iluka Rd to the campground.

WHAT ELSE?

The 2.4 kilometre long Telegraph Creek nature trail (allow
one hour) is a circular route that takes you past colourful
wildflowers (in spring) and a eucalypt forest with a little creek
crossing along the way.

Beach bums have plenty to choose from close to the
campground: Green Patch is the closest, a stunning wedge of
sand accessed by a quaint wooden bridge over the inlet. The
beach has lovely flat rockpools with plenty of crabs and a
gentle sloping beach perfect for paddling and body boarding.
The stretch of sand running north to *HMAS Creswell* Navy
Base on the point includes Iluka and Captains beaches, with
similarly crystal-clear waters and a fringing forest alive with
birds. Heading east from Green Patch, Bristol Point beach
is a little hidden cove accessible via a short walk through
a picnic area and blackbutt forest or along the water at low
tide. Further along, Scottish Rocks Beach is a snorkeller's
paradise with red rock platforms that hide stingrays and
sea dragons. Hole in the Wall, a natural rock formation
jutting out from a curved beach, is between Scottish Rocks
and Murrays Beach at the southern tip of Jervis Bay, which
overlooks Bowen Island.

Booderee Botanic Gardens is 6 kilometres west of the
campground. It is a peaceful place with walking trails and
picnic tables immersed in the greenery.

Jervis Bay township in the great Jervis Bay is a cute coastal hub with restaurants and cafes to satisfy the Sydneysider crowd and much by way of tours, including whale-watching, kayaking and stand-up paddleboarding. It's a 50-minute drive and the closest main town to the campground.

FIRST PEOPLES KNOW-HOW

The Munyunga Waraga Dhugan walking trail, meaning 'white-bellied sea eagle's home camp' in the Dhurga language of the local Wreck Bay people, is a 5.4 kilometre loop walk (allow 2.5 hours) that extends around Booderee National Park. It follows 14 storyboards with information about the local plants and animals, as well as stories about the Wreck Bay First People's culture and history. The ocean views from Governor Head are particularly lovely, with a chance to see marine life including penguins and dolphins. Access the track at Murrays Beach carpark.

WILDLIFE WATCH

There's a penguin rookery on Bowen Island, across from Murrays Beach at the southern tip of Jervis Bay. There's no public access, but you can spot them – and hear their jabbering – from the beach in the evening.

AND ANOTHER THING

Weekend sites at Green Patch are generally booked out up to a month in advance from October to May.

The campground recommends that campers bring their own personal gas barbecues.

ALTERNATIVES

The other two camping areas at Booderee are Bristol Point and Cave Beach. They are suitable for tents only and the sites are walk-in. Cars at Bristol are parked 50 metres from the campground, and at Cave Beach they're 300 metres from it. Both campgrounds are unpowered.

Previous A tranquil sunset casts pastel colours over Murrays Beach *Above* Nearby Bristol Point camping area is walk-in only

Grassy riverside camping, just a 20-minute drive from Canberra.

Cotter

Murrumbidgee River Corridor, ACT

MAP ON PAGE 28

ACTIVITIES

FACILITIES

That you can spy platypus swimming among tree roots near the muddy riverbanks, trace wombat tracks in the dirt and see wallabies nibbling around the corners of your tent, makes this campground pretty special. That you can do this, and be only twenty minutes by car from Canberra, Australia's capital city, puts it in on another level again.

Cotter Campground is a tranquil place sitting on the sandy banks of the pretty Cotter River. It's close to the confluence of the mighty Murrumbidgee River. The catchment area of these two rivers and the smaller Paddy's River, which feed the dam that supplies water to Canberra, has evolved as a leisure precinct. The string of reserves, river-crossings, sandy beaches and the dam provide a weekend escape for Canberra locals and a gamut of family fun activities for campers: from playgrounds, picnic spots and free barbecues to nature-based walks and swims, fishing and canoeing.

Proximity to Canberra, and its popularity, ensure the campground is well serviced with rangers and holiday season in-situ volunteer 'hosts'. That said, the honesty box payment system hints at an atmosphere that feels a long way from any city.

The campground has 50 unpowered campsites spread on grass (for tents) and gravel (for caravans) among tall gums and leafy deciduous trees allowing cool and shade in the summer months. It's a fit for all sizes, from swags and tents,

to camper-trailers and caravans with a maximum of 10 people per site. Sites are first-come, first-served and although it gets bumper-to-bumper in peak season, little rules, such as an entry sign saying no noise between 10pm and 7am, help keep the family friendly vibe. Facilities include:

- An amenities block that has been recently upgraded to include hot showers, drinking water and flushing toilets
- Washing-up area
- Wood fires
- Gas barbecues
- Picnic tables
- Boat ramp

Waterplay is by far the main attraction here. Cotter has its own shallow swimming pool formed by a little concrete weir. Children tend to spend all day here – swimming, skimming stones and floating on inflatables from the footbridge at the other end of the campground back downstream.

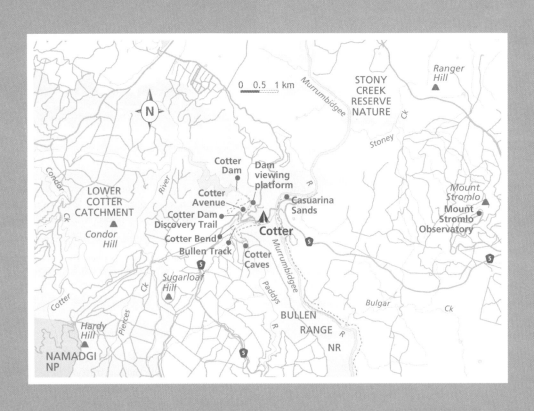

CATEGORIES

Family, Nature, Wi-Fi-Free, No Dogs, Boomers, Nomads

GO DO IT

WHO   Access Canberra; 13 22 81; environment.act.gov.au
WHERE   1691 Cotter Rd, Stromlo, ACT
ACCESS Off Cotter Rd, 25 min west of Canberra city centre
        and 14km from Weston Creek Shopping Centre.

WHAT ELSE?

There are three recreation areas close by the campground.
All of them have grassy picnic areas, tall trees, barbecue and
picnic facilities, toilets and play areas:

• Cotter Avenue, 1 kilometre west of the campground on the
  Cotter River, has an adventure playground with shallows
  perfect for kiddy paddling. It's the access point for the
  Cotter Dam Discovery Trail (*see* Culture vulture).
• Next to it, Cotter Bend, where the Cotter River meets
  Paddys River, has a wide pool and sandy beach – another
  picturesque swimming spot. The Bullen Track (*see* Step it
  up) starts here.
• Casuarina Sands, 1 kilometre north-east of the campground,
  is on the Murrumbidgee River. It is an ideal place to launch
  a canoe, but is equally serene if you want to sit back and
  enjoy the leafy views of the river catchment.

Canberra's Tourist Drive 5 is a loop road that links the
Cotter precinct with inner-city Canberra and parts of NSW.
Follow it east along Cotter Road to explore Mount Stromlo
Observatory, the Royal Australian Mint and the Geoscience
Australia education centre. Follow it south along Paddys
River Road to Canberra Space Centre, Tidbinbilla Nature
Reserve and Gibraltar Falls (the ACT's largest waterfall).
Cyclists whizz past the campground each morning – a nod to
the proximity to Canberra, and a reminder (for me) to bring
my bike next time.

CULTURE VULTURE

The Cotter Dam Discovery Trail near Cotter Avenue
recreation area is a tranquil 1-kilometre stroll towards the
viewing amphitheatre at the base of Cotter Dam, which
contains the drinking water for the ACT. You can learn about
Garrett Cotter, an Irish convict who was banished from a
settlement north-east of Canberra for various misdemeanours.
For five years between banishment and receiving a pardon,
he lived at the head of the river that today bears his name.

STEP IT UP

The 4.5 kilometre return Bullen Track, which starts at Cotter
Bend, is a moderate walking trail that criss-crosses the Cotter
River on little bridges before climbing the Bulleen Range
and heading down to cross Paddys River on stepping stones.
It finishes at Cotter Caves, which was a tourist attraction in
the 1930s and '40s. Today it's closed and all the stalactites
and stalagmites have been broken off by vandals, but there's a
viewing platform where you can read up about its history and
peer into the cavern (it's a better view with a torch). The walk
takes about two hours.

AND ANOTHER THING

Fees can be paid to rangers or left in the honesty box at the
entrance. Site bookings are not available.

Firewood is available for purchase from the ranger or
campground host.

ALTERNATIVES

Woods Reserve Camping Area, 26 kilometres south
of Cotter campground, sits on the banks of Gibraltar
Creek. Gibraltar Falls is located upstream, a 2-kilometre
drive south on Corin Road.

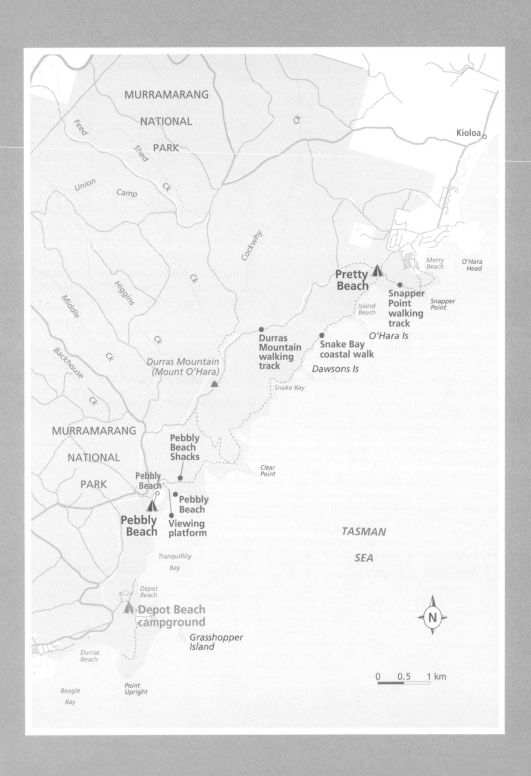

MURRAMARANG

NATIONAL

PARK

Feed

Shed

Union

Camp

Ck

Cockwhy

Ck

Higgins

Ck

Middle

Backhouse

Ck

Ck

Durras Mountain
(Mount O'Hara)

MURRAMARANG

NATIONAL

PARK

Pebbly
Beach
Shacks

Pebbly
Beach

Pebbly
Beach

Pebbly
Beach

Viewing
platform

Tranquillity
Bay

Depot
Beach

Depot Beach
campground

Durras
Beach

Grasshopper
Island

Beagle
Bay

Point
Upright

Durras
Mountain
walking
track

Snake Bay
coastal walk

Clear
Point

Snake Bay

Dawsons Is

O'Hara Is

Island
Beach

Pretty
Beach

Snapper
Point
walking
track

Merry
Beach

O'Hara
Head

Snapper
Point

Kioloa

Ck

TASMAN

SEA

N

0   0.5   1 km

Seaviews, rockholes and swimming in a stand-out setting.

Pretty Beach

Murramarang National Park, NSW

ACTIVITIES

FACILITIES

Wildlife, birdlife, bushland and epic blue stretches of ocean are what make Murramarang National Park special. Covering close to 12,000 hectares, it covers a stretch of to-die-for land between Kiola and Batemans Bay, made up of both coastal hinterland and a forest of spotted gums that, in some areas, extends all the way down to the surf. The park also lays claim to four islands – Dawsons, Wasp, Grasshopper and O'Hara – the latter three of which add a romantic touch to the horizon alongside Gulaga (Mt Dromedary).

Pretty Beach is probably the best of the string of campgrounds in Murramarang National Park, although this might change with the seasons. It's the only one with grass cover, for one, and its hilltop position enjoys full sun – as opposed to deep forest – to get you into beach mode. On hot days, shade can be found on the native bush fringes of the campground, and under a few central eucalyptus trees.

There are 60 sites for tents, trailers, campervans and small caravans, of which 27 are powered. Sites 14–16 are my pick, because they have more space than the sites in the rest of the campground. They also sit close to the walking track that leads down to the beach through lovely grassy soil, loam trees, cabbage palms and native grasses. If you're travelling light and don't need immediate access to your vehicle, nine walk-in campsites in a bushy corner of the campground offer more secluded camping and invite visits from wallabies. Facilities include:

• A shower and toilet block
• A barbecue and picnic shelter (with a nearby fire-ring)
• A recycling area
• A caretaker's office with local info

In addition to these facilities, campers can enjoy picnics at public tables dotted throughout the grassy areas leading down to the beach. There's also a cold outdoor shower here and a wooden viewing platform that shows off Pretty Beach: a lovely arc of white sand protected at both ends by eucalypt-studded slopes and rock cliffs that flatten out into platforms.

The whole campsite empties down to the beach by day to swim, bodyboard, catch sun rays and track crabs in the rockpools. There's a sheltered picnic area and toilet block in this area too, so you really can stay all day.

CATEGORIES

Young Travellers, Family, Nature, Wi-Fi-Free, No Dogs, Boomers, Nomads

GO DO IT

WHO   NSW National Parks & Wildlife Service (NPWS); 1300 072 757; nationalparks.nsw.gov.au

WHERE   Pretty Beach Camping Access Rd, Pretty Beach, Murramarang National Park, about 200km south-west of Sydney, NSW.

ACCESS   Off the Princes Hwy, turn onto Bucks Rd for 5km, turn left onto Dangerboard Rd for 5km, right onto Dangerboard Rd for 5km, right onto Northwood Dr for 400m, then unsealed Pretty Beach Rd for 500m.

WHAT ELSE?

The campground has two basic self-contained cabins with two bedrooms and little front porches.

Humpback and Southern-right whales can be seen from the higher vantage points during their southern migration (May to Nov) along this coastline.

The walk to Snapper Point is a 1-kilometre family trail through bushland to a lookout. It takes about 45 minutes return.

FIRST PEOPLES KNOW-HOW

The local Walbunja people have walked this coastline for thousands of years. Gulaga (Mt Dromedary) that can be seen out to sea has always been respected as a meeting place of the Elders. A fading storyboard at this campsite (which hopefully gets refreshed) shares some of the language of the area's Walbunja people. Gadu means sea, widud widud or marring is sand, manda is bush or forest and bura is rock or stone.

WILDLIFE WATCH

Murramarang National Park boasts a miracle of birdlife. Sit in a quiet spot for long enough and you're guaranteed to see king parrots and kookaburras in the upper tree branches, and satin bowerbirds and eastern yellow robins hopping around the underbrush. Summon your inner birdwatcher and you've a chance to see owls (there are three species in Murramarang), sea eagles and the rufous fantail. All up there are 90 species in the park.

STEP IT UP

The difficult 10 kilometre Durras Mountain Walk starts from the Pretty Beach campground. It takes between three and five hours to get to the summit (and continues onto Pebbly Beach).

The 10.4 kilometre Snake Bay coastal walk also starts at the campground. It takes between three and five hours along rocky coastal terrain. It can only be walked at low tide.

ALTERNATIVES

Also in Murramarang National Park, Pebbly Beach (*see* p. 33) is 9 kilometres south or a 20-minute drive. Depot Beach, is a further 9 kilometres south past the Pebbly turn-off. It also gets an excellent rap.

Camping among spotted gums on an impossibly beautiful beach.

Pebbly Beach

Murramarang National Park, NSW

MAP ON PAGE 30

ACTIVITIES

FACILITIES

We woke up at this campsite to what sounded distinctively like someone tapping on a taut wire, its echoes whipping around the rainforest to haunting effect. Intrigued, we delayed our morning beach swim to see if the perpetrator of this oddly humanised sound revealed itself – it did. An Australian native lyre bird, a male with beautiful curly patterned tail feathers, was practicing the art of mimicry in the bushes nearby. To hear one right here amid the towering trees is pretty special, but it's perhaps not surprising given the natural beauty of this place.

Proximity to Pebbly Beach is key here. And what a beach. The sprawling sand dunes, accessed via a paved path, are grassy and alive with little native flowers so that the place looks and feels like a manicured garden extending down to the sand. Despite all the usual warnings along this coast – submerged rocks, shallow waters, big waves – it's impossible to stand amid this Garden of Eden overlooking the big blue and not want to jump in (which we did).

The campground itself is hidden among a forest of tall spotted gums, that are significant for their longevity. On my visit in autumn, it felt a little dark and damp in the early mornings and afternoons, but it must be wonderfully cool here during hotter months.

The 23 tent sites are functionally laid out on a hard – very hard – dirt surface and are demarcated by pine stumps and platforms edged in timber. You can park your car next to your tent. My only gripe is that there's little by way of privacy between each site. Tent sites 1–17 are near the toilet and shower block, picnic shelter, barbecues and a fire-pit. The camper-trailer, campervan and small caravan sites are further away from the amenities but arguably in a better spot, with just a big old hedge separating them from the beach beyond.

A second sheltered picnic and barbecue area for day-visitor use has a bit of character, with a pitched roof, wooden supports and a corrugate-iron tank. Ducks strut around it and rainbow lorikeets don't mind landing on the roof. It's in a top spot with beach views and a grassy space for kids to play. We gathered here for barbecues, rather than at the one nearer our tent.

Another plus to Pebbly is its roaming kangaroo and wallaby populations. It's a cinch to get that all-Australian Insta pic of a 'skip' nibbling on grass in the foreground with the waves rolling in behind. In nearby coastal towns, it's not unusual to see kangaroos gathered on the urban nature strip and making themselves at home in residential front yards. It's a sight to see. While the little grey-faced roo nuzzling your hand for food seems irresistible, its big brother may not be so friendly.

CATEGORIES

Young Travellers, Family, Nature, Wi-Fi-Free, No Dogs, Boomers, Nomads

GO DO IT

WHO   NSW National Parks & Wildlife Service (NPWS); 1300 072 757; nationalparks.nsw.gov.au
WHERE   Pebbly Beach Rd, Murramarang National Park, about 200km south-west of Sydney, NSW.
ACCESS Pebbly Beach Rd is an unsealed road through thick rainforest. It is signposted off the Princes Hwy.

WHAT ELSE?

Halfway between the beach and the picnic area, a viewing platform has a cold water shower perfect for rinsing off the salty water. It was our go-to at the end of the day for kids' shower-time, too.

Along the Clear Point access trail, four self-catering cabins are dotted through the bush. They're worth strolling by to get a sense of the great Aussie beach shack.

FIRST PEOPLES KNOW-HOW

This is the land of the Walbunja people. North on Murramarang Rd, between Bawley Point and Kiola, Murramarang Aboriginal Area has a walking track point with interpretive signs pointing to middens – and other places of similar cultural significance. The 2.2 kilometre loop takes about 90 minutes and follows a coastal sand track through beautiful grasslands and coastal bush with soul-rejuvenating views toward Brush Island Nature Reserve. There are places to swim and some of the more exposed areas are good for whale-watching in season.

WILDLIFE WATCH

Eastern grey kangaroos, swamp wallabies and red-neck wallabies all call Murramarang home. Dawn and dusk is the best time to spot them. As the sign says: 'Remember that kangaroos and wallabies are wild animals. While the little grey-faced nuzzling your hand for food seems irresistible, its big brother may not be so friendly.'

STEP IT UP

Durras Mountain walking track starts at Pebbly Beach picnic area. Follow the signs to complete the 1.7-kilometre, 35-minute stroll to Clear Point; the 3.9-kilometre, 75-minute walk to Snake Bay; the 3.9-kilometre, 90-minute hike to Durras Mt Summit; or the 8.4-kilometre, 3.5-hour trek to Pretty Beach.

ALTERNATIVES

Also in Murramarang National Park, Pretty Beach (*see* p. 31) is 9 kilometres north or a 20-minute drive away. It's the pick of the park's campsite. Depot Beach, a 9-kilometre drive south, is slightly closer. It also gets an excellent rap.

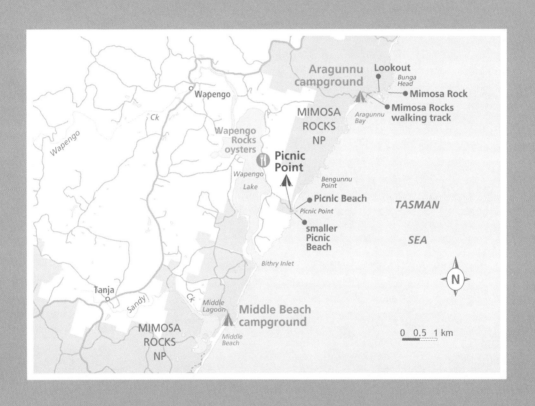

Remote coastal camping with two beautiful beaches to explore.

Picnic Point

Mimosa Rocks National Park, NSW

ACTIVITIES

FACILITIES

The drive out to Picnic Point, especially at dusk when the fading light paints the water with a golden glow, feels like the cinematic opening to a movie set in bucolic Australia. The camera rolls across Wapengo Lake, with its rows of oyster fishing nets, then along a dirt road and onto undulating green paddocks that are dotted not with sheep or cows, but dark ruddy-brown wallabies that stand rigid, eyes glued, as the camera passes them by.

After about 3 kilometres, this enchanting road through private property accesses Mimosa Rocks National Park, via a farm gate (leave the gate as you found it). From here, travel the same distance again along a forested road to Picnic Point, where it loops around a small peninsula jutting east between two arcs of beach.

Picnic Point campground sits right on this point. It feels wonderfully remote and intimate with just 18 sites (and only four of them were occupied on our visit in autumn). They're unpowered and small, so are suitable for tents and camper-trailers but nothing bigger. The central sites are cosied in among stands of banksia trees, while the boundary sites are set in low-lying bushland revealing full and slightly elevated ocean views. Unlike some beachside campgrounds, this one really is only a hop, step and a jump from your tent to the water. The money spot (the sites are unmarked) is on the north side with full water views and a private path leading down a little path to Picnic Beach, a windswept wonder that gets wild when the weather sets in. Two sites on the southern side are also gems, with paths leading directly to smaller Picnic Beach, which is more protected and the friendliest for swimming, rockpooling and cartwheels.

Picnic Point can feel more like a private campground than a national park with thoughtful extras. Facilities include:

• A sizeable recycling station
• Plenty of toilet paper in the two compost toilets
• Chopped firewood (although this could be the generosity of previous campers)

Somewhat erroneously, there is only one picnic table and it's coveted by whoever wants to hear the waves crash onto the striated rock-cliffs and flat platforms at the end of the beach below. But a handful of little concrete seats have been neatly positioned around the place with contemplative ocean viewing and picturesque sundowners in mind.

The little roadside shack of a shop at Wapengo Lake Oysters, part of the mise-en-scene we passed on the way in, sells a dozen small, medium or large unshucked oysters for $8, $10 and $12, respectively. Don't forget a mesh glove, shucking knife and a bag of lemons.

CATEGORIES

Family, Nature, Wi-Fi-Free, No Dogs, Boomers, Nomads

GO DO IT

WHO   NSW National Parks & Wildlife Service (NPWS); 1300 072 757; nationalparks.nsw.gov.au

WHERE Mimosa Rocks National Park is on the south coast, 330km south-west of Sydney near Tathra and Bermagui, NSW.

ACCESS At the end of Wapengo Lake Rd, off the Tathra–Bermagui Rd with 3km of accessible but unsealed private road which accesses Mimosa Rocks National Park via a farm gate.

WHAT ELSE?

The 2 kilometre long Mimosa Rocks track is an easy stroll from nearby Aragunnu Campground carpark with a boardwalk section that crosses an Indigenous midden. It ends at a lookout. Take your binoculars along this track to see the pyramid-shaped Mimosa Rock that marks the underwater grave of the park's namesake, the shipwrecked *Mimosa* paddle steamer, which met its untimely death in 1863.

EAT IT

About 20 kilometres away, historic Bega is home to Bega Cheese Heritage Centre, where you can mug-up on cheese-making production and taste test the local cheddar, the product of dairy cows that feed on the region's lush green grass.

FIRST PEOPLES KNOW-HOW

The Yuin people have inhabited Mimosa Rocks National Park for tens of thousands of years. The storyboards along the Mimosa Rocks walking track tell some of their stories.

WILDLIFE WATCH

Swamp wallabies hop around this campground like they own the place. Take a walk on the beach to see threatened hooded plovers or pied oystercatchers roaming around the rocky platforms.

An easy stroll along Mimosa Rocks walking track

STEP IT UP

About 30 kilometres south, Bermagui is a fishing town with a remarkable Blue Pool built into the wave-swept rocks. Team a swim with local fish and chips or a beer at the charming Bermagui Beach Hotel.

AND ANOTHER THING

The unsealed road to Picnic Point can get slippery in wet weather. Time your run.

You can buy firewood during school holidays and other busy times for $20 per large wheelbarrow load. Call the licenced supplier on 0487 735 259.

ALTERNATIVES

Also in Mimosa Rocks National Park and boasting fantastic beachside locales are Middle Beach Campground, 16 kilometres south, and bigger Aragunnu Campground, 10 kilometres north. They get a great rap.

Spacious bush camping near a romantic beach in a remote coastal wilderness.

Bittangabee

Green Cape, Ben Boyd National Park, NSW

MAP ON PAGE 40

ACTIVITIES

FACILITIES

If you're looking for somewhere to romance someone, the beach cove near the Bittangabee campground is your go. With sloping forests and rock shelves on each side and a moon-thin slip of sand in between, it's picnic rug and bottle of wine territory.

When we visited, a catamaran big enough to live on was anchored in the bay, lending the place a rock-star air. But in reality, this beach and campground in Green Cape, a swathe of wild and rugged coastal landscape in the south of Ben Boyd National Park, is far from the madding crowd. You're more likely to see older people fishing for flathead, kite-flying middle aged folk and kids snorkelling on the peaceful ebb and flow of waves. Kayaks parked along the beach hint at the intrigues to be found around the rocky shoreline.

The beach is tucked away on the southern side of Bittangabee Bay, a sheltered inlet where the Bittangabee Creek meets the South Pacific Ocean. The campground, a five- to ten-minute walk from the beach on a sloping sandy track that winds through the trees, is on land nudging the small ocean-butting rocky headland on the south of Bittangabee Bay. Its 30 unpowered campsites, suited to tents and camper-trailers, are spread out on a flat part-grass, part-sandy area, with plenty of scrubby coastal sheoaks for shade and hammock hanging. It feels a little like a park, with a separate carpark and campsites mapped out with numbers stuck in the sand. Overnighters will do well to find a site next to the carpark for ease of access, but long-stayers will prefer the sites near

the little trails leading down to the beach and around the scenic edges.

Each site has its own fire-pit with a hot-plate or you can join fellow campers at the barbecue (free, gas) and picnic area. MacGyver types might use the sawn-off tree stumps that dot the campground as makeshift tables or chairs. There's also a picnic table at the top of the beach walk which is used mainly for day visitors. Amenities near the campground include compost toilets and tank water.

The beach monopolises much of the time spent camping here, but the bush tracks around the headland are intrigues also. Scramble around rugged black and red rock formations and at low tide explore the pools left in gullies on the smooth wave-washed rock platforms.

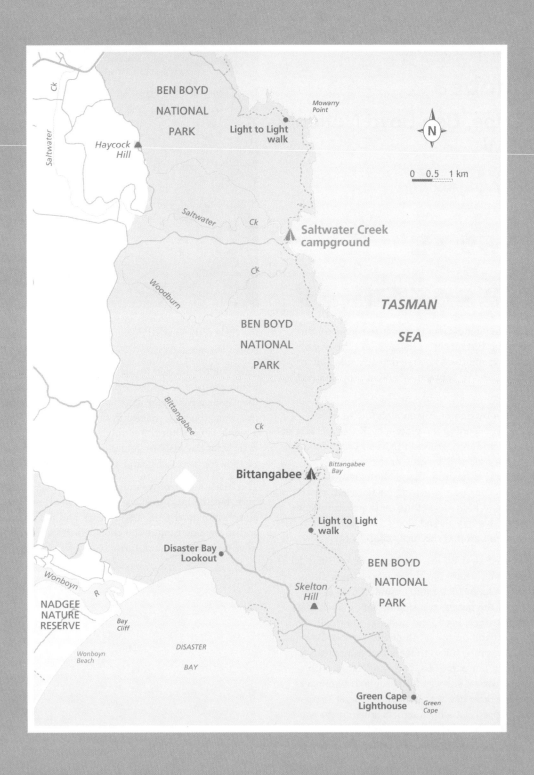

CATEGORIES

Young Travellers, Family, Nature, Wi-Fi-Free, No Dogs, Boomers, Nomads

GO DO IT

WHO   NSW National Parks & Wildlife Service (NPWS); 1300 072 757; nationalparks.nsw.gov.au

WHERE   Ben Boyd National Park is on the south-west corner of NSW near the Victorian border. It is 560km from Sydney and a similar distance from Melbourne.

ACCESS   From Green Cape Lighthouse Rd, turn onto Bittangabee Bay unsealed road for 3km. The campground is at the end towards the right.

WHAT ELSE?

Eden, 43km north, is the closest town to the campground. It's a sweet place with the essential supermarkets, cafes and service stations, plus a lovely port with boats jostling for room at the jetty. Eden takes its status as a whale-watching hot spot seriously with its Killer Whale Museum, whale-watching tour operators and the Eden Whale Festival, held in November.

Green Cape is at the southern end of the so-called Sapphire Coast, which stretches north past Merimbula (69km north, allow one hour and 10 minutes by car) to Bermagui (158km north). It is known for its string of sumptuous beaches and related water activities, including swimming, snorkelling and scuba diving.

In spring, head to Boyds Lookout and Disaster Bay Lookout to see whales, including mothers and calves, migrating south to their Antarctic feeding grounds.

CULTURE VULTURE

Green Cape Lighthouse, built in 1883, is 8 kilometres away from Bittangabee campground down a steep dirt road. Stores and supplies to this prominent white lighthouse and outbuildings, were originally lugged in off ships anchored on Bittangabee Bay. It must have been gruelling work.

Davidson Whaling Station historic site is a nod to the first shore-based whaling station on mainland Australia. It opened in 1828 at Twofold Bay, a 45-minute drive north of Bittangabee campground. It delves into countless stories about the whaling operation and blubber processing. Tours are operated during the Eden Whale Festival.

FIRST PEOPLES KNOW-HOW

The Yuin people, Traditional Owners of Ben Boyd National Park have an important story about the local orca whales. In his incredible book *Dark Emu*, Bruce Pascoe explains that the Yuin had a ritualised interaction with the killer whales. With a ceremony that included lighting fires, the Yuin would 'encourage the mammals to herd larger whales into the harbour where they would be driven into the shallow water and harvested by the Yuin'. The methodology was passed on to European settlers, 'but it ended when a European man shot the lead killer whale [and the] association between man and whale was broken'. Read more about it at Davidson Whaling Station.

WILDLIFE WATCH

Huge lace monitor lizards, also known as tree goannas, stalk this campground. Their heavily camouflaged exterior is no match for the swish-swish noise they make as they walk through camp mid-morning. They look intimidating, but they're harmless if you keep out of their way. Camping in autumn? Keep an eye out for lyre birds performing their fabulous feathered-tail dance.

STEP IT UP

One of the bucket-list walks on Australia's East Coast, the Light to Light walk traverses the red-rock platforms, forests and coastal scenery between historic Boyds Tower and Green Cape Lighthouse. It's a 30-kilometre trail (one way) on mostly flat terrain. Take two or three days stopping at beach campgrounds along the way or bite off small sections. The scenery is epic. Seal and whale sightings are a bonus.

AND ANOTHER THING

The road into Bittangabee is unsealed but suitable for 2WD vehicles. It does get slippery after rain so time your run.

ALTERNATIVES

Also in Ben Boyd National Park, surfers love secluded Saltwater Creek Campground. It's 19km north of Bittangabee.

Green Cape Lighthouse is the endpoint for the 30-kilometre Light to Light walk

Riverside alpine camping close to Thredbo's mountain-biking and hiking routes.

Thredbo Diggings

Kosciuszko National Park, NSW

MAP ON PAGE 44

ACTIVITIES

FACILITIES

Beautiful Kosciuszko National Park is a UNESCO Biosphere Reserve, with more than half the park's 350,000 hectares declared a wilderness area. During winter, this alpine countryside is blanketed white, the snow gums drooping with icy fronds. In the warmer months, it's a different story – the sun-kissed meadows and refined mountain air provide a playground for mountain enthusiasts who choose hiking and biking over skiing.

Thredbo Diggings is located on the curvy road 10–15 minutes north-east of Thredbo, the alpine village and ski resort. Driving along the Alpine Way through Thredbo, we almost u-turned to stay at Ngarigo campground, which is 5 kilometres closer, but going the little extra distance is worthwhile. The unmarked campground is like an alpine parkland, with 20–30 sites, suitable for tents and bigger vehicles, naturally framed by twisted trunks and alpine mint bush. Head right as you enter for sites that overlook an alpine meadow, its grassy – almost manicured – hillocks reach down to Little Thredbo River and the hills rise up behind it. It really has a film set idyll about it. Ducks with jade and purple rear feathers strut around (and steal your food), the water twinkles and burbles over rocks, and lizards scamper about happy in their own national park paradise.

Facilities include:

- Drop-toilets in little corrugated-iron sheds (typical architecture in these parts)
- Picnic tables
- Wood barbecues and fire-pits with hot plates, but they're set high so you'd need a rip-roaring fire to put them to good use (which is unlikely given you need to bring your own firewood)

It is heaven for kids – ours disappeared soon after arrival, following dirt tracks around the water's edge and across logs to little islands in the stream. The water is paddling depth at best, and freezing cold, but worthy of a plunge for the sheer joy of it.

Active adults will be similarly inspired if they care to walk, bike or hike on the trails that pass through the campground.

After dark, be sure to leave the tree canopied camping area for the open meadow for a milky way panorama that Walt Disney would approve of.

Thredbo, a key attraction for this campground, is a self-contained village with the necessary eateries, bars and a supermarket.

Overleaf Admire wildflowers at Blue Lake, catch the chairlift and hike (or bike) down the mountain in Thredbo's warmer months

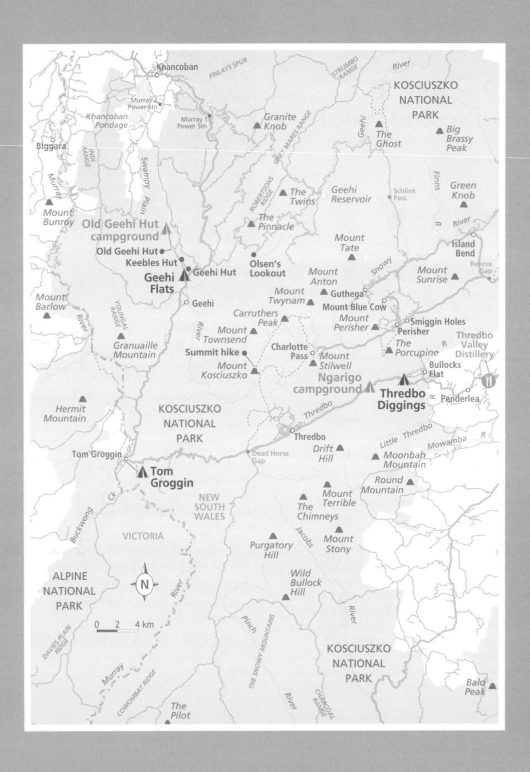

CATEGORIES

Young Travellers, Family, Nature, Wi-Fi-Free, No Dogs, Boomers, Nomads

GO DO IT

WHO   Snowy Region Visitor Centre; 1300 072 757; nationalparks.nsw.gov.au
WHERE   Thredbo area, Kosciuszko National Park, NSW.
ACCESS   Signposted off Alpine way, 12km north-east of Thredbo and 20km west of Jindabyne.

WHAT ELSE?

From November to May, the Thredbo region becomes somewhat of a wildflower-strewn paradise, with the ski slopes transformed into a hiking and mountain-biking fun park. Choose from 20 different walks and hikes and 35 kilometres of mountain-bike trails, ranging from gentle family friendly 12-kilometre rides through flat country to intrepid 35 kilometre long adventures.

You can hook your wheels onto the back of Thredbo's summer scenic chairlift (thredbo.com.au) to get some height (560 vertical metres) on a descent through the gullies and tree clumps formed by ski trails in the winter months. NSW National Parks and Wildlife Service (NPWS) has a great mountain-biking blog page that riders should check out before they come (blog.nationalparks.nsw.gov.au/zero-to-hero-mountain-biking-the-thredbo-valley-track).

Even without wheels, the chairlift is a highlight. The 25-minute round-trip reveals a spectacular rooftop view of the world, featuring mountain peaks including Mt Kosciuszko.

The 3 kilometre long Meadows Nature Track is a pleasant loop walk around Thredbo village.

This is fly-fishing country – try hooking brown and rainbow trout in the shallows.

CULTURE VULTURE

In mid-January, Thredbo blues festival (thredbo.com.au) takes over restaurants, bars and outdoor venues in the village for three days of moody musical fun. Bands hail from Australia and overseas. Book ahead.

EAT IT

Thredbo Valley Distillery (wildbrumby.com) is 15 minutes away on the road towards Jindabyne. It introduced home-grown schnapps to Australia and has now upped the craft offering to include gin made with pristine Alpine water. The cafe and sculpture park make it a perfect pit-stop.

WILDLIFE WATCH

Traipse through the heath and grasslands to spot more than 200 species of alpine flowering plants, including these endemic varieties: alpine sunrays, snow daisies, yellow billy buttons and anemone buttercup.

Kosciuszko is also a habitat for nationally endangered species, including southern corroboree frogs (see p. 48) and broad-toothed rats.

STEP IT UP

The Thredbo Valley track, a 35.1-kilometre trail (downhill), cuts a path through the campground, attracting hikers, walkers and mountain-bikers (whose prized possessions can be seen rigged to the back of their vehicles). Bullocks walking track and Muzzlewood cycle track also pass nearby.

The 13 kilometre long Kosciuszko Summit Hike is one of the bucket-list activities in this region. It's a pilgrimage to the highest point in the country, with 360-degree alpine views.

Other walks include the 19 kilometre long Alpine Lakes hike traversing the area's glacial lakes, including Blue Lake, a rare cirque lake formed by the head of a glacier and recognised for its role in preserving rare and threatened species.

AND ANOTHER THING

This is snow country. Between the Queen's Birthday (June) and Labour Day (Oct) long weekends, 2WD vehicles are required to carry snow chains on the Alpine Way (and it's highly recommended for 4WD vehicles). You can hire them from service stations and ski hire shops in towns including Jindabyne and Khancoban.

ALTERNATIVES

Ngarigo Campground, 5 kilometres away, is a worthy second place if Thredbo Diggings is full. Also Tom Groggin (see p. 47) and Geehi Flats (see p. 50) campgrounds.

An open and spacious campground in a grassy mountain valley on the banks of the Upper Murray River.

Tom Groggin

Kosciuszko National Park, NSW

MAP ON PAGE 44

ACTIVITIES

FACILITIES

Banjo Patterson's classic poem 'The Man from Snowy River', about a lanky, young stockman who drives a herd of wild brumbies through the impassably steep slopes of the Snowy Mountains, resonates in these parts. Patterson visited neighbouring Tom Groggin Station in 1860 and the poem's protagonist was generally thought to be based on Jack Riley, who managed the property at the time. Patterson himself maintained that the character was based on numerous people. Either way the spectacular Snowy scenery described reflects this area.

The campground is located 53 kilometres south of Khancoban and 27 kilometres west of Thredbo. It's on a grassy sprawl of land in a valley that opens up either side of the Alpine Way with a 360-degree view of the surrounding mountain ash forests and lofty peaks. It's a scenic surprise after driving through the windy forested roads to get here.

Just off the dirt road leading into the campground, un-fenced paddocks are ideal for caravans, campervans and camper-trailers who can spread out in the open or keep trailers attached. The money spot, where campers flock to, is a few hundred metres on from this bigger vehicle area in an opening surrounded by mature eucalypts, right on the edge of the Upper Murray River. The river is actually the NSW–Victorian border and this stretch is so narrow that my kids took great delight in picking up pebbles and throwing them 'all the way to Victoria'.

There's a natural sandy ramp leading down to the river, which is mostly shallow, making it easy to paddle in without being swept downstream. It's also a good place to throw a line in. On our stay a fisherperson, up to her knees in gumboots, reported catching trout. The frogs hopping around are another indication of a thriving river ecosystem.

Choose your campsite carefully. The southern side will be in full heat during summer, but will catch some decent rays in spring and autumn. The northern side has handy wooden picnic tables, barbecue pits (BYO wood), toilets and more shaded options, but it might feel the chill in cooler months.

Tom Groggin strikes me as a place where you could set up for a long-term immersion camp. The washing strung between the gum trees is proof that other campers agree. It's also a social spot, with itinerant bushwalkers, mountain-bikers and horse riders passing through.

CATEGORIES

Young Travellers, Free, Family, Nature, Wi-Fi-Free, No Dogs, Boomers/Nomads

GO DO IT

WHO   Khancoban Visitor Centre; (02) 6076 9373;
           nationalparks.nsw.gov.au
WHERE   The Khancoban area of southern Kosciuszko
           National Park, NSW.
ACCESS   From Khancoban Visitor Centre, follow Alpine
           Way into the national park for around 52km.
           From Jindabyne visitor centre drive 3km along
           Kosciuszko Rd towards the national park. Turn
           left on to Alpine Way and follow for 55km.

WHAT ELSE?

Fishing is allowed between the Queen's Birthday (June) and Labour Day (Oct) long weekends.

Bicentennial National Trail (bicentennialnationaltrail.com.au), stretching an extraordinary 5330 kilometres from Cooktown in tropical far-north Queensland to Healesville in Victoria, passes through this campground and Geehi Flats (*see* p. 50). It follows old horse trails through the spectacular alpine and sub-alpine bushland.

There are other trail rides nearby too. Cochran Horse Treks (cochranhorsetreks.com.au) offers guided rides and can give you the low-down on tracks.

CULTURE VULTURE

Given that mountain brumbies still ride wild here, a rendition of Banjo Patterson's 'Man From Snowy River' poem is a fireside must. While you're at it, summon up 'Waltzing Matilda', another Banjo classic.

In nearby Corryong, beyond Khancoban, the Man from Snowy River Festival (April, bushfestival.com.au) attracts about 25,000 people each year.

FIRST PEOPLES KNOW-HOW

Tom Groggin is believed to be a corruption of an Aboriginal word 'tomarogin', meaning water spider, but it's not clear which language it derives from. Snippets of history tell us that this place was a meeting spot for the local Jaitmathang, Dhudoroa, Ngarigo and Wolgal people, who were collectively custodians of the Australian Alps.

WILDLIFE WATCH

This national park is a veritable zoo of Aussie wildlife. Keep an eye out for swamp wallabies and short-beaked echidnas by day, and wombats and brushtail possums by night.

An iconic, endangered species, the tiny bright yellow-and-black-striped southern corroboree frog is found only in Kosciuszko National Park. The Saving Our Species (environment.nsw.gov.au) program aims to prevent this from happening by battling chytrid fungus, protecting frog habitat from pests, and fostering a captive breeding program.

AND ANOTHER THING

This is snow country. Between the Queen's Birthday (June) and Labour Day (Oct) long weekends, 2WD vehicles are required to carry snow chains on the Alpine Way (and it's highly recommended for 4WD vehicles). You can hire them from service stations and ski hire shops in towns including Jindabyne and Khancoban.

ALTERNATIVES

There are plenty of great campsites in Kosciuszko National Park. Along the Alpine Way towards Khancoban, Geehi Flats (*see* p. 50) is another riverside spot close to some of the old hand-built stone huts. If you have a 4WD, Old Geehi Flats is equally appealing and more remote.

In the other direction, Thredbo Diggings (*see* p. 43) is a bucolic spot in the alps.

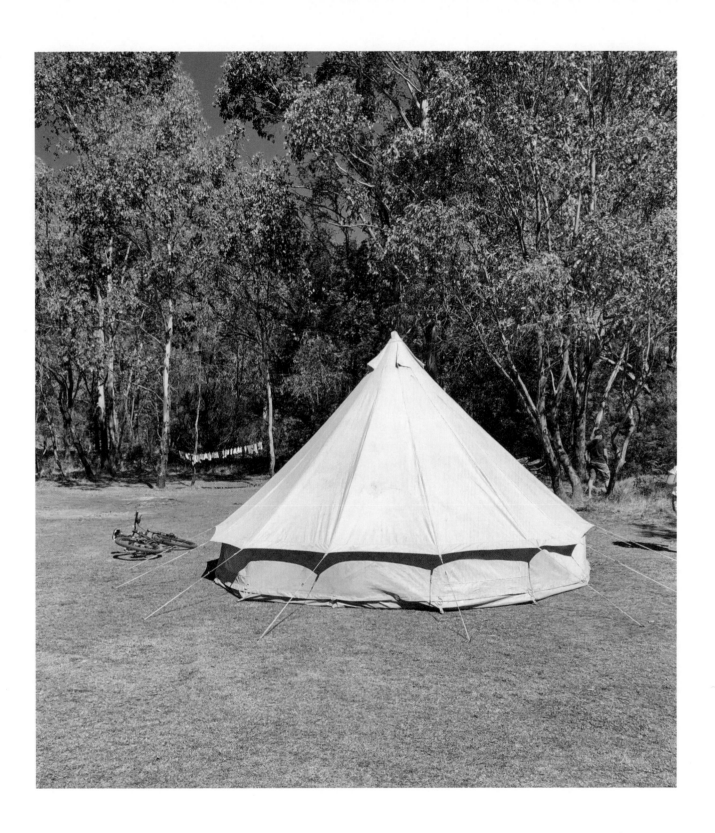

Native and spacious oasis on the banks of the Swampy Plains River.

Geehi Flats

Kosciuszko National Park, NSW

MAP ON PAGE 44

ACTIVITIES

FACILITIES

When I was about 10 years old, my dad, three sisters and I came camping at Geehi Flats, a serene and beautiful savannah woodland, where eastern grey roos sit amid wild flowers right on the edge of the Swampy Plains River. I remember three things vividly. The first was our tent – a big marquee made entirely of mosquito netting. It fascinated us because it was 'see through' and to this day I'm not sure why it was. The second memory is of my sisters and I floating along the river on air mattresses, known as lilos back then. We'd get in at the bridge near the campground entry and float over the smooth-rocked, shallow rapids all the way down to the Geehi Flats hut, with dad watching from a camping chair on the bank. My final memory is of being sunburnt, so much so that the skin on my shoulders bubbled like big dollops of vaseline. It was a long time before we went back.

On this more recent visit, the March sun wasn't quite so harsh and the river was too cold for swimming, but this peaceful place, smelling like a bouquet of eucalyptus, retains its remote and rarified high-country atmosphere. Camping in this pristine wilderness, which is protected as a UNESCO Biosphere Reserve, makes you feel very fortunate indeed.

The campground has 40 sites that are big, unmarked and naturally well-spaced, with respectable drop-toilets and picnic tables dotted around. They're suitable for tents, campervans and camper-trailers. The only thing separating most plots from the Swampy Plains River is a few steps and a narrow path. It runs between the campground and the river and has seats every so often for contemplating current. The water looks so clear (and free of cattle and agricultural run-off)

that we are tempted to drink it without bothering to boil it (although that's not the perceived wisdom). When you throw a line in, as most campers do, you can see your fish fighting for its life a mile off.

Rising 1600 metres behind the campground is the Western Fall of Kosciuszko National Park's Main Range, the highest and steepest part of the Snowy Mountains. You can't quite see the highest peak, Mt Kosciuszko, but the starkness of the sun hitting the rocky range when the campground is in shadow is a sight to behold.

CATEGORIES

Young Travellers, Free, Family, Nature, Wi-Fi-Free, No Dogs

GO DO IT

WHO   Khancoban Visitor Centre; (02) 6076 9373; nationalparks.nsw.gov.au

WHERE   The southern area of Kosciuszko National Park, NSW.

ACCESS From Khancoban, turn left onto Alpine Way and continue along this road for 36km. Turn right into Geehi Flats campground, just before the bridge. From Jindabyne, travel west along Kosciuszko Road for 3km, then turn left onto Alpine Way. Continue for 78km, cross the bridge at Swampy Plains River, and turn left into Geehi Flats campground.

WHAT ELSE?

At the end of the campground, Geehi Hut is a two-room colonial-style cottage hand-built in 1952 with stones hauled up from the river. It was used by stockmen grazing cattle in the high country and today it lends the place a romantic mountain air. You can enter the hut and have a look around, and there's plenty of information on the storyboards outside.

The 8 kilometre return Geehi Huts walk is a great way to see Geehi, Keebles and Old Geehi Huts, all constructed from river rocks. You can also drive it. Be prepared for a couple of river crossings – you'll need a 4WD.

Cycle the Swampy Plain Loop, an easy 10 kilometre round-trip from here with two river crossings.

The 14 kilometre/half hour scenic gravel drive to Olsens Lookout and Geehi Reservoir rewards you with views of Lady Northcotes Canyon and Watsons Crags (no relation to this author) and the steep fall of Geehi River.

FIRST PEOPLES KNOW-HOW

The Australian Alps bioregion is the traditional home of two Aboriginal groups, the Walgal people of what is now Kosciuszko National Park and the Ngarigo people of the region around the highlands. Storyboards at this campground describe how the hakea, rice-flower, mat-rush and banksia, growing in nearby forests, provided a veritable feast of nuts and seeds for the local Jaitmathang, Dhudoroa, Ngarigo and Walgal people. Fruit comes in the form of bushplum

(mountain beard heath), pigeon berry (land beard heath) and bush tomato (rough coprosma).

WILDLIFE WATCH

An iconic, endangered species, the tiny bright yellow-and-black-striped southern corroboree frog is found only in Kosciuszko National Park. The Saving Our Species (environment.nsw.gov.au) program aims to prevent this from happening by battling chytrid fungus, protecting frog habitats from pests, and fostering a captive breeding program.

STEP IT UP

Bicentennial National Trail (bicentennialnationaltrail.com.au), stretching an extraordinary 5330 kilometres from Cooktown in tropical far-north Queensland to Healesville in Victoria, passes near here. It follows old horse trails through the spectacular alpine and sub-alpine bushland.

AND ANOTHER THING

This is snow country. Between the Queen's Birthday (June) and Labour Day (Oct) long weekends, 2WD vehicles are required to carry snow chains on the Alpine Way (and it's highly recommended for 4WD vehicles). You can hire them from service stations and ski hire shops in towns including Jindabyne and Khancoban.

ALTERNATIVES

If you have a 4WD, you can cross the Swampy Plain River and head upstream to camp at the even more remote Old Geehi Hut campsite. It's similarly picturesque, with fewer people. In off-peak times, chances are you'll have it to yourself.

Along the Alpine Way towards Thredbo, Tom Groggin (*see p. 47*) is a spacious and pretty campsite on the banks of the Upper Murray River. Thredbo Diggings (*see p. 43*) is a bucolic spot just beyond Thredbo.

A bush setting on the Murray River next to a characteristic old country pub.

Jingellic Reserve

Upper Murray River, NSW

MAP ON PAGE 54

ACTIVITIES

FACILITIES

My mum's family settled in this region of the Upper Murray, near Holbrook, and my lineage goes back about six generations to the 1830s. While none of them live here now, some have acreage and holiday houses (camouflaged as sheep sheds), where they satiate that nostalgic ancestral urge to get back to the bush. Those of us without a plot return to stay at some of the magical campsites that are strung along the Murray River like kookaburras on a telegraph wire.

The most popular of these is Jingellic Reserve, which is wedged between the Murray River and a characteristic old hotel. As you round a corner on the River Road, the Bridge Hotel (known locally as the Jingellic pub), has a corrugate maroon verandah and cream and green stucco walls. Sitting pretty amid oversized European plane trees and eucalyptus, its Carlton Draught sign sticks out of the roof like a beacon to the thirsty. This place hasn't been gentrified and you'll find hearty steak sandwiches and chicken parma on the menu and you're guaranteed to sip on cold tap beer in chilled glasses, with a host of colourful country characters. With the beer garden so close, the campground can be lively, even rowdy, on the weekends and public holidays, but the mellifluous Murray flowing past the doorstep helps

to balance the lively with the leisurely. The campground facilities include:

• Caravan, motorhome, camper-trailer and tent sites
• River views for all sites
• River's-edge camping for campers with tents
• Grassy and tree-shaded areas
• Picnic tables
• Covered gas barbecue areas
• For toilet facilities and coin-operated showers, head to the pub

There are a couple of concrete ramps for launching kayaks and canoes into the river and a quaint old gate at one end leads down a short path to the creek, which is ideal, depending on how high the river is, for paddling and a game of catch with the dog. Up river, the rusted iron trestles of the old Jingellic bridge provide a good launch pad for adventurous swimmers, while downstream, a view of the newer steel truss ten-span bridge, lined on one side with poplar trees, is the stuff of bucolic landscape paintings.

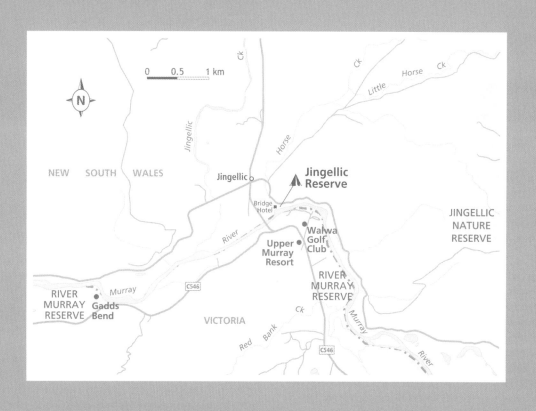

CATEGORIES

Young Travellers, Free, Dog-Lovers, Nomads, Boomers

GO DO IT

WHO   Jingellic Reserve, near the Bridge Hotel, River Rd, Jingellic; (02) 6037 1290; jingellicpub.com.au

WHERE   Jingellic is on the Upper Murray River in NSW, 112km east of Albury on the Victorian–NSW border, and 60km south-east of Holbrook, which is on the Hume Hwy, making this a handy stopover between Sydney and Melbourne. It's also a gateway to the Snowies.

ACCESS River Rd is off Jingellic Rd, Jingellic when coming from the Hume Hwy. On the Victorian side, the Murray River Rd is the scenic route option where you turn left onto Jingellic Rd over the Jingellic Bridge.

WHAT ELSE?

Upper Murray Resort on the Walwa side of the river rents canoes, which can be launched in the river at Walwa for a daytrip down the river to Jingellic.

Care to swing a golf club among the wallabies? The Walwa Golf Club is a 13-hole riverside course just over the border in Victoria.

About 30 kilometres away, Bluff Falls in Burrowa–Pine Mountain National Park (18,400 ha) is a worthy outing. The water cascades off the park plateau, over Cudgewa Bluff and into a tranquil grotto below. Also here is the Bluff Creek Nature Trail, a short walk (4km return) that meanders through moist ferny gullies and tall stands of Blue Gum trees as it links the Bluff Creek visitor area with Bluff Falls. The Lookouts walking track is a steep walk from Bluff Falls that climbs past Campbells Lookout (700m) to Ross Lookout (6km return); it offers excellent views of the park and surrounding countryside from vantage points along the way. Pine Mountain, also in the national park, is a largely geographical unknown, a gigantic rock monolith reputedly one and a half times as large as Uluṟu. The walk to the top over imposing rock outcrops (12km return) is difficult, but good views are available from Rocky Knob after 1 kilometre.

Bring your kayak or canoe for some great adventures on the water

ALTERNATIVES

There are some seriously scenic campsites accessed along the Murray River Road near here. Gadds Bend is the antidote to Jingellics Reserve's atmosphere. It's a swathe of paddock on a big sweeping bend of the river, where you can skim stones, swim, hear cattle and sit in the shade under the river gums.

Also try Clarke's Lagoon Wildlife Reserve, between Walwa and Tintaldra, for a similar riverside setting. Neither of these have amenities.

Main Camp

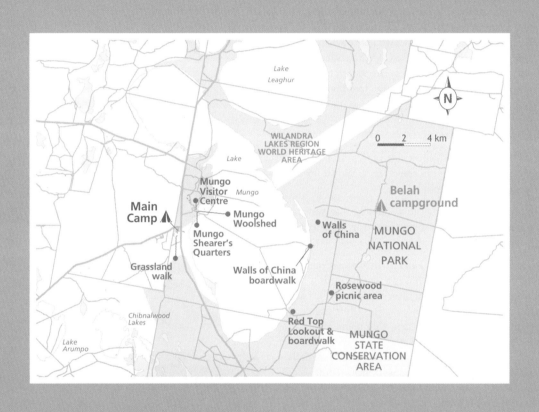

Outback camping on the doorstep of one of Australia's most significant Indigenous heritage sites.

Main Camp
Mungo National Park, NSW

ACTIVITIES

FACILITIES

There's nothing quite like flying over Mungo National Park in outback NSW. Setting out from the NSW–Victoria border towns of Echuca and Moama, the muted green and brown of Murray River country turns creamy yellow through the agricultural belt, then gradually picks up a red tinge. Then the rooftops disappear and all you can see through the round Cessna windows is red dirt and dots of spinifex. Just when you think the arid, flat landscape could go on forever, the pilot dips the wing of the little Cessna and points out Mungo Lake. This ancient dry lakebed, a feature of Mungo National Park, is made of dune fields, sand formations and, on the eastern side, the Walls of China's spectacular crescent-shaped lunettes. These clay and sand formations, which go from dull grey to a glowing red in the setting sun, have been carved and cragged over thousands of years by wind and water. Even from the air, the ridged edifices are like works of art in an alien landscape.

They're just as special on the ground: Mungo Lake is part of the Willandra Lakes Region, an ancient dry-lake system and one of only four places in Australia to be UNESCO World Heritage–listed for both natural and cultural values. Given that the other three sites are the famed Uluṟu-Kata Tjuṯa National Park, Tasmanian Wilderness and Kakadu National Park, makes this place pretty special. In terms of

comparable visitor numbers and popularity, you could call it a hidden gem.

Main Camp, a remote outback campground on the south-west side of Mungo National Park, is the ideal place to soak up this unique landscape and indulge in Indigenous culture. It has 33 unpowered campsites suited to tents, camper-trailers and caravans. They're generously spaced along a gravel loop road, in bays with posts separating the camping area from the natural landscape. The land is dry and flat but shaded intermittently with established eucalypt, pine and peppercorn trees. It's a first-come, first-served basis, so get there early to nab the shadiest campsites or those with sheltered picnic tables and/or fire-pits, depending on your needs. Other facilities include:

• Amenities block with compost toilets
• Picnic tables
• Barbecue facilities
• Fire-pits (at some sites)

You'll need to bring your own firewood and water, for both drinking and cooking. On the upside, the visitor centre (*see* p. 58), 2 kilometres north-east, has hot showers and flush toilets that campers can use.

CATEGORIES

Family, Nature, Wi-Fi-Free, No Dogs, Boomers, Nomads

GO DO IT

WHO   NSW National Parks and Wildlife Service (NPWS, Buronga office); (03) 5021 8900; nationalparks.nsw.gov.au/visit-a-park/parks/mungo-national-park

WHERE   Mungo National Park is in south-west NSW, 875km west of Sydney and 600km north of Melbourne.

ACCESS   From Sturt Hwy, take Silver City Hwy south of Mildura, turn right into Arumpo Rd and follow to the end. Main Camp is on the right shortly before the T-intersection

WHAT ELSE?

From the southern end of the campground, Grassland Walk is an easy 1 kilometre circuit walk through grasslands and shrubs with signs pointing out native bushes and belah and wilga tree varieties. It's unshaded so go early in the day.

Located near the entry to Lake Mungo, 2 kilometres north-east of the campground, Mungo Visitor Centre has excellent tourist information, displays, a phone and general information about the local Indigenous cultural heritage. Campers need to fill out a self-registration form here on arrival (even if the centre is unstaffed). You can also sign-up for a Willandra Lakes guided tour or pick up a 'Driving the Mungo Story' pamphlet, which is a self-guided driving tour taking in the Walls of China (*see* below), the dunes and Mallee country. Stops along the way include Red Top Lookout, and Rosewood picnic area. The visitor centre always has information available, but it's only staffed in the school holidays.

The Walls of China walk, accessed from the Walls of China carpark, 12 kilometres east of the campground, is an easy 500 metre long boardwalk (allow 30 minutes minimum). It's a must-do at sunrise and sunset when the sun paints the view with a rose-coloured hue. There is signage along the walk, but better still, join a Discovery Ranger tour to go beyond the boardwalk into the lunette landscape. The visitor centre has details.

CULTURE VULTURE

Next to the visitor centre and Mungo Shearer's Quarters, the historic Mungo Woolshed and sheep yards takes visitors

Main Camp

back to the property's former life as a pastoral station, when it was run by European settlers and Chinese labourers. It was constructed in 1896.

FIRST PEOPLES KNOW-HOW

The Paakantji, Ngyiampaa and Mutthi Mutthi people are the three traditional clans of Mungo. Their cultures have survived in this landscape for at least 45,000 years. You can meet members from all three tribes on Discovery Rangers walks, talks and tours that explore the ancient local cultural and archaeological treasures. The Walls of China tour is one of them. With your own vehicle, tag-along behind a guide for a 2.5-hour adventure beyond the boardwalk to hear these stories first-hand. Bookings are made through the visitor centre.

One of the tales you're likely to hear much about is that of Australia's oldest-known inhabitants, the human remains of Mungo Woman and Mungo Man, said to be 42,000 years old. They are the oldest human remains to be found outside of Africa and their 'survival' owes much to this unique landscape.

WILDLIFE WATCH

Mallee country is home to emus, western red kangaroos and hundreds of noisy pink cockatoos, a sound that always brings to mind the Australian bush. There are significant bird species here, such as wedge-tailed eagles, brown goshawks and greeny-gold Mallee ring-neck parrots.

AND ANOTHER THING

Unsealed roads to the campground are generally suitable for 2WD cars, but definitely not in wet weather when the route turns into a mudslide. A 4WD is advised.

ALTERNATIVES

Secluded Belah campground, 30 kilometres east of Main Camp, is really basic outback camping. It has 12 campsites with picnic tables and drop-toilets.

Also near the visitor centre, Mungo Shearer's Quarters provides budget heritage accommodation in five rooms with various bunk and bed combinations.

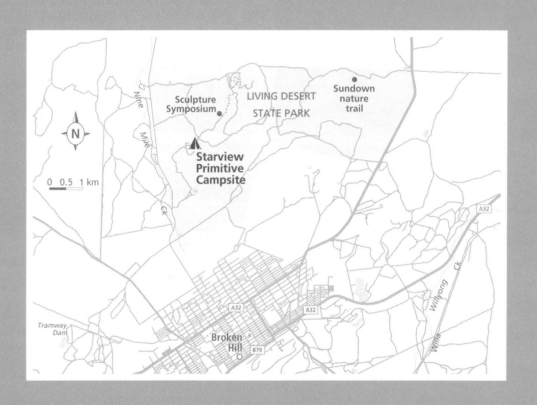

Bush camping in a desert oasis with a sculpture park and nature walk.

Starview Primitive Campsite

Living Desert Reserve, Broken Hill, NSW

ACTIVITIES

FACILITIES

Rain falling in the desert is a wonderful thing, the parched yearning earth breathes each drop of water as it darkens the dusty ground, the wildflowers perk up, even the wallabies look to have a little more spring to their step. Perhaps the rain rose-coloured my stay at this wonderful place, but I don't think so. A well-maintained bush campground in a desert oasis, within walking distance to one of the best sunsets you'll ever see is heaven-sent in any weather.

Starview is part of Living Desert, a 12,400 hectare flora and fauna reserve alive with wildflowers, desert trees, wildlife and wild and unique mineral-rich ecologies. It was established in 1994 to promote a knowledge of Australia's arid zones, an astonishing place where flora, including wattles, saltbush and wallaby grass, grows in extreme conditions. The Sculpture Symposium (*see* p. 62) within the Living Desert, is its key attraction. Visitors to Broken Hill come here for barbecues under the shade of eucalypts, one of the best sunsets in Australia, and to explore.

The campsite has its own entrance, less than 1 kilometre from the public picnic area and you'll need a key for entry. It opened in 2017 and has been set out on a flat expanse of land, with gentle hills on three sides. While it's called 'primitive', the facilities are well-maintained by the local council. Facilities include:

- A separate parking area for caravans and bigger vehicles, with shade trees
- A small tent section laid with tanbark, which provides a softer alternative to the arid desert surface (though it's not ideal for tent pegs)
- A sheltered barbecue area
- Covered picnic tables
- Rubbish bins
- An arbitrary secondary shelter (which we moved the swag under when it rained)
- Seats for stargazing
- The small, corrugated-iron amenities block between the camper area and the tents sites, to our great delight, has a hot-water shower and is wheelchair friendly

Trees newly planted around the border of the tent area will hopefully grow large enough to provide essential shade on hot desert days.

CATEGORIES

Free, Family, Nature, Wi-Fi-Free, No Dogs, Boomers, Nomads

GO DO IT

WHO   Broken Hill Visitor Centre; 08 8080 3560;
         brokenhill.nsw.gov.au
WHERE   Nine Mile Rd, Broken Hill, NSW.
ACCESS   Head north out of Broken Hill on Kaolin St,
         which becomes Nine Mile Rd for 8km. The right-
         hand turn into the Living Desert is signed.

WHAT ELSE?

From the public day-use area about 1 kilometre from the campground, a nature walk leads through the bushland to Indigenous etchings (which are actually quite hard to find – see how you go).

The 2.2 kilometre long Sanctuary Cultural Trail is a one-hour meander from the public day-use area and follows dirt paths through a flora and fauna sanctuary protected by a predator-proof electric fence. It has educational stops at intrigues, such as a simulated Indigenous yapara and an animal viewing hide.

CULTURE VULTURE

The main attraction is undoubtedly the Sculpture Symposium, a collection of 12 eclectic pieces created by local (many Indigenous) and international artists, including Antonio Nava Tirado, from Mexico, whose identifiable sculpture is based on the music of Jarge Reyes. The artworks sit atop a hill rising magnificently out of the flat surrounding desert. There's something very spiritual about this place, especially at sunset when gold washes over the landscape and the sculptures, carved out of huge blocks of sandstone that were transported from Wilcannia, take on elongated shadowy forms. It's possible to drive to the Sculpture Symposium, but the 900-metre walk from the picnic ground sets the scene nicely.

Nobody should visit quirky Broken Hill without watching *The Adventures of Priscilla, Queen of the Desert*, an iconic movie starring Hugo Weaving, Guy Pearce and Terence Stamp – two drag queens and a transgender woman who road-trip across the Australian Outback from Sydney to Alice Springs in a tour bus called 'Priscilla'.

Nearby Silverton, 33 kilometres west of the campground, is another star of the silver screen where *Mad Max*, starring Mel Gibson, was filmed. It's oh-so-much-more than that, though. This one-donkey, red-earthed outback town, with a handful of nostalgic red-brick houses and the charismatic Silverton pub at its heart, is one of Australia's quirkiest and iconic towns. There are a couple of art galleries here, whose artists riff off the novelty of the local community (emus are a theme), plus an old school and church that you can stroll around. A cold draft beer at the bar in the pub is essential, but be warned that some of the blokey 'humour' decorating the walls is dated in a rather cringe-worthy way.

FIRST PEOPLES KNOW-HOW

The arid landscape is alive with bush tucker. The local Bulali or 'uplands people' of the Barrier Ranges are a sub-group of the Wilyakali people who occupy the region from Broken Hill to Olar, 100 kilometres west in South Australia. The Bulali harvest acacia seeds to grind into flour. They also eat the fleshy taproots of plants found along creek beds and the leaves and fruit from wildflowers such as hopbush and ruby saltbush. You'll see all these plants growing in this harsh environment and can marvel at their life-sustaining properties.

WILDLIFE WATCH

Wallabies and emus blend into the landscape here and Euro and wedge-tailed eagles can be seen up high.

Also watch for the Western brown snake, or gwardar to the Bulali people. Its slim glossy upper body ranges in colour from light brown to black.

STEP IT UP

Sundown Nature Trail is a 2.8 kilometre return walk through the hilly, arid terrain of the larger Living Desert State Park, with far-reaching views over the spectacular red desert landscape. It takes about 90 minutes and is best appreciated before sunset or after sunrise. For access, you need to follow the Silver City Highway towards Tibooburra

for 10 kilometres. Look for the signed turn-off to the trail and follow the 2.2 kilometre graded track to the carpark. It's a good one for families.

AND ANOTHER THING

Gates to the Living Desert open at 6am in summer (Dec to Feb), until approximately 30 minutes after sunset. In other months, gates open at 8.30am until half an hour after sunset (around 6pm). There's a $6 entry fee payable at the Tap 'n Go pay bay.

ALTERNATIVES
The new Broken Hill Outback Resort has 80 large powered and unpowered caravan and camping sites, an amenities block and a camp kitchen.

Victoria

Wild coastal landscapes, rainforested national parks and scenic rivers that meander through eucalypt-infused bushland — Victoria's campgrounds are nature's bounty

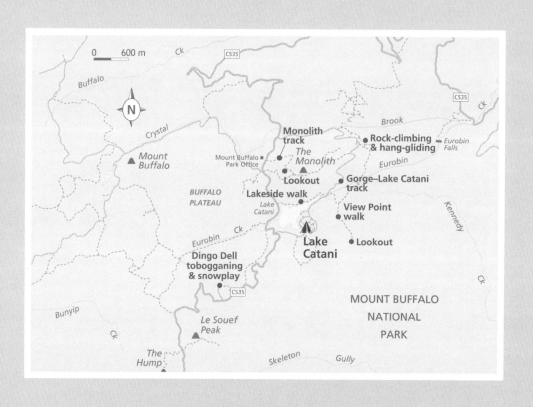

Sub-alpine lakeside camping among the snowgums, with kayaking, walking and adventure sports.

Lake Catani

Mount Buffalo National Park, Vic

ACTIVITIES

FACILITIES

If you're an adventurer looking for an adrenaline-hitting rock-climb or hang-glide, Mount Buffalo National Park is for you. If you're seeking a peaceful paddle around a lake, a tranquil wildflower walk or a quiet moment throwing a line in off a jetty, same goes.

Mount Buffalo plateau sits at a lofty 1723 metres above sea level in the west of Victoria's alpine region. The incredible foothill-tickling national park that protects it is the traditional land of the Mitambuta and Taugaurong Indigenous people and one of Australia's oldest national parks. It covers a total of 31,000 hectares and celebrates diverse sub-alpine landscapes formed at different altitudes. This is a Pandora's box of drooping snow gum and alpine ash woodlands, heathlands, pounding waterfalls, massive granite bluffs, tors, sheer cliff-faces and exquisite native wildflowers.

Immersing yourself on a day-adventure from the popular nearby towns of Bright and Porepunkah is a cinch, but an overnight in the cool alpine air with the warmth of a woodfire, the hoot of an owl and the promise of an inky starry-strewn night is hard to beat.

The campground sits on the shores of Lake Catani, a pretty alpine lake that has blended winsomely with the natural environment since it was artificially constructed more than a century ago. Its waving shoreline is kissed by tall eucalypt forests in some parts, and billowing water reeds in others. Grassy clearings, that give the lake the appearance of a garden pond, allow campers to swim, launch a kayak or fish from the water's edge. A characterful timber jetty jutting into the water near the lake's visitor day-use area is the perfect place to feel the fading light on your face, accompanied by the serenade of birds and frogs.

The 49 unpowered campsites are suitable for tents mostly, but also caravans and campervans. They are nestled among the forest of snow gums, not far from the water's edge on the south side of the lake. They're well-spaced along a one-way road on grass and leaf-littered dirt patches with numbered posts and timber poles for boundaries.

As a general rule, the lower your site number, the closer to the amenities block. That said, the lower numbers are also close to a special area (sites 22–29) set aside (from Monday

Previous Pausing to take in the view from Mt William, Grampians (Gariwerd) National Park

to Thursday) for school groups during the Victorian school term; it's worth ringing ahead to ask whether a school has booked in. Seven walk-in sites (42–49) for small tents are nicely secluded and some are on raised timber platforms that you can secure ropes to. For a small secluded campground, the facilities are excellent. They include:

• Toilets
• Water (untreated natural supply – BYO drinking water)
• Hot showers
• Washing-up area
• Basic laundry (no washing machines)
• Shared outdoor fire-pits
• Solar panel lighting in amenities building

Adjacent to the amenities building there's also a rustic stone shelter or mess hall with communal tables and fireplaces. It's perfect for cosy dinners on cold nights and card games on rainy days.

Opposite Kayaking on Lake Catani

CATEGORIES

Family, Nature, Wi-Fi-Free, No Dogs, Boomers, Nomads

GO DO IT

WHO   Parks Victoria (Mt Buffalo Park Office); 13 1963/ (03) 5755 1466; parks.vic.gov.au

WHERE   Mount Buffalo is 28km east of Porepunkah, the nearest town, and 330 kilometres north-east of Melbourne along the Hume Hwy.

ACCESS From the Hume Hwy, take the Snow Rd C522 exit towards Milawa/Taminick for about 45km, turn right onto Great Alpine Rd (B500) for 31km, turn right onto (slow and winding) Mount Buffalo Tourist Rd (C535) for 27km and follow signs to Lake Catani Campground and Lakeside Day Visitor Area.
During winter, the main road from McKinnons Corner through to Cresta Valley is often snow-covered. Snow chains must be carried within the park during snow season.
The Reservoir, Lake Catani and Horn roads are unsealed and closed during winter or after heavy rain. The Horn and Reservoir roads are not suitable for caravans.

WHAT ELSE?

The campground has an information shelter and a friendly on-site 'host' in high season for payments and local tips. The neighbouring visitor day-use area has information, plus picnic tables, toilets, showers and (in peak times) kayaks for hire (visitmountbuffalo.com.au). Mount Buffalo park office is 1.5 kilometres north and has park information, maps and info on track conditions. Firewood can be purchased from rangers.

There are 90 kilometres of walking tracks, both easy and challenging, that wend through all corners of the park. From the campground:

• The easy 3-kilometre Lakeside walk begins near the day-use area and is a one-hour circuit around lovely lake vistas.
• The 4-kilometre Gorge–Lake Catani track accesses the gorge through Alpine ash woodlands (allow 90 minutes return). This track also accesses the 4-kilometre View Point walk (allow 2 hours return) to a lookout over the Buckland Valley.

• The 1.8-kilometre Monolith track starts 1.5 kilometres north of the campground at the parks office. It leads to a superb rocky outlook with panoramic views across the plateau. From up here you can take in a bird's eye view of Lake Catani (allow one-hour, one-way).

Bike riders can take to vehicle tracks within the park. Check out great routes along the Reservoir Road and the Gorge–Lake Catani track, which is accessible from the campground (*see* p. 68).

The park's extraordinary granite gorge has single-pitch and multi-day rock-climbing for all grades of climber, and a ramp launch suitable for experienced hang-gliders.

When it snows (and that's never guaranteed in these parts), the park has 14 kilometres of wonderfully undulating marked and groomed cross-country ski trails, plus unmarked trails and back country ski touring. They start at Cresta Valley carpark. The kids can build snow-people and go tobogganing at Cresta Valley and Dingo Dell (where there's a year-round day visitor centre and cafe), depending on snowfall. Check online (ski.com.au or vicsnowreport.com.au).

WILDLIFE WATCH

The different altitudes of the national park allow for diverse fauna. At the campground look for lyrebirds, crimson rosellas, wallabies and wombats. In the wider park, you might see peregrine falcons, the endemic Alpine Silver Xenica butterfly found only on the Buffalo plateau, native rats, possums and gliders and, especially around Easter, Bogong moths, with their patterned wingspans.

AND ANOTHER THING

The campground is seasonal: open from November until April, with peak periods during Melbourne Cup Day weekend (Nov), Christmas school holidays, Labour Day weekend (Mar) and Easter school holidays. Bookings open at 10am on 1 September each year and it's first-in, best-dressed so don't miss the date. Campsites must be booked in advance, but outside these times there's usually space at short notice.

Weather conditions are fickle in alpine country, and temperatures sit well below lower lying areas. Pack for cold weather any time of year.

In the winter ski season, when snow turns the mountain plateau white, there are five sites open (and free) to hikers and ski-ins. They are huddled around the stone shelter, which can be used for fires and protection from the elements. A pit-toilet is the only other amenity open. Access is 1 kilometre away from the closed gate on Mount Buffalo Road.

ALTERNATIVES

The national park has remote bush camping at Rocky Creek and Mount McLeod for hikers. Pit-toilets are available and fuel stoves are permitted.

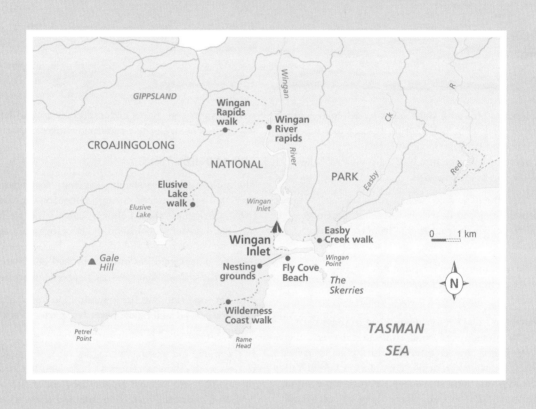

A secluded and peaceful coastal campground so remote that only the most intrepid campers will venture to it.

Wingan Inlet

Croajingolong National Park, Vic

ACTIVITIES

FACILITIES

Many of the campsites in this book are remote or secluded but they're not crazy far from a sealed road. Wingan Inlet is a bit different. It is down a 35-kilometre dirt road that takes about an hour to traverse in a 2WD. But intrepid campers will reap the rewards. Taking into account Cape Conran Coastal Park to the west and Nadgee Nature Reserve to the east, this stretch of land, with Wingan Inlet right in the middle, is the largest continuous coastal protected area on the south-eastern Australian mainland. Furthermore, the star attraction Fly Cove Beach – one of the south-east coast's most untouched beaches – is a 2-kilometre walk from the campground. You'll likely find yourself solo on it at some point during your stay.

Wingan Inlet, where Wingan River snakes into the south Pacific Ocean, is a peaceful body of water with a fringe of thick forest and pandanus trees that give it the appearance of a lake. Standing on its shore at the campground, you can look across the glassy surface to see the golden sandbars of Fly Cove Beach which protect the inlet from the pummelling ocean swell beyond.

The campground sits right next to the inlet. It has 23 unpowered campsites suitable for tents, campervans and camper-trailers, and includes an area dedicated to overnight hikers completing the Wilderness Coast walk (*see* p. 72). All of the sites are fully shaded by a 60-foot canopy of bloodwood trees and each site – on a rectangle of cleared

hard ground – is separated by smaller trees and shrubbery. It would be cool among the trees in the winter months, but it is blissfully protected during summer. Shared fire-pits at campsites 21 and 16 (my picks) make for sociable camping. We got chatting to some local fisherpersons who have been making this place their own every Easter for almost a decade. It's also tempting to snap-up site number 15, which is next to the 'beach access' sign, but otherwise the sites are similar in size, shape, accessibility and aspect. Facilities include:

• An amenities block with compost toilets
• Shared picnic facilities, including three barbecues

For a quick swim from the campground, Wingan Inlet has a silty black sand beach, which is down the picnic end of the campground. It has a mud-clay bottom with little fish darting around. The tidal nature of the lakes means it's not too salty. Slipping into these waters with a kayak would be pretty special indeed (*see* p. 72).

CATEGORIES

Family, Nature, Wi-Fi-Free, No Dogs, Boomers, Nomads

GO DO IT

WHO   Parks Victoria Information Centre; 13 1963;
       parks.vic.gov.au
WHERE West Wingan Rd, Croajingolong National Park,
       East Gippsland, Vic, approximately 450km east
       of Melbourne and 500km south of Sydney.
ACCESS Off the Princes Hwy at the end of West Wingan Rd
       along a 36km stretch of dirt and gravel.

WHAT ELSE?

Fly Cove Beach is 2 kilometres from the campground along a signed walking track. And what a walk it is. The wooden boardwalk flanked by paperbark trees, skirts the edge of the inlet, its reeds and ferns endowing the place with a swampy, croc-country feel. (Never fear, there's nothing remotely like that around, unless of course you count the monitor lizards: metre-long giants that roam the campsite). The boardwalk gradually becomes a sandy path as you near the beach, the sound of the waves giving its proximity away. Towards the end there's a short climb over sand dunes and then, wow, beautiful Fly Cove Beach spreads north and south, the sand gently rippled by the wind, the seaweed jetsam left behind in the tide's wake and not a footprint in sight. We had first tracks on this beach at 3.30pm, and with access limited to boats and walk-ins, there's nobody coming in from anywhere else. Bring lunch and spend the day here.

With a canoe or kayak, explore Wingan Inlet and the mesmeric Wingan River further upstream. A two-hour paddle to Wingan River rapids is worthwhile for a swim in the pools. You can also walk here via Wingan Rapids walk, which begins from Boundary track, a short drive from the campsites.

From the east side of the inlet at Fly Cove, take part of Easby Creek walk 950 metres one-way through bushland to the coast where there's a private little beach.

Elusive Lake, west of the campground is accessed via the 2.4 kilometre one-way Elusive Lake walk (allow 30 minutes). It's accessed via West Wingan Rd, 4 kilometres from the campground. This deep dune-blocked clear water lake is surrounded by sandy banks and tall eucalypts.

CULTURE VULTURE

Historic Point Hicks Lightstation, the tallest lighthouse (37m) in mainland Australia, is 35 kilometres west of the campground (allow an hour by car). It was built in 1887 and first started guiding ships through these treacherous seas in 1890. A reminder of the dangers can be seen in the hull of *SS Saros*, just behind the lightstation, which ran aground in heavy fog in 1937. The lighthouse is open to the public, with tours running Monday to Friday. Or you can stay the night; accommodation is available in the two lighthouse keepers cottages or in a bungalow.

WILDLIFE WATCH

On rocky islands off the coast there's a colony of Australian and New Zealand fur seals. Their wails, which you can hear when it's not too windy, sound like noisy revelling footballers. That they've found a home here indicates the bounty of the marine life, which also attracts serious amateur fisherpersons looking to hook bream, perch and salmon.

The dunes at Fly Cove are a natural nesting ground for Hooded Plover, which are nearing extinction. Keep to the walking tracks to help keep their nest eggs safe.

STEP IT UP

Isolated beaches, river estuaries and rocky headlands are some of the varied landscapes on the 100 kilometre long Wilderness Coast walk, which stretches from the eastern shores of Sydenham Inlet to Wonboyn in the Nadgee Nature Reserve. It passes through Wingan Inlet campground along the way.

ALTERNATIVES

Also in Croajingolong National Park, tiny Shipwreck Creek Campground has five sites and is 300 metres from a secluded beach.

Opposite top left Strolling along Fly Cove Beach *Opposite bottom right* Shipwreck Creek is an alternative option for camping

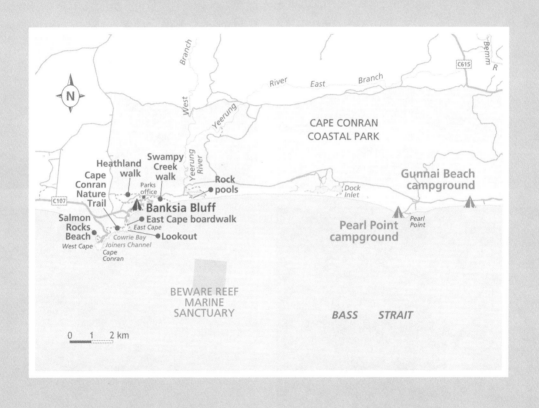

Camping in a landscape of timeless beauty, minutes from the beach, with walks, swims, surf and wildlife.

Banksia Bluff

Cape Conran Coastal Park, Vic

ACTIVITIES

FACILITIES

Cape Conran Coastal Park is extraordinary. Its remoteness (420km east of Melbourne and 620km south of Sydney) might belie its popularity. But you'll understand when you go there.

The 11,700-hectare expanse of wilderness stretches 60 kilometres along Victoria's far-east coastline, south of the NSW border. Its beautiful landscape encompasses vast orange beach boulders, heath-covered hinterland, dense mahogany and eucalypt forests, and untrodden beaches decorated with pearlescent shells and gnarled white driftwood. The place is so untouched, relatively speaking, that the wildlife seems to dominate. A stay here is a promise of potoroos and bandicoots, wombats and wallabies, echidnas, kookaburras and monitor lizards. Just like it should be.

The unassuming campground is blissfully located in this woodland beauty among remnant eucalypt trees and canopies of flowering banksias that run adjacent to the beach. There are a lot of campsites, to be sure, but they're strung around 10 little loop roads spaced along a kilometre of land. Every campsite is nicely placed within 100 metres of the beach, via little sandy communal trails. To camp here is to sleep to the pound of wild Southern Ocean surf by night then play in it, fish in it and surf in it by day.

The 135 unpowered campsites are all suitable for tents and many are suitable for camper-trailers, campervans and caravans. They have compacted sandy groundcover and are mostly flat, but vary in size and shape according to the surrounds. During the summer period this place is crazy popular – you have to enter a ballot mid-year (*see* p. 77) and

sites are allocated prior to arrival. Outside of the summer peak season, campers can choose their campsite on arrival. Take note that campsites 1–67 are dog-free while campsites 68–135 are dog-friendly (but dogs must be on leashes). Also, 30 of the campsites do not have fire-pits so choose accordingly. Other facilities include:

- Flushing toilets (stocked daily with loo paper)
- Cold water showers
- Picnic tables (not many – best to BYO)
- Bore water taps (not for drinking)
- Designated fireplaces with hotplates to cook on
- A communal fire

That the facilities are so basic, tends to take city campers, who might be expecting hot showers, by surprise. But the toilet and shower facilities are clean and evenly spread around the campground 'loops'.

Other accommodation at Cape Conran includes seven timber cabins which are a short walk from the beach and have private front verandahs and pot-belly stove heating. There's also a lodge for large groups with a kitchen, barbecue and wood oven.

If creature comforts really are your thing, the campground's safari tents or 'Wilderness Retreats' make for luxe, low-impact bush camping. The have timber decks, queen-sized beds with linen and towels, a small fridge, a nearby toilet and shower block and a communal kitchen.

CATEGORIES

Young Travellers, Dog-Lovers, Family, Nature, Wi-Fi-Free, No Dogs, Boomers, Nomads

GO DO IT

WHO   Parks Victoria Information Centre/Cape Conran office; 13 1963/(03) 5154 8438; parks.vic.gov.au

WHERE Cape Conran Coastal Park is 19km east of Marlo in eastern Vic, 420km east of Melbourne and 530km south of Sydney.

ACCESS From the Princes Hwy at Orbost turn left onto Lochiel St for 450m, then left turn onto Marlo Rd (becomes Marlo–Conran Rd then Cape Conran Rd) for 33km. From Cann River, turn right onto Princes Hwy for 45km, left onto Cabbage Tree–Conran Rd for 13km, left onto Cape Conran Rd for 450m.

WHAT ELSE?

The on-site office and activity centre has plenty of information about walks and activities, including surf lessons, night walks and kayaking tours. During the busy summer periods, the campground has activities for kids (including ranger talks and talent nights). It also sells gas, water (pricey), firewood and ice. There's a coffee van in the summer holiday season, too.

The closest town is Marlo, 19 kilometres west, which has a hotel and general store.

The beach is the showstopper for entertainment and activity, but in keeping with the uninhabited remoteness of the place, it is not patrolled. On days when it's choppy or the waves are dumping, head to the rockpools on the Yeerung River inlet, 3.3 kilometres east of the campground.

Salmon Rocks Beach, 2.9 kilometres south, over West Cape, is serene at sunset with lovely cresting waves. West Cape is the place to cast a line for salmon and flathead.

Banksia Bluff

Short and inspiring walks direct from the campground include the 3-kilometre return (one-hour) Heathland walk through flowering grass trees to see rosellas and parrots feeding on the area's native nectar plants. The 1.6 kilometre one-way Swampy Creek walk (allow 30 minutes) follows woodland and the creek bed to the coast. Both walks start near the activities centre opposite the parks office.

FIRST PEOPLES KNOW-HOW

Cape Conran is Krowathunkooloong country. Krowathunkooloong is one of the five clans of the Gunaikurnai people. According to batalukculturaltrail.com.au, the viewing platform at Salmon Rock is built above a visible Aboriginal shell midden. West Cape provided an abundance of food for the Gunaikurnai people, with many important sites and middens found along the beaches of the Cape Conran areas. East Cape was the traditional border of the lands of the Gunaikurnai, and the Bidawal and Monero people. The East Cape boardwalk (*see* Step it up) was constructed by the Moogji Aboriginal Council to protect the important Aboriginal sites beneath it for all Australians.

WILDLIFE WATCH

Kangaroos, echidnas, possums, long-nosed potoroos, bandicoots, wombats and goannas (monitor lizards) can be seen at this campground. Keep an eye out for snakes lazing in sunny spots on the hinterland walks. You'll also keep camp with parrots, rosellas and cheeky kookaburras. Southern-right and humpback whales frolic off the coast here from May to October, as well as dolphins. South-west off the coast, Beware Reef Marine Sanctuary is a known spot for experienced divers with a rainbow of sea creatures and fish species.

STEP IT UP

From the East Cape day-visitor area, 500 metres south-west of the campground, the 2.3-kilometre Cape Conran Nature Trail (allow one-hour, one-way) follows a coastal boardwalk route past Cowrie Bay to Joiners Channel. Also from here, the 400-metre East Cape boardwalk (allow 15-minutes, one-way) passes over East Cape to the lookout. From here, walk along the beach to find the track that links to the Cape Conran Nature Trail. At the T-intersection, head right to follow the trail back to East Cape day-visitor area, or left to continue on to West Cape and beautiful Salmon Rocks Beach.

AND ANOTHER THING

Check the website in July to go in the ballot for campsites at Christmas. Easter bookings can be made up to one year in advance.

Remember to bring your own drinking water.

If bringing your dog read up about paralysis ticks, which can be a problem here.

ALTERNATIVES

Also in Cape Conran Coastal Park, Gunnai Beach and Pearl Point are bush campgrounds. They have fire-pits, but no toilets.

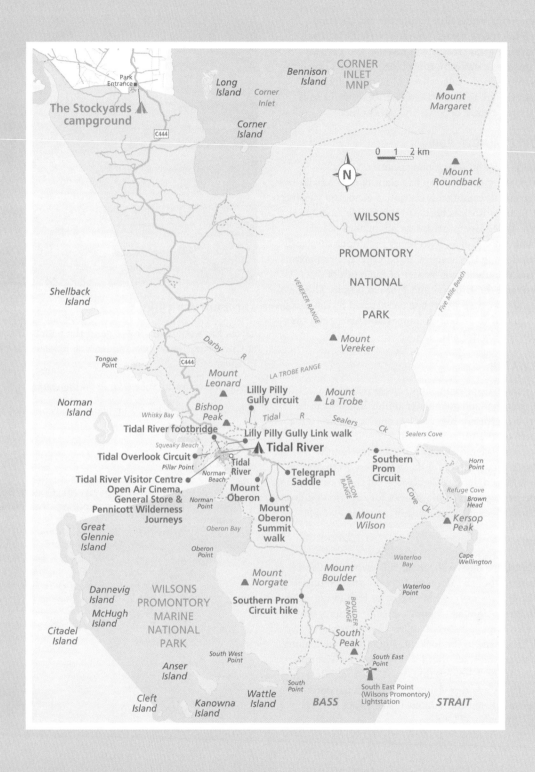

One of Victoria's best and much-loved campgrounds surrounded by beach, ocean, mountains, river and rainforest.

Tidal River

Wilsons Promontory National Park, Vic

ACTIVITIES

FACILITIES

Catching some dinner on Tidal River

If someone asks you to The Prom, don't go rushing out to buy a taffeta dress. The invitation is not for your hand at a formal dance, rather for your company at one of Victoria's most-prized natural wilderness areas, Wilsons Promontory. That it has a short-form nickname says much about its popularity. For Melburnians especially, The Prom is a well-known nature-based getaway, a place for families on summer holidays, couples on romantic overnight hikes and daytrippers on a scenic immersion.

Located on the southern-most tip of Victoria on a triangular-shaped land mass jutting into Bass Strait, The Prom is almost entirely made up of national park and is a diverse landscape of mountains, temperate rainforest, tidal rivers, squeaky sand beaches and granite peaks.

Tidal River, home to the Tidal River Visitor Centre and most of the accommodation, including the campground, is the national park's main hub. It sits midway along the south-west coastline, about 30 kilometres from the entrance to the park. The stretch of land has clumps of native bush, gnarly gumtrees and natural grassy clearings where wallabies, emus and wombats feel at home among the camper hubbub. The sandy flats and clear waters of Tidal River run along its north-west boundary. Hugged by Pillar Point on one side and Norman Point on the other, Norman Beach's yellow sands, sapphire blue waters and island views extend along its south-west boundary. Looking north-east, the hazy blue mountain range including the lofty summit of Mt Oberon completes the idyllic picture.

With 484 campsites, Tidal River easily hosts the most campers of any campground in this book. That it retains its reputation as one of the best camping spots in Victoria says oodles about the surrounding landscape. That said, you'll experience it best outside of summer holidays, Easter and long weekends. You'll also side-step the influx of daytrippers that stream in from about 10am 'til 4pm during these peak times.

The campground is divided into two sections: surfers, bodyboarders and sunbakers will enjoy the sites among the tea trees running adjacent to Norman Beach, while families, kayakers and paddleboarders will appreciate the gentle waters and sand play of the area closer to Tidal River. The loop access roads (Main Rd and Ring Rd) are sealed, but the minor unsealed roads between the rows of tents are in a more natural setting.

There are 20 powered campsites and 455 unpowered campsites (the nine other sites are presumably for overnight hikers). The powered campsites are 8x8m long (four sites are a little bit longer) and are located at the eastern end of Second, Third and Fourth avenues in the Tidal River section. The unpowered sites are found in both the Tidal River and Norman Beach sections and are sized according to position – some are tight and others are spacious but they're all quite close together. Thus, no more than six people (including children) and one vehicle are allowed in each campsite. You'll need to pay more for an extra vehicle or, with more than two vehicles, book an extra campsite.

The campground's many facilities are spread fairly evenly through both sections of the campground and include:

• Mobile device charging stations (at the visitor centre and in some laundries). A $2 coin is required and will be returned when finished.
• Toilet and (hot) shower block
• Picnic areas with free gas barbecues
• Laundry facilities
• Washing-up area
• A dump point (at the overnight hikers' carpark)

Wherever you are in the campground, the natural world is just beyond. Walk over the gorgeous curved Tidal River footbridge and head right to Lilly Pilly Gully Link walk (1km) to access Lilly Pilly Gully circuit (5.8km). Alternatively, turn left after the bridge and walk along part of the Tidal Overlook Circuit to Squeaky Beach, named for the white quartz sand that squeaks underfoot.

CATEGORIES

Young Travellers, Family, Nature, Wi-Fi-Free, No Dogs, Boomers, Nomads

GO DO IT

WHO   Parks Victoria/Tidal River Visitor Centre; 13 1963/
           (03) 8427 2122; parks.vic.gov.au
WHERE   Wilsons Promontory National Park entrance
           is 195km south-east of Melbourne, Vic.
ACCESS   Follow Monash Fwy (M1) to join South Gippsland
           Fwy (M420/A440) to Meeniyan. Take the
           Meeniyan–Promontory Rd (C444) to the Wilsons
           Promontory entrance. Tidal River is a further
           30km, or about half an hour, from the entrance.

WHAT ELSE?

Tidal River General Store is next to the visitor centre. It sells grocery and camping essentials (ice, gas refills, batteries, sunscreen, mozzie spray). The nearby cafe sells dine-in and take-away food. There is no fuel – the closest fuel is at Yanackie just before you enter the national park and 30 kilometres from Tidal River.

A free shuttle bus operates between Tidal River and Telegraph Saddle during summer and Easter school holidays, and on weekends from November to April. Departure points include the Tidal River Visitor Centre carpark, the overnight hikers carpark at Tidal River and at Telegraph Saddle

There are plenty of nearby trails and hikes for campers to explore

carpark. Grab a timetable from the visitor centre or check times at bus stops.

Other accommodation options at Tidal River include safari-style wilderness retreats, self-contained riverside cabins and huts and lodges for big groups. These mostly sit between the two camping areas and are often booked a year or more in advance.

Pennicott Wilderness Journeys (promcruises.com.au) has amazing yellow amphibious boats. The daily 2.5 hour Wilsons Prom cruise explores the island and inlets, including the eerie facade of Skull Rock. It has an office at Tidal River.

CULTURE VULTURE

The gorgeous Tidal River Open Air Cinema has been operating here for more than 50 years, playing everything from vintage films and art-house classics to blockbusters. The cinema now has a tarpaulin cover, permanent screen, 200 sling-type deck chairs, lush grass and a kiosk selling popcorn and choc-tops (of course). Adult-size beanbags are also available for hire. It runs from 26 December through to end-January, and then for two or three nights on weekends and weeknights until after Easter.

WILDLIFE WATCH

Wallabies, wombats, emus and crimson rosellas are common at Tidal River and you might see the odd snake too. The

wombats are cute but they're hungry critters and have been known to tear through tents to get to food. Best to keep it hidden in eskies or your vehicle. The crimson rosellas are equally cheeky and think nothing of pinching food from your hand.

Victoria's largest marine protected area is found in the water off Norman Beach. Snorkellers and scuba-divers will spot red velvetfish, eastern blue groper, fan-shaped Georgian corals, sea-tulips, lace corals and, for the lucky few, the rare weedy seadragon.

STEP IT UP

Do a twirl on the 558-metre summit of Mt Oberon and you'll see Tidal River's winding journey to Bass Strait and a spectacular panorama of forests, mountains, beaches and offshore islands. Mt Oberon Summit walk is a 6.8 kilometre return hike (allow two hours) that starts at Telegraph Saddle carpark. During peak holidays and summer weekends, the carpark closes and the road is barricaded but you can catch a shuttle bus to the carpark from Tidal River.

The Southern Prom Circuit is a three-day, two-night trail traversing lush fern gullies, golden beaches, secluded coves, temperate rainforests and mountain saddles. The loop starts at Telegraph Saddle carpark and continues 10.3 kilometres (3 hours) to Sealers Cove for the first night, then 13.6 kilometres (4.5 hours) to Waterloo Bay for the second night, then another 12 kilometres (4.5 hours) back to Telegraph Saddle carpark. For a more laidback itinerary,

you can add an extra night at beautiful Refuge Cove, between Sealers Cove and Little Waterloo Bay. Adventurous families can hike into Sealers Cove from Telegraph Saddle carpark for an overnighter then return on the same track (my six and nine-year-old did it no problem). Double the timings above with kids. There are pit-toilets along the way but everything else – camping equipment, food, water, cooking gear, first-aid, etc – needs to be carried in.

Another overnight option is the walk direct to South East Point (Wilsons Promontory) Lightstation, which sits windblown and moody on the southern tip of mainland Australia overlooking Bass Strait. It is accessible on foot only, which accentuates the remoteness. The 19.1 kilometres (one-way) from Tidal River (allow six hours one way) follows the southern route of the Southern Prom Circuit (*see* above). Stay in a cottage or shared accommodation, then hike back the next day.

Visitors booked on any of the overnight hikes at the national park must sign-in at the visitor centre before setting out.

AND ANOTHER THING

During most of the year, the campsites are unallocated and work on a first-come, first-served basis. A ballot is held for bookings for the five weeks from Christmas until late January and you'll have to contend with an allocated spot. Applications are open between 1 and 15 July. Advance bookings (and minimum stays) are required for Labour Day weekend (Mar), Easter weekend and Melbourne Cup weekend (Nov).

You'll need to check in at Tidal River Visitor Centre (on Ring Rd adjacent to the main campground) to pay for park and camping permits and book overnight hikes. The staff here really know their stuff. It's open daily, 8.30am–4.30pm. Check notices outside the centre when arriving after hours.

ALTERNATIVES

If you miss out on spots in the national park, The Stockyards is a small bush campground 30 kilometres north of Tidal River near the national park entrance. It has 20 unpowered campsites, a toilet and shower block and picnic tables. It is not on the beach but Whisky Beach is nearby.

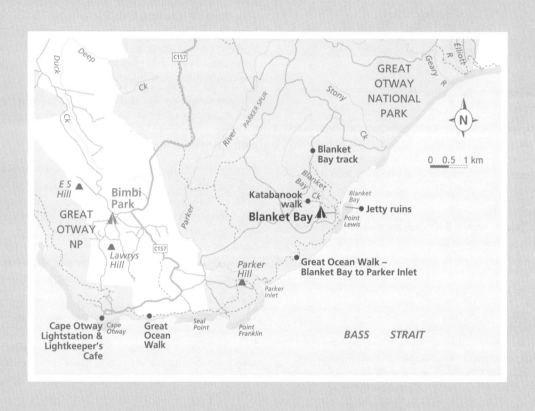

Bush camping on a reef-protected beach, backed by a forest of koalas.

Blanket Bay

Great Otway National Park, Vic

ACTIVITIES

FACILITIES

Some call it grunting, others call it purring ... very heavy purring. However you hear it, the eclectic sounds of the koalas in the eucalypts around this campground at night always raises an eyebrow, if not the hairs on the back of your neck. Fortunately, they're as cute as pie by day, and seeing them wandering on all fours on the dirt roads around Blanket Bay, or gently swaying in the leafy branches above, is one of the privileges of camping here.

Blanket Bay is located on the eastern coast of Great Otway National Park, on the traditional land of the Gunditjmara people and the Gadubanud people before them. It stretches from the surf town of Torquay, along the world-famous Great Ocean Road and up through the magnificent Otways hinterland. The park's natural wonders include wind-whipped rocky headlands, a wavering blue coastline, picturesque waterfalls and lofty scented rainforests. The coastline at Blanket Bay is backed by a huge tract of manna gum – tall eucalypts recognised by the streaky bark that peels off their lower trunk and the tasty thin green leaves favoured by our aforementioned furry friends.

Sheltered amongst this beautiful wooded area, just 10 metres from the beach, is brilliant Blanket Bay campground. While naturalists can appreciate the wildlife, the spring wildflowers and criss-crossing hinterland trails, swimmers, snorkellers and rock-poolers will take full advantage of a beach protected by a rocky intertidal reef. Lying in the shallows, exploring the seaweedy depths and adventuring along the rugged rocks north to Blanket Bay Creek inlet is all part of the fun.

The campground is super popular and needs to be booked well ahead (*see* p. 84). It has 22 unpowered campsites; 12 for tents only, and 10 suitable for tents, campervans and camper-trailers. The sites are in bush clearings with hard dirt and gravel floors. They vary in size from the biggest 19x6 metres (site number 1) to a cosy 4x5 metre site (number 14), but all sites have a maximum of six people and one vehicle. (Additional cars can be parked in the day-use carpark). Sites 1–8 are at the rear of the campground, away from the cooking areas, with more privacy. Sites 12 and 15–18 are near the picnic shelter. These sites, along with sites 19–22 are also close to the steps leading downhill to the beach. Some of these sites have ocean vistas. You can choose which site when booking online. Facilities are basic but include:

- Five drop-toilets
- Communal fireplaces
- Tank water
- A basin for washing-up
- Picnic tables
- Boat launching area

You'll need to BYO firewood for the three communal fireplaces – a sure-fire way to get to know fellow campers. As the embers die down, turn your attention to the night sky for a sea of stars.

There is a separate designated camping area at Blanket Bay for users of the Great Ocean Walk (*see* p. 84).

CATEGORIES

Family, Nature, Wi-Fi-Free, No Dogs, Boomers, Nomads

GO DO IT

WHO   Parks Victoria Information Centre; 13 1963;
parks.vic.gov.au

WHERE   Blanket Bay Campground, Great Otway National
Park, 233km south-west of Melbourne, Vic.

ACCESS From the Great Ocean Road, 20km west of Apollo
Bay, take Cape Otway Lighthouse Rd for about
9km and follow the signs onto Blanket Bay Rd for
6km. This narrow gravel road is 2WD accessible
but you'll need to take extra care after heavy rain.
The campground is at the end past the turn-off to
the day-use carpark.

WHAT ELSE?

Campers can bite off small chunks of the Great Ocean Walk
(*see* Step it up) direct from the campground. The signed and
shaded Katabanook walk connects with the Blanket Bay
track that continues north towards Elliot River. The signed
3.5-kilometre walk to Parker Inlet (allow 90 minutes one-
way) follows the track south-west. You're almost guaranteed
to spot koalas on both these walks.

About 60 kilometres north of the campground, Otway Fly
Treetops Adventures (otwayfly.com.au) features a 600-metre
walkway that ascends 25 metres into a beautiful, sweet-
scented, cool-temperate rainforest. It's a remnant from
Gondwana days when dinosaurs roamed the Earth and is
very worthwhile, especially for families.

CULTURE VULTURE

Remains of the 1880s jetty that was built to handle supplies
headed to the Cape Otway Lightstation (lightstation.com) can
still be seen at Blanket Bay at low tide. The Lightstation,
10 kilometres south-west, is the oldest surviving lighthouse
on the Australian mainland. Built in 1848, it had a pivotal
role in assisting ships – often occupied by 19th-century
migrants, who had spent months travelling to Australia – on
their course to land along the treacherous Shipwreck Coast.
It's open daily for visitors and the Lightkeeper's Cafe means
you can have a coffee and eat local produce, while gazing at
the lighthouse and the coast.

WILDLIFE WATCH

Koalas are the star-players but you'll also see possums and
wallabies (who might try to snack on your food, so keep it
hidden). Little blue-tailed wrens flit around the bush and
rosellas soar through the trees. If you're lucky, you might
glimpse an echidna shuffling through the undergrowth.

STEP IT UP

The campground is on the route of the 8-day, 100-kilometre
Great Ocean Walk (greatoceanwalk.com.au), which
extends along coastal heathlands, estuaries, clifftops and
beaches between Apollo Bay and the Twelve Apostles near
Princetown. If you're up for the walk, it has some cracking
oceanfront campsites, including a designated camping area
at Blanket Bay.

AND ANOTHER THING

This is a popular spot. Advance online bookings apply for
Easter, Labour Day weekend (March) and Christmas peak
periods. Check the website: parks.vic.gov.au for release dates,
mark it in your diary, then scramble for a first-in, best-
dressed booking.

Don't forget to bring your own drinking water and firewood.

ALTERNATIVES

Bimbi Park (bimbipark.com.au) on the road to Cape
Otway Lightstation is a bush-setting campground, with
tent sites, various cabin styles, including eco-cabins,
good amenities, pony rides, a rock-climbing tower, mini
golf and a playground.

For a nearby surfer-cool campground experience, head
to Johanna Beach (*see* p. 85). To find your zen in a
rainforest setting try The Source (*see* p. 89).

A wild and windswept coastal campsite close to surf, lighthouses and tales of shipwreck.

Johanna Beach

Great Otway National Park, Vic

MAP ON PAGE 86

ACTIVITIES

FACILITIES

At Cape Otway Lightstation (*see* p. 87), half an hour's drive from Johanna Beach, salty looking types with the sea in their bones, regale visitors with stories of the Shipwreck Coast, how at least 700 shipwrecked vessels have gone down in these dangerous waters and how only 240 of them have ever been discovered. Stunning Johanna Beach, just a sand dune or two from the campground, was named for a boat shipwrecked here in the early 1800s. It's a fitting tale for a wild and remote place on its knees to the elements, a mood amplified by the fact that we are the only campers here in winter.

When you think of camping along the Great Ocean Road, this is the kind of scene that comes to mind. Its low-key approach and limited facilities are outweighed by the dramatic locale. Twenty-five well-spaced and fastidiously kept grassy campsites are set in a sheltered hinterland of native shrubs and coastal vegetation and in an open space that edges onto farming land. The sites don't have beach views, but there's a picnic table on the rise before the sand dunes where you can see the ocean while munching on lunch.

Facilities are limited: there are non-flushing toilets, no showers and campers will need to bring their own drinking water. Pet owners will be chuffed that dogs are allowed on leash here, a rarity in a national park.

The beach, with a roar that can either lull you to sleep or keep you wide-eyed at night, is just beyond the bush-covered dunes. It's unpatrolled and off the beaten track. Chances are, campers will mostly mingle with the surfers who come here, as Johanna Beach's west-facing breaks are legendary (*see* p. 87), but it's not for the inexperienced. In summer, the surf scene is a drawcard – think boards strapped to rooftops, groups of mates and tinny music.

For non-surfers, the 3.5-kilometre beach is an explorer's paradise, with crabs busy in the rock pools at low tide, sand cliffs hiding nesting birds and the Johanna River inlet, primed for little people water play and beach cricket.

About 400 metres from the adjoining day visitor area, north-west of the campground, Joanna Beach Great Ocean Walk campground, for hike-in campers only, has rocking views. There are eight sites. Three of them, on the rough sloping ground near a little information shelter, have views stretching right down the beach so you can wake up, check the surf conditions, and go back to bed if necessary. The other five are tucked into the bush. Even if you can't camp here, it's a little eyrie worth hiking to.

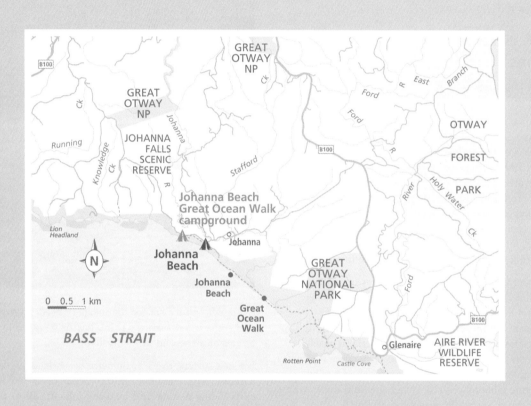

CATEGORIES

Young Travellers, Dog-Lovers, Family, Nature, Wi-Fi-Free, Boomers, Nomads

GO DO IT

WHO   Parks Victoria Information Centre; 13 1963; parks.vic.gov.au

WHERE   Old Coach Rd, off the Great Ocean Road, near Glenaire, Vic.

ACCESS It's a 3-hour drive from Melbourne, via the direct inland route through Colac. Alternatively, it's a 4-hour drive from Melbourne via the scenic Great Ocean Road. From here turn onto Red Johanna Rd, after 5km turn left onto Old Coach Rd. The campground is 500m along.

WHAT ELSE?

This is a good surf (*see* Surf) and surf-fishing beach for experienced fishing enthusiasts (the waves are serious here). Try your hand at catching a mullet or salmon for dinner.

Otway Fly Treetops Adventures (otwayfly.com.au) features a 600-metre walkway that ascends 25 metres into a beautiful, sweet-scented, cool-temperate rainforest, a remnant from Gondwana days when dinosaurs roamed the Earth. It's very worthwhile, especially for families.

CULTURE VULTURE

Cape Otway Lightstation (lightstation.com) is the oldest surviving lighthouse on the Australian mainland. Built in 1848, it had a pivotal role in assisting ships – often occupied by 19th-century migrants, who had spent months travelling to Australia – on their course to land along the treacherous Shipwreck Coast. It's open daily for visitors and the Lightkeeper's Cafe means you can have a coffee and eat local produce, while gazing at the lighthouse and the coast.

STEP IT UP

The campground is on the route of the 8-day, 100-kilometre Great Ocean Walk (greatoceanwalk.com.au), which extends along coast heathlands, estuaries, clifftops and beaches between Apollo Bay and the Twelve Apostles near Princetown.

AND ANOTHER THING

Johanna is an unpatrolled beach and the waves are suited to experienced surfers only – so take heed. The nearest patrolled beach is 26 kilometres away in Apollo Bay.

SURF

According to beachsafe.org.au, Johanna Beach is the best-known surfing location west of Cape Otway, with famous left- and right-breaks. The beach faces south-west and receives waves averaging 1.5 metres. The most noticeable features of the surf zone are the distinct bar (250m wide) and deep rip channels (spaced every 350m), forming eight bar-rip systems, each capable of holding waves from 1 to 3 metres. The result is the production of bars with deep channels to either side, forming left- and right-hand breaks off each bar. Because the channels are deep, the beach can hold relatively high, surfable waves before closing out.

ALTERNATIVES

Bimbi Park (bimbipark.com.au) on the road to Cape Otway Lightstation is a bush-setting campground, with tent sites, various cabin styles, including eco-cabins, good amenities, pony rides, a rock-climbing tower, mini golf and a playground. For a nearby national park experience, head to Blanket Bay (*see* p. 83).

South-west of Lorne on the Great Ocean Road, Cumberland River Holiday Park (cumberlandriver.com.au) is a scenic spot, with tent and campervan sites and cabins, backing onto a magnificent tree-topped cliff-face.

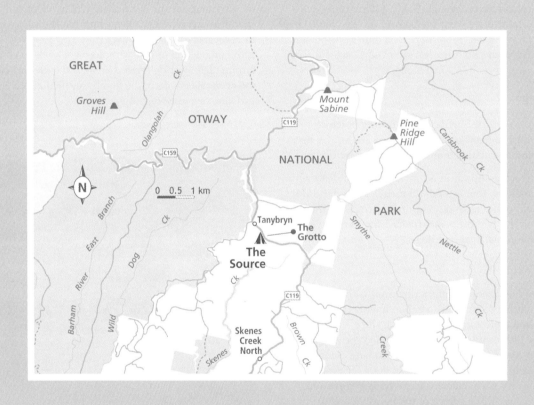

A barefoot rainforest immersion with waterfalls, wildlife, meditation and the sweet smell of eucalypt in the air.

The Source

Great Otway National Park, Vic

ACTIVITIES

FACILITIES

Great Otway National Park is rainforest meets ocean – a verdant hinterland of fern-filled rainforest, blue-tinted mountains and cascading waterfalls that meet wave-washed beaches and rugged rocky sea cliffs. It is home to some of Victoria's most popular beachside getaways and to tourist icons, including the Great Ocean Road and Great Ocean Walk, both of which take advantage of the magnificent Bass Strait views.

In the hilly hinterland, about 15 kilometres behind the beachside enclave of Apollo Bay, The Source is a private campground on an exceptionally beautiful property boasting 300 acres of rainforest. Waking here is to breathe pristine eucalypt-scented air, listen to birdsong, spot wildlife and revel in a slice of nature that feels nurtured and cherished. There's something very holistic about it.

The eight campsites – with names including The Meadows, Sunset and The Sanctuary, are dotted around the property and mostly located in open native-grass clearings that back onto rainforest. There's plenty of room, with each site hosting up to 20 people. There are no facilities, which plays to the natural immersion, so it's essential to bring your own camp toilet. Owners Vita and Fabian, who commute from Melbourne, allocate the best campsite according to group size and needs (but if you prefer a certain site, you can request it).

We stayed in the Secret Garden, a cosy spot hidden in the forest on the edge of a clearing. It has a fire-pit, like all the sites, where campfire stories took on magical and mystical themes to suit the misty, moody and ethereal surrounds. Secret Garden is also close to The Grotto walk. This mossy boardwalk wends through a forest of towering ferns and thick-trunked old-growth mountain ash and myrtle beech trees.

It then extends over a little bridge, with a babbling brook below, to the base of a beautiful 20 metre high amphitheatre of rocks, ferns, eucalypt trunks and trickling water. (So serene is this place, I did a sound recording for future meditative purposes). The Grotto is one of three private waterfalls on the property, the highest of which reaches 30 metres. Easily navigable and well-maintained routes extend through the rainforest to all three. There's also a whimsical timber 'rainforest pavilion' bridging a tiny creek, where visitors can sip on thermos tea surrounded by chirruping frogs and the pitter-patter of water dripping on leaves.

Vita and Fabian also cater to campers without the kit. Visitors can pre-book camp chairs, a two-person pop-up tent (waterproof with black lining for sleep-ins) or a six-person dome tent (waterproof and windproof) with a side verandah and room enough to stand in. There's also a two-person eco-pod for hire (it looks like a glammed-up dog kennel).

CATEGORIES

Young Travellers, Dog-Lovers, Family, Nature, Wi-Fi-Free, Boomers, Nomads

GO DO IT

WHO   The Source; 0416 877 994;
        youcamp.com/view/the-source-otways

WHERE   1255 Skenes Creek Rd, Tanybryn, about 185km
        south-west of Melbourne in Great Otway National
        Park, Vic.

ACCESS From Apollo Bay, head east on Hardy St, then
        take the Great Ocean Rd for 6km before turning
        left onto Skenes Creed Rd for 12km. The property
        is on the left and is signed.

WHAT ELSE?

Forrest is 20 kilometres north of the campground; it's a quaint little town in the hills and a handy pit-stop. Forrest General Store is a cafe mostly, with great coffee and toasties, but it also sells essentials and gourmet produce, and has tourist information and a post office. Next door there's a bike hire shop.

For a more substantial shop, Apollo Bay, 18 kilometres south of the campground, has two supermarkets, take-away shops, pubs and Apollo Bay Bakery, known for its plump scallop pies.

Otway Fly Treetops Adventures (otwayfly.com.au), 28 kilometres west of the campground, features a 600-metre walkway that ascends 25 metres into a beautiful sweet-scented cool temperate rainforest, a remnant from Gondwana days when dinosaurs roamed the Earth.

Vita and Fabian offer wellness experiences in this slow traveller's paradise. Their Forest Bathing/Walking Meditation and Shamanic Drum Journey is a 'deeply nourishing, powerful and transformational' immersion in the rainforest surrounds. The focus is on tapping into spiritual and energetic levels to create positive change.

CULTURE VULTURE

Cape Otway Lightstation (lightstation.com), 50 kilometres south-west of The Source, is the oldest surviving lighthouse on the Australian mainland. Built in 1848 it has had a pivotal role in assisting ships – often occupied by 19th-century migrants, who had spent months travelling to

Australia by ship – on their course to land along the treacherous Shipwreck Coast. It's open daily for visitors and the Lightkeeper's Cafe means you can have a coffee and eat local produce, while gazing at the lighthouse and the coast.

AND ANOTHER THING

A 4WD is essential in wet weather conditions.

Vita and Fabian ask that guests make a conscientious effort to leave no trace on departure.

Guests can pre-order firewood (one-day's supply is about $30) so that it is all ready for you next to the fire-pit. BYO marshmallows.

Barry White is The Source's resident koala. He can be spotted up close at the cottages near the front gate.

The property has a five-person cottage and a six-person homestead that are available for holiday rentals.

ALTERNATIVES

There are plenty of great campgrounds in the Great Otway National Park, including at Johanna Beach (*see* p. 85) and Blanket Bay (*see* p. 83).

South-west of Lorne on the Great Ocean Road, Cumberland River Holiday Park (cumberlandriver.com.au) is a scenic spot backing onto a magnificent tree-topped cliff-face.

The Source – Battersbys

A small, lush national park oasis overlooking the Glenelg River.

Battersbys

Lower Glenelg National Park, Vic

MAP ON PAGE 92

ACTIVITIES

FACILITIES

'Ngatanway wartee pa kakay teen Gunditjmara mirring', reads the rusted metal sign on the dirt road entry to this campsite – 'Welcome brothers and sisters to Gunditjmara country'. Battersbys (or Bocara as it's known to Gunditjmara people) makes you feel that the only people to have been here are the Traditional Owners of the land and a lucky camper or two, myself included. This really is an untouched natural bush oasis.

The Glenelg River rises in Gariwerd (Grampian) Ranges and wends its 400-kilometre path through Lower Glenelg National Park to the sea at nearby Nelson. The Lower Glenelg part of the river is where it's at its botanic finest, a native garden of stringybarks, blackwoods and banksias, with bountiful wildlife to match.

Battersbys campground takes full advantage of this ancient scenery. It has just two vehicle-based campsites and an unmarked grassy area for walk-ins, but it's best-used by kayak-based campers on the Glenelg River Canoe Trail (*see* p. 96), a 75-kilometre meander, via 17 riverside campgrounds, from the rural town of Dartmoor to the coastal port of Nelson (one of them is Pattersons, *see* p. 95). Battersbys' two campsites are hemmed in by shady trees

and thick bush on three sides and the river on the other. Facilities include:

• A toilet
• Fire-pit
• Picnic tables

Like all of the campgrounds on the Lower Glenelg, Battersbys has a pretty little wooden jetty, two in fact, where fisherpersons languidly sit to set a line and boaters come and go as the tidal waters flow up and down. The jetties are also swimmer-friendly. Launching yourself into the beautifully clear water from these characteristic wooden structures helps to avoid the thick silty black mud typical along the shorelines. But I have to warn you, without a ladder it's hard to climb back out once you're in the water, without calling on inner-core strength you never knew you had. If there's no ladder, accept, like I did that knee-high socks of mud might play a part in your getting wet.

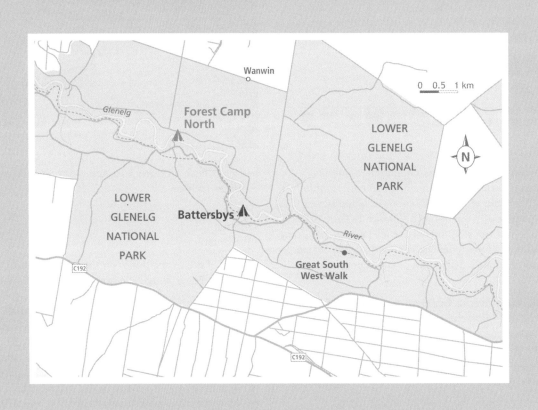

CATEGORIES:

Family, Nature, Wi-Fi-Free

GO DO IT

WHO — Parks Victoria Information Centre; 13 1963; parks.vic.gov.au

WHERE — Lower Glenelg National Park is in south-west Vic adjoining the SA border, about 420km from Melbourne and 490km from Adelaide.

ACCESS — The 300m access track to Battersbys is signposted off Glenelg Dr some 16km east of North Nelson Track.

WHAT ELSE?

Landlubbers won't be short on exploring. A pretty little bridge over a narrow dirt track marks part of the Great South West Walk, a 252-kilometre loop that begins and ends in Portland, traversing a dozen or so campsites on its way. A billboard in the shelter of the walk-in campsite shares details of the next stage of the walk, the 13 kilometres to Pattersons campground (*see* p. 95).

About 30 kilometres north-west, Princess Margaret Rose Cave is a resplendent limestone formation – complete with stalactites and stalagmites. It is worth a tour if you can forgive the gift shop with its 1950s-style tea-towels and blokish Aussie paraphernalia. It's accessible by road from Battersbys. If you're on the Glenelg River Canoe Trail (*see* p. 96), there's a titular jetty for canoes to tie up to and it's only 300 metres from the river up a little path. There's also a 3.3-kilometre walk from Laslett's campground, one of the last stops on the Canoe Trail.

CULTURE VULTURE

If you're travelling with kids, get your hands on Trace Balla's award-winning children's book *Rivertime*. It's a beautifully illustrated coming-of-age story about a 10-year-old boy who heads off on a canoe trip down the Glenelg with his bird-watching uncle. After a reluctant start, he begins to find a connection with the land, its creatures and, ultimately, his inner-self.

WILDLIFE WATCH

It's a who's who of Australian birds and animals, including kangaroos, emus, wallabies and kookaburras, alongside lesser-known wrens, azure kingfishers, platypus and potoroos. You can spot koalas in trees along the river, and hear them at night.

AND ANOTHER THING

Despite the minimal number of campsites, the facilities also cater to day-use visitors.

ALTERNATIVES

There are plenty of great campgrounds in Lower Glenelg National Park, including nine vehicle-based and seven canoe-access or hike-in sites. They're mostly hidden away in bushland on the riverbank, with amenities including tank rain water, fire-pits and pit-toilets. Forest Camp North and Hutchessons are good alternatives. Also, Pattersons (*see* p. 95).

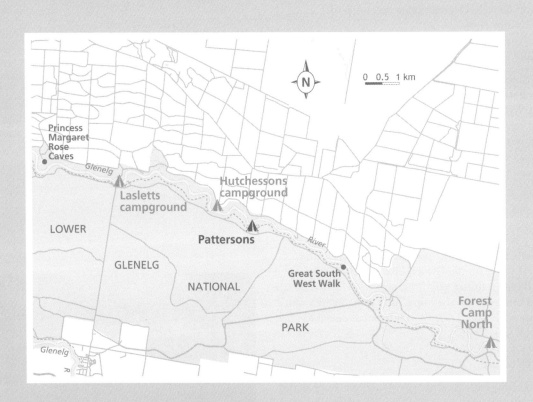

Princess
Margaret
Rose
Caves

Glenelg

Hutchessons
campground

Lasletts
campground

LOWER

Pattersons

GLENELG

River

NATIONAL

Great South
West Walk

PARK

Glenelg
R

Forest
Camp
North

N

0   0.5   1 km

An idyllic riverside locale with scout huts and kangaroos on the Glenelg River Canoe Trail.

Pattersons

Lower Glenelg National Park, Vic

ACTIVITIES

FACILITIES

In this book, I've mainly stuck to campgrounds that are accessible in a 2WD, if not a 4WD, but this river idyll is one of the exceptions I had to make. The campground, sitting pretty on a bend in the Lower Glenelg River, is part of the Glenelg River Canoe Trail (*see* p. 96) and has no road access. It is ideally accessed via a canoe, kayak, tube – or even snorkel and flippers if you're really keen – but you can also hike in (*see.* 96).

Whichever way you get here, the scenery makes it worthwhile. Patersons's characteristic scout huts, oversized shade trees, wooden jetty and idyllic riverside locale are the stuff of children's literature. If Enid Blyton had ever wanted an Australian setting for a *Famous Five* novel, Pattersons would be a contender.

The Canoe Trail is a scenic 75-kilometre meander from the rural town of Dartmoor to the coastal port of Nelson along the Glenelg River on the Victorian–South Australian border. It's a four-day trip from end to end, but it can be shortened by beginning further downstream. The only inhibiter for longer journeys is the fact the campgrounds are limited to one-night-only stays. There are 17 campgrounds along the trail, but only seven of them are set aside for canoes-only (Pattersons is the fifth of these). The lack of road access means it's likely you'll have the place to yourself. And with pre-bookings essential for Canoe Trail planning, you're unlikely to have anyone pull-up last-minute.

I've done this trip twice – once with family and again with friends. Both times we did three nights and started at Battersbys (*see* p. 91) in the Lower Glenelg River section.

The scenery in this part of the park is beautiful and dramatic, with chalky white limestone cliffs fringing the wide bends on one side and banksia and blackwood branches tickling the current on the other. Drifting along on the current to a soundtrack of kookaburras, crickets and the trickle of water is slow travel at its finest.

The campground extends along the left-hand side (heading downstream) of a wide section of the river. With mostly mature eucalypts and native trees, it's open to a grassy flat expanse, backed by white cliffs.

On my first trip here, the three green door-less corrugated iron scout huts with wooden floors were a life-saver in unexpected rain. The second time, when the sun shone, they served as cubbies for the kids to play in. They form an amphitheatre around a fire-pit, which has little log seats suited to sipping hot tea around the fire. Facilities include:

- Two long picnic tables sitting end-to-end that cater to festive group meals
- A water tank
- A compost toilet in a private spot up the far end of the campground

Shaded by an old gum tree, the jetty is a lovely launchpad for river swims and a peaceful place to throw a line in. Unlike most of the Canoe Trail campgrounds, you can also pull your canoes up onto the riverbank here, which helps with unpacking.

CATEGORIES

Family, Nature, Wi-Fi-Free, No Dogs

GO DO IT

WHO   Parks Victoria Information Centre; 13 1963;
        parks.vic.gov.au
WHERE   Lower Glenelg National Park is in south-west
        Vic adjoining the SA border, about 420km from
        Melbourne and 490km from Adelaide.
ACCESS The major access roads into the national park are
        the Portland–Nelson Rd and Wanwin Rd. The
        300m access track to Battersbys where we started
        the Glenelg River Canoe Trail is signposted off
        Glenelg Dr some 16km east of North Nelson
        track. It's about 14km paddling from Battersbys
        to Pattersons.

WHAT ELSE?

About 30 kilometres north-west, Princess Margaret Rose
Cave is a resplendent limestone formation complete with
stalactites and stalagmites. It is worth a tour if you can
forgive the gift shop with its 1950s-style tea-towels and
blokish Aussie paraphernalia. It's accessible by road from
Battersbys (see p. 91). If you're on the Canoe Trail (see Glenelg
River Canoe Trail), it's 17 kilometres downstream. There's a
titular jetty for canoes to tie up to and it's only 300 metres
from the river up a little path. There's also a 3.3-kilometre
walk from Laslett's campground, one of the last stops on the
Canoe Trail.

WILDLIFE WATCH

Keep your eyes open for the Glenelg's swimming wallabies.
I thought this was an outrageous bush myth, but two
fishermen in the site next to us spotted what they thought
was a dog in the water, but on closer inspection was a wallaby
having a little freshen up as the sun was setting.

STEP IT UP

The Great South West Walk (greatsouthewestwalk.com), a
252-kilometre trail beginning and ending in Portland, does
pass near this campground, so hiking here, and carrying all
your stuff in, is another option.

AND ANOTHER THING

Mind you tie the canoes up properly. We had to send a search
party out when one of ours disappeared downstream.

GLENELG RIVER CANOE TRAIL

With seven of the Lower Glenelg's 17 campgrounds set aside
for canoe-access only, you'll see plenty of canoers, their rigs
piled high with camping gear. The highlight when we canoed
was the enormous white limestone cliffs that rise up on
either side of the river, a result of the water having carved
out the rock over 20 million years to create a mesmerising
gorge. If a canoe trip does float your boat, canoes can be
hired from the nearby towns of Dartmoor, Winnap or Nelson.
Many hire shops also offer drop-off and pick-up at various
points along the river, depending on your itinerary. We are
grateful to the lovely local couple – Ross and Marg – who
own Paestan Canoe Hire (canoehire.com.au), where you can
stay overnight in a bunkhouse, or camp on the property, and
be up and on the river nice and early. If you're keen to know
more about the Canoe Trail, the aforementioned website
has a link to an amateur movie my friend and travel guru
Michael Cameron made of one of our trips down the Glenelg.
It will give you a good idea of what to expect. The website:
nelsoncanoehire.com.au is another good source of info.

ALTERNATIVES

There are plenty of great campsites in Lower Glenelg
National Park, including nine vehicle-based and seven
canoe-access or walk-in sites. They're mostly hidden
away in bushland on the riverbank, with amenities
including tank rain water, fire-pits and drop-toilets.
Forest Camp North and Hutchessons are good
alternatives. Batterbys is my other pick (see p. 91).

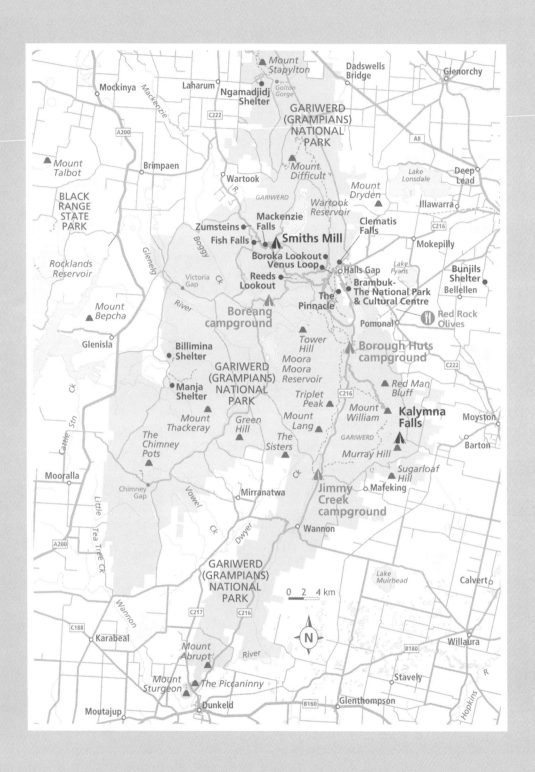

Free bush camping with walks and waterfalls on the doorstep.

Kalymna Falls

Gariwerd (Grampians National Park), Vic

ACTIVITIES

FACILITIES

Gariwerd (Grampians National Park) is a series of rugged and ridge-backed sandstone mountains that rise unexpectedly from the surrounding flat and largely treeless agricultural plains, like a sleeping giant. Its eponymous national park, home to dense forests, rocky outcrops, wildflowers, waterways and eye-popping panoramas, has made it one of Victoria's most popular destinations; it's a place to bushwalk, hike, rock-climb and generally get into nature, with wineries and produce stores thrown in for good measure.

The park is big and it takes time to get around to all corners so it's best to do your homework on an activity, then pick the most proximate of the dozen or so campgrounds. That said, it's hard to beat tiny Kalymna Falls campground for a remote, free bush-immersion and you'd do well to make it your starting point for activities. It's in the east of the park on an unsealed road that ends at the base of the spectacular Mt William range, boasting the park's highest peak, Mt William at 1167 metres.

From the sealed section of Waterhole Road, travelling at 50km/h, it takes about 20 minutes to get to the campground in dry conditions (the road, particularly at the end, does get slippery when wet so avoid in a 2WD). The jagged rocky escarpment, which rises beyond the canopy of the campsite's trees is the dramatic drawcard – it's either mysteriously covered in passing cloud or standing glorious against a blue sky.

The tiny campground has six sites, all sitting just off the main road and joined by a sweet little trail through the bush. The campsites are big enough for two small tents and each site has a roadside carpark. Number 1 is closest to the road – meaning easier access to gear, but none of them are more than a few metres away. If I had to pick, number 5 is the least favourable as it is furthest from the road. Even so, there's enough glorious native bush, complete with beautiful flowering bottle brush trees, to wrap each space in its own private bush paradise.

A trail through the bush leads campers to a single toilet in a corrugated-iron shed. Over the road and down near the tranquil creek, there's a little picnic area. It has two picnic tables and a metal fire-ring, which, according to the ranger, was put there by accident. That's likely why you'll see conflicting notices about whether fires are allowed, but check with the rangers. Certainly, the remains of fires lit in the dry creek bed are a no-no, given recent bushfire seasons.

Also, straight from the ranger's mouth: the campsite has been free for three years, so it attracts more visitors than would otherwise be the case – given the limited sites and unsealed road access. To counter that, it gets just as much service and upkeep as a paid campground – the toilets are cleaned daily and rangers make regular appearances.

CATEGORIES

Young Travellers, Free, Family, Nature, Wi-Fi-Free, No Dogs, Boomers, Nomads

GO DO IT

WHO   Parks Victoria Information Centre; 13 1963; parks.vic.gov.au

WHERE Gariwerd (Grampians National Park) is about 270km north-west of Melbourne, Vic. Kalymna Falls is in the Pomonal region, in the east of the park.

ACCESS From Ararat-Halls Gap Rd, turn onto Waterhole Rd for 3.7km, then right onto Long Gully Rd for 1.3km, right onto Redman Rd for 750m, left onto unsealed Mitchell Rd for 10km and right onto Mount William Picnic Ground Rd for 1km.

WHAT ELSE?

The 1.5-kilometre walk to Kalymna Falls begins at the campground picnic area and follows a rough 4WD maintenance road, with the creek bed on your right-hand side. A sign showing 0.1km marks the smaller walking track down to the falls. On our visit, the falls were enough to wet the rocks, but after rain the water flows freely over the rocks and pummels the creek below sending mist into the air. It's about a one-hour return journey.

Gariwerd's (Grampians National Park) main town is Halls Gap, located in a scenic spot surrounded by a ridge of mountains. The town's architecture lacks character, but it's a functional hub, with eateries and ice-creameries, alongside stores selling all sorts of serious paraphernalia for hikers and essentials for campers. Think spare pegs, billies, frypans, batteries. From the grassy central playground area and carpark, there are some worthwhile easy walks, a taster for what's available elsewhere in the park. Venus Baths Loop is a 2.3 kilometre easy circuit to picturesque rockpools. Clematis Falls is a 2.4 kilometre return easy walk to a tranquil waterfall (best in winter and spring).

EAT IT

Red Rock Olives (redrockolives.com.au) on the Ararat-Halls Gap Rd has a charming farmgate cafe (open Thurs–Mon), serving antipasta platters laden with olives, fresh bread, cheese and charcuterie. Taste the olives and buy a bottle of EVOO for gourmet camp cooking.

FIRST PEOPLES KNOW-HOW

Known as Gariwerd, a name derived from either the local Jardwadjali or Djab Wurrung language, the national park has the largest number of significant and ancient Aboriginal rock-art paintings and shelters in southern Australia. Five rock-shelters are open to public viewing; Ngamadjidj, Gulgurn Manja, Billimina, Manja and Bunjils Shelter (Black Range Reserve, near Stawell). Pick up a copy of Aboriginal Culture of Gariwerd at Brambuk – The National Park & Cultural Centre – in Halls Gap.

WILDLIFE WATCH

There are plenty of wallabies bounding around the bush and the native flowering trees are a paradise for more than 200 species of birds, including little blue finches.

STEP IT UP

The maintenance road, which begins at the campground picnic area, is also the starting point for more strenuous walks (suited to experienced hikers), including the Mt William (Duwul) peak and the overnight Major Mitchell Plateau hike. Check in with Brambuk – The National Park & Cultural Centre – in Halls Gap, for maps, bookings and to log your details.

AND ANOTHER THING

Bring a hammer. The gravel in the campground is hard as rock and you'll need heft to get tent pegs in the ground.

ALTERNATIVES

The national park has 12 vehicle-based campgrounds, all with varying native scenery and basic amenities, including pit-toilets, fireplaces and picnic tables. The closest are Borough Huts (the biggest with 35 sites) and Jimmy Creek (one of only three with showers), but Smiths Mill (see p. 101) stands out.

Bush camping within easy reach of an iconic Gariwerd (Grampians) waterfall.

Smiths Mill

Gariwerd (Grampians National Park), Vic

MAP ON PAGE 98

ACTIVITIES

FACILITIES

If I had to choose my favourite Gariwerd (Grampians National Park) hang-out, it would be a toss-up between The Pinnacle and Mackenzie Falls (*see* p. 103). The Pinnacle is a panoramic lookout on a cliff-hanger rock that juts out at an unnerving angle into the blue yonder. From up here you can have an 'I'm the king of the world' moment looking out over western Victoria. Mackenzie Falls is a magnificent waterfall that cascades over sheer cliff-faces and rocky ledges to land in a gob-smackingly gorgeous waterhole at the bottom. Visitors can take it in from a viewpoint at the top, but the steep trail to the bottom, with little hook turns and lookouts, engenders a real sense of its height and power. It's the only Grampians waterfall guaranteed to run year-round, too.

What tips me towards Mackenzie Falls is its proximity to Smiths Mill campground. From the campground, you can access Mackenzie Falls by car on the 1 kilometre sealed main road or – even better – on a walk direct via unsealed Old Moss Road. The scenic wonder of the falls and the native bushland at Smiths Mill makes for a unique and special combination and the resident emus (*see* p. 103) are just a bonus.

Smiths Mill is the second biggest of the Gariwerd campgrounds, with 28 spacious non-powered sites in configurations suitable for tents, caravans and larger vehicles, and groups. It must get busy here with a maximum of six people per site, but on my visit at the start of summer

there were just a handful of other campers – and we were spread out so we hardly crossed paths.

The sites are delineated by pine-log stumps and are spread across a flat expanse of native grass studded with black-trunked eucalypts. Some of the sites have wooden picnic tables and fire-rings, others are close to the toilet block and shower, which is pretty quirky. It is in a roofless corrugated-iron room that looks like a water tank from a distance. Inside, a shiny silver bucket hangs from a hook, with a small shower head at the bottom. Campers can heat their own water (putting it in a black plastic bag for the day works) and pour it into the top of the bucket for an al fresco shower with trees and clouds for company.

Towards the rear of the campground, there are remnant saw mill artefacts dotted around and a bridge crossing the Millstream Creek, which burbles away in the background. It's a good place to throw a line in and, if you're lucky, spot a platypus.

Above One of the best hang-outs, Mackenzie Falls

CATEGORIES

Young Travellers, Family, Nature, Wi-Fi-Free, No Dogs, Boomers, Nomads

GO DO IT

WHO   Parks Victoria Information Centre; 13 1963; parks.vic.gov.au

WHERE   Gariwerd (Grampians National Park) is about 270km north-west of Melbourne, Vic. Smiths Mill is in the Zumsteins region, in the central part of the park.

ACCESS   From Halls Gap, head north-west on Grampians Rd for 1.3km, then turn left onto Mt Victory Rd for 17km, right onto Wartook Rd for 1km, then right onto Old Mill Rd for 350m where you'll see the campground.

WHAT ELSE?

Gariwerd's (Grampians National Park) main town is Halls Gap, located in a scenic spot surrounded by a ridge of mountains. The town's architecture lacks character, but it's a functional hub, with eateries and ice-creameries, alongside stores selling all sorts of serious paraphernalia for hikers and essentials for campers. Think spare pegs, billies, frypans, batteries. From the grassy central playground area and carpark, there are some worthwhile easy walks, a taster for what's available elsewhere in the park. Venus Baths Loop is a 2.3 kilometre easy circuit to picturesque rockpools. Clematis Falls is a 2.4 kilometre return easy walk to a tranquil waterfall (best in winter and spring).

There's something for everyone at Mackenzie Falls. The Lookout walk and the Broken Falls walk are 1.9-kilometres return and 500-metres return, respectively. They're wheelchair friendly and take in gorge and cascade views through shady stringybark forest. Stepping it up a notch, the Mackenzie Falls walk is a steep 2-kilometre descent down 264 stairs. Unfortunately, swimming is not permitted in the waterhole at the bottom. Settle instead for a refreshing water spray. Mackenzie River walk is for hardier walkers. It's a 7-kilometre return waterside rock-hop past Fish Falls (4km) to Zumsteins historic picnic area, which has a pretty boardwalk and old huts, a hangover from its days as a holiday retreat in the 1930s.

Nearby Boroka Lookout has two platforms for viewing Halls Gap valley, Mt William range and the farmland plains to the east. Reeds Lookout faces the southern Grampians and the Victoria Valley. Boroka is best for sunrises, and Reeds' picture-perfect sunsets are not to be missed.

The Pinnacle Lookout is about 20 kilometres south-east of the campground. It is accessible via an easy-to-medium 2.1-kilometre walk (allow 45 minutes) from Sundial carpark, a more challenging 2.1-kilometre climb (allow 90 minutes) through rocky terrain from Wonderland carpark, or a moderate 9-kilometre extended route (allow 5 hours return) from Halls Gap caravan park (via Wonderland carpark). Both routes pay off in the form of mesmeric views including Halls Gap, Lake Bellfield and the silhouetted distant Gariwerd (Grampians National Park) terrain.

CULTURE VULTURE

Smiths Mill gets its name from its former days when Horsham man Harold Smith's sawmill was here. It operated for about 20 years from the early 1930s and was one of a number of mills working in Gariwerd (Grampians National Park) before the national park was established in 1984. Only a few relics of the mill remain today, such as a rusty old set of wheels, but with the help of storyboard information and on-site signs, campers can read about the history and workings of the mill.

EAT IT

Grampians Grape Escape (grampiansgrapeescape.com.au) is a decades-old wine, food and music festival held annually in Halls Gap on the first weekend of May. Check out what's on offer from local producers and wine-makers, cruise the food trucks and sign-up for masterclasses and cooking demos.

FIRST PEOPLES KNOW-HOW

Known as Gariwerd, a name derived from either the local Jardwadjali or Djab Wurrung language, the Grampians has the largest number of significant and ancient Aboriginal rock-art paintings and shelters in southern Australia. Five rock-shelters are open to public viewing; Ngamadjidj, Gulgurn Manja, Billimina, Manja and Bunjils Shelter (Black Range Reserve, near Stawell). Pick up a copy of Aboriginal Culture of Gariwerd at Brambuk – The National Park & Cultural Centre – in Halls Gap.

WILDLIFE WATCH

Black-legged emus are nicely camouflaged in the bush at this campground, but you'll be sure to catch a glimpse of them, especially on the other side of the Millstream Creek. Also keep an eye out for platypus in the river at dawn and dusk and, up above, endangered black and red gang gang cockatoos. You'll hear them before you see them.

STEP IT UP

The new Grampians Peaks Trail is expected to be finished in 2021. According to Parks Victoria it will take inspiration from Tasmania's Three Capes Walk: a 'once-in-a-lifetime 13-day hike through the backbone of a mountain range famed for its dramatic scenery and Aboriginal heritage'.

ALTERNATIVES

The park has 12 vehicle-based campgrounds (and a handful of hike-ins), all with varying native scenery and basic amenities, including pit-toilets, fireplaces and picnic tables.

The closest is Boreang, on an unsealed road, but Kalymna Falls (*see* p. 99), in the east, stands out.

South Australia

Follow the wild and wondrous coastline, catch a ferry to Kangaroo Island or head inland to South Australia's wine country

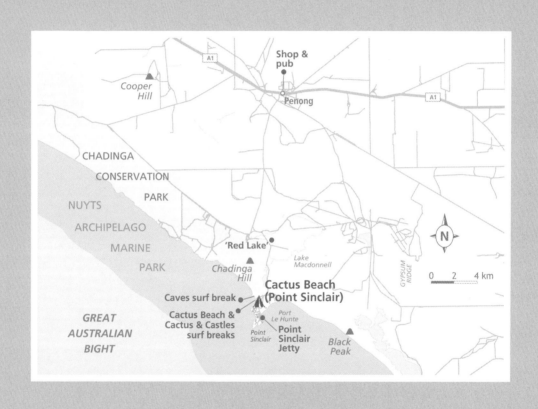

A remote campground with serious waves, big horizons and raw natural coastal beauty.

Cactus Beach (Point Sinclair)

Eyre Peninsula, SA

ACTIVITIES

FACILITIES

In the '70s surfers road-tripping across the Nullarbor Plain, their boards and tents occy-strapped to Holden rooftops, would stop at Cactus Beach to surf Cactus, Castles and Caves – some of the best left- and right-hand breaks in the country. There is plenty of reminiscing about these trips online, and the resounding sentiment of those who have returned more recently is that the place hasn't changed. Its barrel waves and crimson sunsets, its community of sun-kissed and salt-crusted surfers, its untouched arid and coastal landscapes still have a pulling power like no other.

If you're a surfer wanting to catch an iconic Aussie wave with an international reputation (*see* p. 108), a traveller looking to bare your soul to the coastal wilderness, or indeed a camper searching for an off-the-beaten track adventure, then Cactus Beach is for you.

Officially known as Sinclair Beach, Cactus is located near the eponymous beach on the Eyre Peninsula's Point Sinclair, an extremely remote part of Australia on the eastern side of the Great Australian Bight. It is accessed via a signed but unsealed road off the Nullarbor's Eyre Highway (A1). The 20-minute drive from the highway to the campground is pretty special (*see* p. 108), but it's no match for the view on arrival at the campground. A vast brilliant blue ocean stretches the length of the horizon and rocky cliffs, white quartz sands and hardy native heath populates the foreground. It is wild, raw and outrageously beautiful.

The campground's 30 or so designated campsites sit behind the sand dunes amid clumps of low-lying coastal bush with clear ocean views. The sites are unpowered, and it's basic camping, but you'll find some thoughtful and nicely tended-to perks. A rustic open-air A-framed corrugate shelter with internal tree trunk columns sits towards the rear of the camping area. It is surfer-cool with bumper stickers slapped on the inner walls and homemade signage. There is space for food prep (without a barbecue so you'll need to BYO a gas cooker), a washing-up area and a separate sink for clothes washing. Other facilities include:

• Bore-water showers (more lukewarm than hot) but BYO drinking water
• Flushing toilets (in an outhouse with a half-rock wall and a pitched roof)
• Communal campfires with stone and wood wind breaks
• A clothes line

The 550-hectare property is privately owned and operated by Ronnie Gates who was one of those who arrived in the 1970s. Difference is, he never left and eventually bought the property in the mid '80s. He has lived on the property ever since (along with a small community of long-term surfers) and sees to its day-to-day running. He collects the camp fees (you'll need cash), sweeps out the fireplaces each day, replenishes the firewood (although it's in short supply so bring your own if you can) and empties the rubbish bins daily. He's also good for a story or two.

The beach is just over the dunes via a boardwalk.

Previous On the Yorke Peninsula, Hillocks Drive campground's wild coastline includes rocky wave-washed swimming holes (*see* p. 109)

CATEGORIES

Young Travellers, Dog-Lovers, Family, Nature, Wi-Fi-Free, Boomers, Nomads

GO DO IT

WHO   Point Sinclair campground; (08) 8625 1036; no website.

WHERE   Off the Nullarbor along the Eyre Hwy, 21km south of Penong, 71km west of Ceduna and 870km north-west of Adelaide, SA.

ACCESS   The Point Sinclair Rd turn-off south to Cactus Beach is well signposted at Penong near the school. The 20km road is unsealed but easily done in a 2WD. Allow 20 minutes one-way, more if you stop to admire the pink lake (*see* below).

WHAT ELSE?

If you're not a surfer, Cactus Beach is an excellent spot for chilling with the sand between your toes. A seat overlooking the surf is a good place to meditate and check out the action. At the southern end of the beach there are some scenic cliffs and rock pools, perfect for paddling in at low tide.

Point Sinclair juts into the ocean south of the campground. On its east coast, tucked into a sheltered curve of Port Le Hunte, the Port Sinclair Jetty stretches 190 metres into the big blue. The former shipping jetty now provides a pleasant place to stroll and throw a line in. There is a place to launch boats on the beach here, plus picnic tables, toilets and a swimming enclosure so you can swim without fear of great white sharks. It's 1.8 kilometres from the campground (allow 20 minutes on foot).

Penong has a pub, shop and garage. The nearest supermarket is in Ceduna, 71 kilometres east.

The unsealed road from Penong to Cactus Beach has an unexpected surprise: Lake McDonnell's 'Red Lake' is a body of water with a combination of high salinity levels, salt-loving algae and pink bacteria, which make it appear bubble-gum pink (and red sometimes I imagine – given the name). The road passes through the lake via a causeway. On a blue sky day the luminous pink on one side of the road contrasts with the green and blue on the other side making it extremely Insta-worthy.

CULTURE VULTURE

According to info at the campground: 'Pioneering South Australian surfer Wayne Dale brought film-maker and original owner Paul Witzig here in 1969. At that stage Cactus was only known to a few surfers and there was no facilities. Living conditions became "feral" and the fragile environment was being damaged. In 1976 Coastal Protection officer and surfer Jeff Edwards drew up the plans on which the current camp is based. Ron Gates has been owner manager since 1986.'

FIRST PEOPLES KNOW-HOW

The Wirangu First People lived here for thousands of years and their middens are still visible – if you know where to look. Aboriginal cultural shell middens are protected by law, so tread lightly.

AND ANOTHER THING

The caretaker will collect your camping fees and it is strictly cash-only. You can't book, but you can ring ahead to check availability.

The facilities use bore water but you'll need to BYO drinking water.

Bring an annex or shade covering, especially in the summertime.

SURF

In 2012 this surfing mecca was declared a National Surfing Reserve due to the reverence held for three sensational breaks: Cactus (left-hander) and Castles (left-hander) at Cactus Beach and Caves (right-hander) at neighbouring North Castle Bluff Breaks. This is no place for amateur surfers. Part of the kudos of anyone getting on a board here is their daring. It's not myth or legend, Cactus Beach has its share of great white shark (white pointer) sightings. At least three attacks have been recorded, one of them fatal. On one of the cliffs there's a plaque laid in memory of Cameron Bayes, who tragically died as a result of a shark attack on 25 September 2000, while surfing on his honeymoon.

ALTERNATIVES

There are roadside camping areas heading east 60 kilometres away at Kooniba, and west 35 kilometres away at Goodwood on the Eyre Highway. Scott Bay Campground, 96 kilometres west at Fowlers Bay, is accessible only with a 4WD along the beach.

Private camping with endless ocean, rockpools and beach fishing.

Hillocks Drive

Yorke Peninsula, SA

MAP ON PAGE 110

ACTIVITIES

FACILITIES

One of the best-known campgrounds on the Yorke Peninsula is this privately owned tract of land extending a bewildering 7 kilometres along a wild ocean escarpment. The rugged cliffs, wave-pummelled beaches and rawness of the landscape are the attraction. So too are the commercial conveniences – hot showers, a kiosk, toilet blocks, rubbish facilities – and the somewhat relaxed rules, such as being able to bring your dog (on a leash), come in a group and make a bit of noise, and turn up without a booking. It's an intriguing landscape, with an impressive choice of more than 100 unpowered sites in varying landscapes. At the western end of the campground, an agricultural scene of dusty yellow wheat fields abuts the coastal environment. Great hillocks of sand the size of desert dunes are held together by the root system of peppermint gums and a cast of what look like coastal succulents. At the back of these dunes, 20 or so sites, including The Arch where we camped, are shaded by a low canopy of trees and protected from the wind. They're suited to swags, one-tent sites and smaller groups who prefer a bit of privacy.

On the coastal side of these dunes, the sites around Butlers Camp are close together but they're the most popular, with some shade and wind shelter, a nearby toilet block and access over the dunes to Butlers Beach. This main beach had small waves on our visit, but they were rough and not great for swimming. Rather, groups and families with big, long line-fishing rods spend leisurely days waiting for mulloway, salmon and snapper to bite.

For campers looking for a more secluded getaway, the eastern end is less populated and wilder. Sites dotted sporadically throughout the low-lying coastal heathlands might bear the brunt of the wind but they have incredible views over the Investigator Strait and Kangaroo Island beyond. Campers here have a backyard of small coves, beaches and rocky outcrops that can be explored via sandy paths and natural stairways through the crumbling limestone escarpment.

Given the expanse of land, it's a good idea to base yourself somewhere for the day. Treasure Cove Beach is more rock reef than sand. It's good for snorkelling or throwing a line in. Meteor Bay, at the far end of Hillocks Drive, has a steep bank creating an amphitheatre of black rock around the beach, making it look like the hole of an ancient meteor. It's a rockpooling paradise.

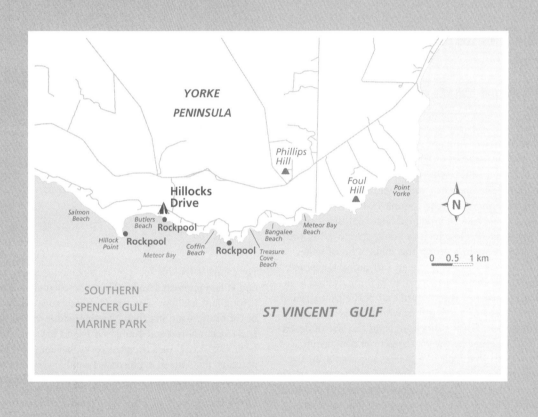

YORKE

PENINSULA

Phillips Hill

Foul Hill

Point Yorke

Hillocks Drive

Salmon Beach

Butlers Beach

Rockpool

Bangalee Beach

Meteor Bay Beach

Hillock Point

Rockpool

Coffin Beach

Rockpool

Meteor Bay

Treasure Cove Beach

N

0   0.5   1 km

SOUTHERN

SPENCER GULF

MARINE PARK

ST VINCENT   GULF

CATEGORIES

Young Travellers, Dog-Lovers, Family, Nature, Wi-Fi-Free, Boomers, Nomads

GO DO IT

WHO   Hillocks Dr; (08) 8854 4002; hillocksdrive.com
WHERE   Warooka is 230km west of Adelaide on the Yorke Peninsula in SA.
ACCESS   Follow signs on South Coast Rd, 14km from Marion Bay and 16km from Innes National Park.

WHAT ELSE?

Follow the signs on the main road within the campground to 'Rock Pool', where great swathes of rock have been pulled askew by geological forces so that lines of granite sparkle in horizontal lines. In one such crevice, a sandy bottom aquamarine rockpool is home to seaweed, small stripy fish and sizeable orange crabs. At the right time of day, the waves lap the edge of the pool, leaving it calm enough for us to jump off the surrounding rock walls and snorkel around.

What's that hip-blip on the horizon? The property has two eco ocean pods to stay in, one on a hilltop at the eastern end and the other close to Butler's Beach. They're fit for four guests and offer an upsized glamping experience with all the mod-cons.

CULTURE VULTURE

Nearby Innes National Park has a visitor centre and plenty of wildlife, culture and activities. Spot whales from the Cape Spencer Lighthouse (*see* p. 117), explore the *Ethel* shipwreck (*see* p. 117), surf Chinamans break (*see* p. 115) and check out the historic old town of Inneston.

WILDLIFE WATCH

Look out for grey kangaroos, western pygmy possums, goannas and sleepy lizards, Yorke Peninsula's most common reptile. Birdwatchers might spot blue wrens, hooded plovers, wattle birds and peregrine falcons. Australian sea lions and long-nosed fur seals bask on the rocks here and you can spot seasonal Southern-right whales (June to Sept) and pods of dolphins.

STEP IT UP

Walk the Yorke (yorkepeninsula.com.au/walk-the-yorke) is a system of trails, covering more than 500 kilometres of the Yorke Peninsula coastline. One of the most rewarding and challenging sections is the 25.3-kilometre walk from Foul Bay to Marion Bay, which passes through Hillocks Drive campground. The track is signed or you can grab a map (in sections or as a complete set of 10) from the Yorke Peninsula visitor centre. You can also get maps for other short walks, day walks, multi-day walks, 'hero' walks and cycle trails in the region.

AND ANOTHER THING

During busy periods, Hillocks Drive has four- and five-day minimum stays. Enquire ahead.

ALTERNATIVES

Innes National Park, 16 kilometres away, has similarly wild and adventurous campsites at Cable Bay (*see* p. 116) and Shell Beach (*see* p. 113).

Basic bush camping with a nearby beach and natural blue swimming hole.

Shell Beach
Innes National Park, SA

ACTIVITIES

FACILITIES

If asking directions to Shell Beach campground, you'll inevitably be told to look out for Shepherds Hut (*see* p. 115), which is hard to miss near the turn-off to the campground, and equally hard not to love. The campground is 100 metres or so past Shepherds Hut, on the right-hand side. It's a charming little hideaway among the vegetation, but the best bit about this campground is its proximity to the beach.

There are eight sites that are spread around a central circular road and hidden in eucalyptus trees and smaller coastal bush, that offer some shade and shelter from the wind. Campsites 2, 4 and 5, are good spots because they are a little set back off the dirt road. Campsite 3 is the biggest. All sites have space for one vehicle, and are close to the toilet block.

Take a five-minute walk down the sandy access road to the carpark, then you'll hit the well-maintained wooden boardwalk and staircase, which leads over the dunes to the spectacular sight of Shell Beach. It's about 300-metres long, with protruding granite rock platforms at each end, a slight arc and a backing foredune, all of which make it feel self-contained – like your own little private beach. The end closest to the stairs (west) is the gentlest, with plenty of sand and small waves for body boarding. The middle of the beach has flat platforms of rock. The far end has rocky outcrops perfect

for climbing and rockpooling. Head a little further beyond this eastern end point to reach the famed Shell Beach Rock Pool (keep going beyond the one that feels like it might be the rock pool but isn't). This sensational blue swimming hole, about 20 metres from shore, is bordered by high-rock boulders. It's deep enough to have its own aquarium of fish. On a still day, you can don goggles and spend time in the serene underwater as the waves wash over the top.

Keep your eyes out for the pods of dolphins that swim quite close to shore.

CATEGORIES

Young Travellers, Family, Nature, Wi-Fi-Free, No Dogs, Boomers, Nomads

GO DO IT

WHO   Innes National Park – Natural Resource Centre; (08) 8854 3200; naturalresources.sa.gov.au; parks.sa.gov.au

WHERE   Innes National Park is located on the south-western tip of the Yorke Peninsula, approximately 300km on the Yorke Hwy from Adelaide via Port Wakefield, Ardrossan, Minlaton and Warooka, SA.

ACCESS   Via Yorke Hwy, which becomes Pondalowie Bay Rd within the national park, then unsealed Browns Beach Rd, which you stay on for about 10km.

WHAT ELSE?

The simple single-room limestone Shepherds Hut, with a sweet little balcony, a towering gum tree out back and a corrugated water tank to one side, personifies much of what there is to love about Innes National Park – the isolation, the wild landscape, the tough European settler history. While camping over the summer holidays, we 'upgraded' to Shepherds Hut for a couple of nights over Christmas. It's a squeeze of a place with two bunk beds (with decent mattresses), a table and chairs, fire place and a tap with a bucket for a sink. (Toilet facilities are shared with the campground.) We put our camp table on the front verandah and at the end of each day had visits from tammar wallabies, one with a joey in her pouch. It made for a very Australian Christmas. Book through the campground.

You'll see little, if any, road-kill in Innes National Park – help out by sticking to the 40–60km/h road limit and you'll be rewarded with snapshots of emus eating on road verges.

Innes is building a global reputation for owning some of SA's best surf breaks (see p. 118).

WILDLIFE WATCH

In 2004 tammar wallabies were reintroduced to the Australian mainland and Yorke Peninsula, after becoming extinct on the mainland in the 1920s. Evidence of the project's success can be seen hopping in the hinterland around the campground. The growing population of the endangered mallee fowl is another good-news story.

STEP IT UP

Walk the Yorke (yorkepeninsula.com.au/walk-the-yorke) is a system of trails covering more than 500 kilometres of the Yorke Peninsula's coastline. Grab a map (in sections or as a complete set of 10) from the Yorke Peninsula visitor centre for the low-down on short walks, day walks, multi-day walks, 'hero' walks and cycle trails. The Innes National Park section, from Marion Bay to Gleeson's Landing, has seven walks including the three-hour return Thomson–Pfitzner Plaster Trail Hike along the old wooden rail line.

AND ANOTHER THING

When you arrive at Innes National Park check in at the visitor centre to pay the entry fee. Also grab a couple of maps from the front desk for a detailed overview of the park.

ALTERNATIVES

Innes National Park's other campgrounds are Browns Beach, Casuarina, Gym Beach, Pondalowie Bay, Stenhouse Bay and Cable Bay (see p. 116).

Opposite There are plenty of trails and beaches to explore throughout Innes National Park

Barefoot camping on a wild southern peninsula close to surf.

Cable Bay

Innes National Park, SA

MAP ON PAGE 112

ACTIVITIES

FACILITIES

At the tip of the Yorke Peninsula, with wind-buffeted views towards Kangaroo Island, Innes National Park is an untamed and pristine wilderness, with blonde beaches, bush-covered dunes, rock-clifftops and crags that take a never-ending beating from the Southern Ocean weather systems.

Its iconic native inhabitants – kangaroos, tammar wallabies and emus among them – are evolutionarily tuned to the wild environment, and part of the magic is seeing them up close in their natural habitat.

The crystal-clear water provides opportunities to surf (*see* p. 118), swim, snorkel and scuba dive in a designated marine park – the playground of dolphins, red octopus, schools of salmon and other marine life.

Adding to the drama, there's a lighthouse, shipwrecks and an historical mining town (*see* p. 117) – all the fodder for tales of maritime and settler woe.

Camping at Cable Bay campground really embraces this wild remoteness; you can pitch a tent here and expect to feel all the elements and – with just nine sandy-bottomed campsites – an invigorating sense of isolation, too.

Of the five Innes National Park campgrounds, Cable Bay is closest to the beach and handy to the surf. You can be tent-to-tide in less than a minute, via a short wooden path straddling a dune. Tents in nicely spaced sites surrounded by greenery sit just below the line of vision, but caravan occupants in the right position will enjoy a view of islands. There's a single long-drop toilet, and all sites are unpowered. The beach, which runs adjacent to the campground, is small with sand-cliffs and pockets of seaweed. It's bookended by rugged cliff-faces that can look foreboding on a stormy day but are worth exploring on a sunny one.

Just east of the campground, a viewpoint takes in the impressive Cable Bay panorama, a sweeping vista, with conical-shaped Chinamans Hat Island (the popular surfing spot, *see* p. 118) and Althorpe Island Conservation Park in the foreground. Kangaroo Island sits on the horizon.

Opposite Stenhouse Bay jetty is a relic from mining days

CATEGORIES

Young Travellers, Family, Nature, Wi-Fi-Free, No Dogs, Boomers, Nomads

GO DO IT

WHO   Innes National Park – Natural Resource Centre; (08) 8854 3200; parks.sa.gov.au

WHERE   Innes National Park is located on the south-western tip of the Yorke Peninsula, approximately 300km by Yorke Hwy from Adelaide via Port Wakefield, Ardrossan, Minlaton and Warooka, SA.

ACCESS   Via Yorke Hwy, then Pondalowie Beach Rd within the national park.

WHAT ELSE?

Jutting into the beautiful blue, the Stenhouse Bay jetty is a relic from mining days. The old mine is still here, but its chalky ramparts are off-limits. The jetty on the other hand is the domain of hand-holders, sight-seers and fisherpersons who sink a line to haul in squid, the black ink marks of which have left stains along the wood. We spent an afternoon fishing here and the locals were happy to share their fishing know-how.

Beach fishing is big here, too. Throw a line for mullet, tommy ruffs, garfish, sweep, mulloway and whiting. Browns Beach is one of the state's best salmon fishing areas. Check out marine park fishing restrictions at: marineparks.sa.gov.au

CULTURE VULTURE

On the western side of the campground, a 2 kilometre long unsealed road leads to Cape Spencer Lighthouse. It was built in the 1950s so it is not an historic lighthouse, but the ocean views make a visit worthwhile especially when Southern-right whales (May to Oct) are cruising by.

Also off Pondalowie Beach Road, the abandoned historic village of Inneston is an homage to South Australia's mining and pioneer history, and the only surviving example of an early 20th-century gypsum (used to make chalk) mining complex. It's a heat-trap in summer, when the glaringly white roads and old limestone buildings are best avoided, but in cooler months its short exploratory walks will add intrigue to your itinerary.

Follow a scenic boardwalk to one of Innes National Park's highlights, the *Ethel* wreck, the remains of a 711-tonne, three-mast iron ship, which has been resting on the shores here since 1904. Sometimes the sand and tide hide its rusting beached skeleton, other times its great hulk is exposed. It's one of many ships lost to the area's wild coastline.

EAT IT

Marion Bay pub, next to the general store just outside the national park, has a nice outdoor area and cooks up pizza topped with local prawns and calamari.

Cable Bay – Vivonne Bay

FIRST PEOPLES KNOW-HOW

The Narungga people have lived on the Yorke Peninsula for many thousands of years. The Narungga nation was made up of four clans: the Kurnara in the north of the peninsula, Windera in the east; Wari in the west; and Dilpa in the south. The Narungga people still maintain important cultural links to the region.

AND ANOTHER THING

When you arrive at Innes National Park, check in at the visitor centre to pay the park entry fee. Also grab a couple of maps from the front desk for a detailed overview of the park.

SURF

Innes is building a global reputation for owning some of SA's best surf breaks, with the Yorkes Classic Surfing Competition (May) piquing the interest each year. The most popular surf spot is Pondalowie Bay, which according to the yorkepeninsula.com.au/surfing website is: 'a very good quality combination of beach and reef break, a fast, hollow left up to 1 metre and a long walled right up to 3 metres'. When only the left is working at Pondalowie, Richards, 250 metres north, 'is a good quality beach/reef combination right-hander that breaks up to 1.5 metres'. The *Ethel* wreck (*see* p. 117) is a summer break only. It's 'fickle but can get very good. Usually a powerful right-hander up to 2 metres'. Similarly, West Cape has 'a left- and occasional right-hand beach break up to 2 metres'. Chinamans is 'a hollow, very powerful left-hand reef break of excellent quality, complete with hair-raising take-off and a sharp, shallow ledge'. It's for experienced riders only. Further east, Baby Chinamans is 'an average quality left-hand reef-break up to 2 metres. It is suitable for beginners'. For more surf info see: yorkepeninsula.com.au/surfing. Contact surfandsun.com.au for information on surf lessons and equipment hire.

ALTERNATIVES

Innes National Park's other campgrounds are Browns Beach, Casuarina, Gym Beach, Pondalowie Bay, Stenhouse Bay and also Shell Beach (*see* p. 113).

Top Sharing the road with some wild emus

A small campground with mind-boggling beauty and dunes, inlet and ocean.

Vivonne Bay

Kangaroo Island, SA

MAP ON PAGE 120

ACTIVITIES

FACILITIES

Vivonne Bay with its serene river inlet, its white-sand beach, its endless blue water, its barrelling waves, is a place where you'd expect the small plot of land right next to it to be home to a luxury resort, one that only the moneyed few have the privilege of staying at. That it's a small campground, available to anyone who gets there early enough or chances a spot, makes it somewhat of a 'golden ticket' in terms of Australia's beachside camping options. The bay is located on the southern side of Kangaroo Island and faces south into the often tempestuous Southern Ocean, but is sheltered from westerly waves by Point Ellen, from where a magical wave-shaped arc of beach stretches uninterrupted for 5 kilometres.

The campground sits behind coastal dunes at the sheltered western end of the beach next to the mouth of the Harriet River. It is basically a big, red-dirt carpark with two amenities blocks down one end and no more than 20 sites (8 of them powered) spread around the perimeter at the other. A boundary of low-lying coastal bush provides protection from wind and tall central trees provide some shade.

It's the most well-equipped of Kangaroo Island's council-run campgrounds. Facilities include:

• Central picnic table
• Toilet
• Solar hot water shower ($2 coin for five minutes)
• Water tanks
• Sheltered picnic area with four tables, two barbecues and a sink
• Children's playground

The campground can get a little hot and dusty when the sun is overhead, but nobody in their right mind would be hanging out too long here given the proximity to the beach. From the campground, a wood plank path extends 20 metres over a dune revealing Harriet River inlet in all its glory. With the gentle flow of crystal clear water, this is a fantastic playground for swimming and snorkelling in the shallows, collecting (but not keeping) abalone and cowrie shells, digging for sand crabs and chasing pelican shadows. You can kayak along the river or try surfing – the waves have a reputation for amateurs as they're small but consistent.

Walk north-east along the beach to get to the publicly accessed Vivonne Bay Beach, which has similar surf conditions. In the other direction, the characteristic wood-plank town jetty has trolley rails to assist fishing boats when they pull into shore. The picnic area with barbecues on the foreshore here has heavenly views.

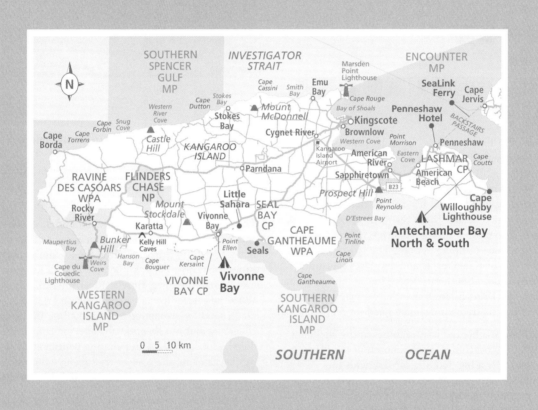

CATEGORIES

Young Travellers, Dog-Lovers, Family, Nature, Wi-Fi-Free, Boomers, Nomads

GO DO IT

WHO — Kangaroo Island Council; (08) 8553 4500; kangarooisland.sa.gov.au/recreation/camping-facilities

WHERE — Vivonne Bay is 100km from Penneshaw (Kangaroo Island's main township) ferry terminal and 55km from Kingscote airport, SA.

ACCESS — From South Coast Rd, turn south onto Jetty Rd for 2km and left onto Samedi Dr for 3km. The campground is at the end.

WHAT ELSE?

Little Sahara is a small desert, 8 kilometres from the campground. It is teen central, with dune activities including hiking, quad-biking and sand-boarding. You can rent a toboggan or a sand-board from the general store in Vivonne Bay.

About 25 kilometres south-east of Vivonne Bay campground, Seal Bay Conservation Park is home to Kangaroo Island's most well-known attraction – a sea lion colony. A self-guided tour along a beachside boardwalk (900m return) will give you eyes on sea lions sunbathing and playing in the waves. For a closer view (and at the other end of the budget) the Sunset Experience Tour (sealbay.sa.gov.au/home) allows visitors to walk among the colony with an experienced guide.

Also, check out the new behind-the-scenes research tour. Boffins will delve into the latest sea lion research and learn how to scan sea lions to collect valuable information about their habits.

WILDLIFE WATCH

South-west of Vivonne Bay campground, just beyond the jetty, Vivonne Bay Conservation Park is an 887-hectare nature reserve. Its closure from 1 May until 31 December each year is a measure to help preserve the breeding area of native animals, including the South Australian endangered white-bellied sea eagle.

AND ANOTHER THING

Camp fees can be paid via the onsite ticket machine.

SeaLink vehicle and passenger ferry (sealink.com.au) operates between mainland Cape Jervis (2 hours south of Adelaide) and Penneshaw, Kangaroo Island, daily (except Christmas Day). The journey takes 45 minutes for the 16-kilometre crossing. Booking ahead is essential, especially in peak times.

ALTERNATIVES

Many of Kangaroo Island's great campgrounds were hit by the 2019/20 bushfire season. Antechamber Bay South (see p. 122) is another great campground that was not impacted.

Picturesque riverside camping handy to kayaking, swimming and a beach.

Antechamber Bay South

Lashmar Conservation Park, Kangaroo Island, SA

MAP ON PAGE 120

ACTIVITIES

FACILITIES

Antechamber Bay South doesn't usually get a mention on Kangaroo Island's 'best campground lists', because it's not metres from the beach, but I say it deserves to. Its location, on the pretty Chapman River, which flows into the sea at Antechamber Beach a pleasant ten-minute walk away, offers campers the best of both fresh water and beachside nature and activities.

The campground's 12 unpowered campsites are strung along the banks of the river in the natural clearings between the bush and trees. We booked late and scored site 4 in a lovely small grouping of campsites sitting tucked beneath the melaleuca tree canopy. These sites are well shaded and sheltered with dirt and samphire (*see* p. 124) groundcover and a clearing where you can access the river. Sites 5–12 get gradually closer to the beach end of the campground and the facilities. They are more spacious and open to the elements with drier, grassier groundcover – if a little less private. Along this section there is wide sandy-bottomed river access so clear you can see little fish darting around. Facilities at this campground are at the northern end and include:

• Tank water
• A large sheltered picnic area with tables, bench seats, barbecues and boathouse ambience

The toilet block is actually located across the river at Antechamber Bay North campground (*see* p. 124) – you can see it sitting tantalisingly across the water. Don't let that defeat you. It's a 2-minute drive back onto the main road and around to it, or do what we did and swim/paddle across for your daily ablutions (this is bush camping after all).

For the most part, the river is slow-flowing, serene and shallow. In some parts you can wade out to the middle and the water is still only up to your belly-button, making it great for young families. Bring kayaks, tractor tubes, inflatables, fishing rods, snorkels and goggles to really explore it. Alternatively, pull up a camp chair to see black swans gliding by and pelicans soaring overhead.

Large sections of the water are muddy with an intriguing saline ecology of slippery green seaweed (which our kids covered themselves in in a game of 'creature from the deep'). As you move along the inlet, the mud and seaweed give way to white sand and shallow tracts of blue water. The gently rolling blue waves of beautiful Antechamber Beach, protected by the bay, are just beyond.

CATEGORIES

Dog-Lovers, Family, Nature, Wi-Fi-Free, Boomers, Nomads

GO DO IT

WHO   National Parks and Wildlife South Australia;
         (08) 8553 4444; parks.sa.gov.au
WHERE Lashmar Conservation Park is located 40km
         south-east of Penneshaw, on Kangaroo Island, SA.
         The campground is on its southern end.
ACCESS Unsealed Creek Bay Rd is accessed off Chapman
         River Rd (east), which is signposted off Cape
         Willoughby Rd.

WHAT ELSE?

Lashmar Conservation Park is a small triangle of land located 40 kilometres south-east of Penneshaw. It stretches along Antechamber Bay, with little dangly offshoots that include the Chapman River and Lashmar Lagoon. All its waterways are designated marine park.

One of the advantages of this campground is its proximity (19km south or a 20-minute drive) to the island's main town of Penneshaw. It's the hub of information and amenity and has a fantastic IGA supermarket laden with the local gourmet produce that the island has become known for. The lovely old brick Penneshaw Hotel has one of the best beer gardens in Australia with big sun umbrellas and a killer cliff-top view.

CULTURE VULTURE

Cape Willoughby Lighthouse, 11 kilometres south of the campground (in the titular conservation park) is South Australia's first. The domineering structure, built in the 1850s, has steered many a ship away from the shoreline, but the coast still has its tales of shipwreck and ruin. Learn about them in the small on-site museum.

EAT IT

The saline ecology along the Chapman River has some intrigues, including the campground's samphire ground cover. This native bright green and fleshy succulent, which looks like a sea asparagus or beans (and is spongy to walk on) is in season from October to March and is found in many of southern Australia's salty flat regions. It has a crunchy texture and, with a salty flavour, is very snackable. We were literally picking it near our tent and munching on it, but this is not advised unless you know what you're doing. A man I got chatting to on the beach told me that locals are bemused by the fact samphire has become a trendy ingredient. He and his family have been eating it since they were kids. 'Douse it in olive oil and lemon juice and serve it with fish,' he recommended.

AND ANOTHER THING

SeaLink vehicle and passenger ferry (sealink.com.au) operates between mainland Cape Jervis (2 hours south of Adelaide) and Penneshaw, Kangaroo Island, daily (except Christmas Day). The journey takes 45 minutes for the 16-kilometre crossing. Booking ahead is essential, especially in peak times.

ALTERNATIVES

Antechamber Bay North campground, located across the river, has 11 campsites grouped together under native trees. It is closer to the beach (without being on it) and the all-important toilet block, but it lacks the charm of its southern neighbour.

Many of Kangaroo Island's great campgrounds were hit by the 2019/20 bushfire season. Vivonne Bay (see p. 119) is another great campground that was not impacted.

Rural camping with thoughtful facilities and a winery on the doorstep.

Bellwether Winery

Coonawarra, SA

MAP ON PAGE 126

ACTIVITIES

FACILITIES

When passing through the historic Coonawarra wine region, famed for its heavy reds, it behoves travellers to pop into a winery and try the local drop. If you can camp the night, well, now you're twisting my arm.

Bellwether is a charmer of a winery in the beautiful old stone 'Glen Roy' shearing shed, a relic from the prosperous 1800s. Sheep were shorn on the property right up until 2009, but since then owner and winemaker Sue Bell has given the place a new twist. The old windmill and sheep yard fencing remains but shiny, corrugate-iron outhouses have been added to host a wine cellar, an outdoor kitchen for campers, along with a 'posh' bathroom that has seven showers, six toilets and even a room with a claw-foot bath. (It's easily the loveliest amenities block in this book.)

The sheep might be gone (except for a couple that cruise around the campground), and the vines for making the house cab sav are grown elsewhere in the region, but the property is still rich in pastoral history.

The campground, 50 metres from the winery, is essentially a paddock with six stylish bell tents and six tent sites (three powered), dotted among the centuries-old red gums. The campground has some eclectic touches that give it warmth and humour. Tap water is plumbed into an antique basin that leans up against an old tree trunk. A central fire-pit and barbecue area has logs for seats and wine barrels for resting your glass of shiraz on – winter-warmer heaven.

Visitors to the winery ring a bell at the front door if there's nobody around.

The camp kitchen feels more like the al fresco dining area of a (rustic) boutique guest house, with lovely timber furnishings and country kitchen lino chairs. Bowls of homegrown lemons, bunches of herbs and baskets lined with a teatowel and filled with sourdough have little help-yourself-notes on them. Breakfast is included and it's a case of retrieving eggs and thick-cut fresh, local bacon from the fridge and cooking it up yourself.

As the posters that plaster the bathroom walls attest, Bellwether has its share of winery events, from intimate cook-ups to music gigs and the annual Sips in the Sticks, held in July, with inspiring local producers on the mike and talented chefs in the kitchen. It's popular so book ahead.

CATEGORIES

Young Travellers, Dog-Lovers, Family, Nature, Wi-Fi-Free, Boomers, Nomads

GO DO IT

WHO   Bellwether Winery; 0447 334 545; bellwetherwines.com.au

WHERE   Coonawarra, SA.

ACCESS   14183 Riddoch Hwy, 7km north of Coonawarra

WHAT ELSE?

One of the biggest and bushiest old red gums here has a spectacular treehouse in it – the stuff of childhood fairytales.

The verdant produce garden, sprawling with oversized spinach leaves, seeding fennel and out-of-control rosemary bushes has been grown from the sheep poo salvaged from the shearing shed.

If you're camping with a group, book in for one of Bellwether's 'Table of Twelve' dinners held in the shearing shed around a spectacular old wool sorting table, which has been glass-topped for diners. Local and seasonal menus are the aim so expect a unique degustation menu with wine pairings from a chef and winemaker.

CULTURE VULTURE

Sue Bell doesn't grow her own vines, rather she buys parcels of grapes from grape-growers – both near and far, as muses for her own oenological interests. Sip on heavy-set locally grown cabernet sauvignon and cabernet or take your palate on a terroir journey with a Tamar Valley chardonnay or Heathcote vermentino. Hear it from the winemaker herself on a tasting in the shearing shed. Groups are limited to five. Cost is $10.

EAT IT

There are dozens of wineries throughout Coonawarra, some big-name, some boutique, where you can indulge in cellar door tastings. Royal Oak Penola (royaloakpenola.pub) is my pick for eating with a menu paying homage to the produce found on the Limestone Coast.

AND ANOTHER THING

Learn from our mistake: check in before 4pm so you don't miss out on a wine tasting and the chance to buy some camp wine.

Western Australia

Australia's biggest state stretches along an endless surf-camp coastline from Southern Ocean waves to Ningaloo Reef. Up north campers will feel the magnetism of the Kimberley

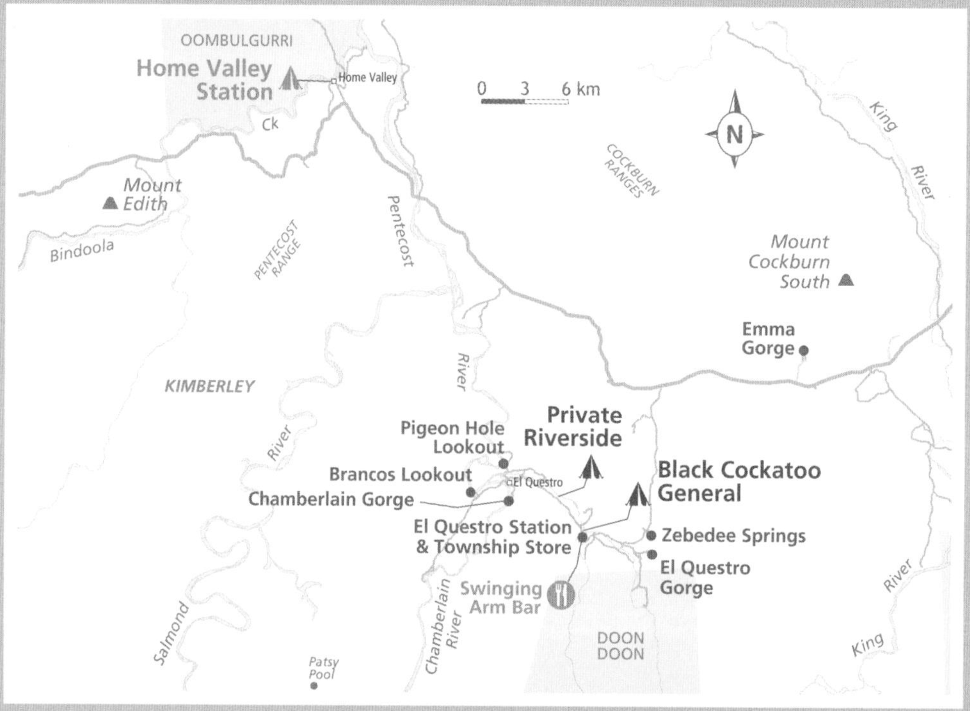
OOMBULGURRI
Home Valley Station
Home Valley
Ck
0 3 6 km
N
King River
COCKBURN RANGES
Mount Edith
Bindoola
PENTECOST RANGE
Pentecost River
Mount Cockburn South
Emma Gorge
KIMBERLEY
River
Pigeon Hole Lookout
Private Riverside
Brancos Lookout
El Questro
Black Cockatoo General
Chamberlain Gorge
El Questro Station & Township Store
Zebedee Springs
El Questro Gorge
Swinging Arm Bar
Chamberlain River
Salmond
Patsy Pool
DOON DOON
River
King

Previous Camping tents at El Questro Station (*see* p. 131)

Camping in the heart of iconic Kimberley country,
with swimming holes, gorges, waterfalls and lookouts.

El Questro

Kununurra, the Kimberley, WA

ACTIVITIES

FACILITIES

If you're travelling the East Kimberley's famed Gibb River Road between the junction of Wyndham, Kununurra and Derby, then El Questro Station will likely be either your first or your last stop. Whatever you do, don't miss it – it's as much an attraction as any on this iconic road trip. The former cattle station-turned-tourist drawcard is a magnificent property that stretches 283,279 hectares through stunning Kimberley savannah. The landscape of ancient red earth, rock ridges and escarpments is striped by brilliant green trees, both established and stunted, and framed by far-off blue-tinged mountain ranges. It boasts a natural ecosystem of wild-flowing rivers where crocodiles roam, towering red and black rock gorges where gushing fresh waterfalls either plunge or trickle, depending on the time of year, and swimming holes where fringing pandanus trees, palms, ferns and eucalypt form natural tropical oases. There is enough to see and do at El Questro to keep you busy for a week.

This extraordinary wilderness attracts thousands of people each year and El Questro has the facilities, activities and creature comforts to match all budgets and itineraries. Guests can stay in luxurious suites, air conditioned rooms and bungalows, permanent canvas tents (with beds and fans), or at an extensive campground where nothing is lacking.

Black Cockatoo General is the main campground with about 200 unmarked powered and unpowered sites. It's in the thick of the action next to the Station (the main amenities and restaurant hub – or 'township'), and has a caravan park-vibe, with sprawling manicured grass spaces and the kind of uniformity needed to host so many tents, camper-trailers and

bigger 4WD vehicles (smaller vehicles are not advised along the access road to El Questro, *see* p. 132). Facilities include:

- Toilet blocks (both flushing and compost)
- Hot shower blocks (avoid peak time queues or the hot water runs out)
- Camp kitchens
- Barbecues
- Laundry facilities (coin-operated)
- Fire-pits

When the main campground is brimming with people (and it almost always is), the best sites are, I think, on the boundary near to the river. But if big-crowd camping really isn't your scene and power and showers aren't a necessity, keep going 2 kilometres past the main site to the start of a string of 30 private campsites sitting along the Pentecost River. These beautiful and private little nooks, named after the local bird species (wren, quail, kookaburra, mopoke, etc) are spaced well apart, with shady trees and plenty of bush in between – ensuring you won't bother your neighbours. If you're fortunate enough to nab one of the first five campsites, you'll have access to the water and an opportunity to swim (but take heed of croc signs elsewhere on the property). Fires are allowed in pits here and there are eco-toilets dotted every few campsites. Another coup: these private campsites can be booked in advance. For everything else, head back to the main campground at Black Cockatoo General (1 kilometre from the closest private campsite, 8.2 kilometres from the furthest).

CATEGORIES

Young Travellers, Dog-Lovers, Family, Nature, Boomers, Nomads

GO DO IT

WHO   El Questro Wilderness Park; 1800 837 168; elquestro.com.au

WHERE   75 Coolibah Dr, Kununurra, 110km west of Kununurra, in WA.

ACCESS From Kununurra, take Great Northern Hwy 58km towards Wyndham, then 36km on a sealed section of the Gibb River Road. El Questro is signed down a 16km gravel road that you will need a 4WD to access, given the rough road corrugations and two river crossings (solid bottoms and approximately 300–500mm in depth). Only high-clearance caravans should take this road.

WHAT ELSE?

If you only do two things at El Questro make it the gorgeous swimming holes and waterfalls of Emma Gorge and El Questro Gorge. At the former the water plunges over the side of a 65 metre high red cliff-face, at the latter there's a series of blissful waterholes framed by fern fronds and livistona palm trees that you discover one by one on a memorable wilderness adventure.

At El Questro's 'The Station', Township Store has groceries plus everything you ever needed or forgot on a camping trip. There are also ATM machines, payphones, bags of firewood, fuel (unleaded and diesel), and a garage for repairs and tyre sales (perish the thought). At reception grab yourself a map for self-guiding adventures or ask one of the rangers for advice on activities. Wi-fi access can be purchased online for a fee.

Take a cruise along the high escarpment walls of Chamberland Gorge, a 3 kilometre long waterhole only accessible by boat.

Head to Brancos Lookout or Pigeon Hole Lookout for the sunset – El Questro has open-topped safari jeep tours, or self-drive for a 4WD adventure.

Take a morning outing to Zebedee Springs. These palm-fringed thermal swimming holes are naturally heated to between 28 and 32°C. The earlier you get here the better – it's popular and closes at noon.

Horse-lovers can indulge in one- and two-hour station rides or a full-day ride, including a picnic by a waterhole.

There are over 200 kilometres of well-signposted tracks for walks suited to different abilities. Ask for maps at reception.

Specialist barramundi fishing, bush culture and history, and birdwatching tours are also available.

There are a dozen or so helicopter tour options, including a private flight to one of the property's secluded waterholes, and a two-hour Bungle Bungle and Lake Argyle flight.

EAT IT

Swinging Arm Bar is also at The Station. It is a rock-walled venue with a huge outdoor area and long share-tables where you can gather to tell fellow travellers a yarn or two. It serves breakfast (bacon and egg rolls, for example), lunch (beef burgers) and dinner (freshly caught battered barramundi and chips). On Saturdays it's particularly good fun with an outdoor barbecue and live country music.

WILDLIFE WATCH

El Questro is home to hundreds of species of birds, fish and native animals. You'll definitely see barramundi, catfish and archer fish in Chamberlain Gorge; and wallabies at sunrise and sunset – and echidnas, if you keep quiet. One friend spotted an olive-coloured snake near El Questro Gorge. Sadly, cane toads, considered a pest, have made it this far west of Queensland.

Opposite Emma Gorge is a popular swimming spot
Right A campfire performance at Swinging Arm Bar

AND ANOTHER THING

El Questro Station is seasonal. Depending on the weather, it opens at the start of April and closes mid-October. To get the most of the waterfalls and swimming holes, the earlier you come in the season the better. Bookings are essential in June and August.

All campers are required to purchase a visitor permit. The permit gives visitors access to all the gorges, waterholes, thermal springs and lookouts. You pay per adult/child, and permits are valid for seven days. For a one-night stay buy a daypass. The permit is similar to a national park pass in that it pays for general maintenance, fire management, development of new tourism areas and protection of the unique environment. It will be automatically added to online bookings.

ALTERNATIVES

The Gibb River Road has a range of campgrounds, from similarly commercial places like Home Valley Station, about 50 kilometres north-west of El Questro, to more intimate bush camps, such as Ellenbrae Station, 160 kilometres west. For more Kimberley camping in this book, head to Kooljaman (*see* p. 135).

Kooljaman at Cape Leveque

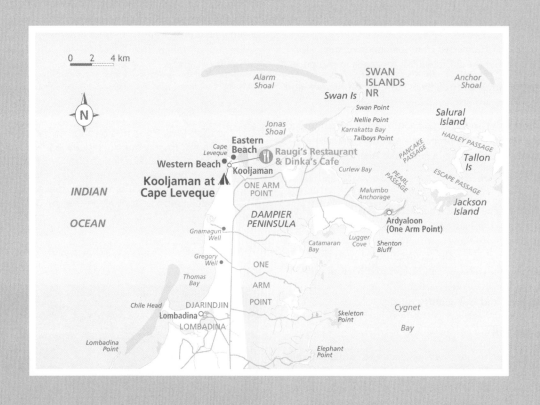

Red dirt wilderness camping with Indian Ocean views and spectacular Dampier Peninsula scenery.

Kooljaman at Cape Leveque

Dampier Peninsula, WA

ACTIVITIES

FACILITIES

Broome in the Kimberley region of northern Western Australia feels like a far-off land, especially to anyone living on the east coast. That Kooljaman lies 200 kilometres north at Cape Leveque on the northern point of Dampier Peninsula, with 4WD access only, gives you some sense of how heart-stoppingly remote and out of the ordinary this place is. Up here, the unique Kimberley landscape of rust-red pindan soil stretches across luminous green country to rugged cliff-faces, before ending abruptly on a coastline of long white sands and jade water that turns blue as it nears the horizon. The vastness of the place, the almost surreal isolation and the endless beauty is mind-bending stuff – you'll want to stay a while.

Kooljaman at Cape Leveque Wilderness Camp is on Native Title land of the Bardi Jawi people (*see* p. 136), and is totally immersed in this raw and rugged environment. Kooljaman is the Bardi Jawi name for Cape Leveque. The property sits on the north-pointing tip of Cape Leveque with Western Beach facing the Indian Ocean on one side and Eastern Beach on King Sound on the other. The accommodation, which ranges from basic campground, to shelters, cabins and tricked-up safari tents, is spread across the red landscape in bushy treed areas, on clifftops and by the water's edge. A fab boardwalk links the main reception, restaurant and campground on the western side with the cafe on the eastern side near the short path to Eastern Beach. Everything else branches off this thoroughfare, making it easy to get around. Eastern Beach is your swimming and snorkelling beach where you'll likely spend the majority of your time. Western Beach is the go-to for red-washed sunsets and sundowners.

The campground has powered and unpowered campsites suited to tents and smaller campervans and camper-trailers (that will need to fit within a 4x6m site – no caravans or motorhomes). The 20 powered campsites are in a grassy area with shade and greenery. Kooljaman is off-the-grid, but solar power allows for one car fridge per campsite and lighting (no kettles, microwaves or air conditioning units). There are 16 unpowered sites. Ten of them have a prime cliff-top location with jaw-dropping ocean views (accordingly, they book out early). The six other campsites sit under the eucalypts and are shaded. Both the powered and unpowered camping area facilities include:

- Shared toilet and shower amenities blocks (bore water)
- Camp kitchen with fridge, gas stove and barbecues
- Communal fire-pits
- Sheltered picnic tables (with incredible ocean views)
- Laundry (with two coin-operated washing machines)
- Bore water (drinkable)

Four mini safari tents catering to two people are also in the campground. They each have twin or double beds, linen and towels, a fan, lighting and a little front balcony with chairs, plus access to the camping facilities listed above.

Another cool option for campers are the basic 'beach camp shelters' sitting right on the water's edge near Eastern Beach. They're made of palm fronds and wood, with sand floors and are for adventurous souls who don't mind rolling out a swag on the dirt, showering outdoors and cooking dinner on an open fire. Facilities include:

• Shared toilet block
• Picnic table
• Firewood (first night of firewood is free)

Non-camping accommodation includes rustic bush-immersed cabins and beachfront log cabins. They're well-equipped with linen and towels, ensuites, kitchen facilities and front balconies with a dining table and barbecue.

CATEGORIES

Young Travellers, Family, Nature, No Dogs, Boomers, Nomads

GO DO IT

WHO   Kooljaman at Cape Leveque Wilderness Camp; (08) 9192 4970; kooljaman.com.au

WHERE   Cape Leveque, 210km north of Broome, 2416km north-east of Perth, WA. It's also 2058km south-west of Darwin and 4148km north-west of Melbourne (just to make the point!).

ACCESS From Broome, take the Broome–Cape Leveque Rd about 210km north to Cape Leveque. It is the only road and it cuts right up the centre of the peninsula. It's sealed for about half the journey. A 4WD is essential.

Kooljaman at Cape Leveque

WHAT ELSE?

Kooljaman reception is open year-round, 8am–5pm (until 4pm Nov to Mar). It has a desk for booking local tours and experiences and has board games for hire. The Dampier Peninsula is a restricted Dry Zone so Kooljaman does not sell alcohol but BYO is welcome. Eftpos is available.

Venture into the Ardyaloon (One Arm Point) and Djarindjin community shops where you can buy fresh meat, fruit and vegetables. Ardyaloon (One Arm Point) has 24-hour fuel.

Kooljaman has upmarket Raugi's Restaurant (*see* Eat it). Dinka's Cafe, which overlooks Eastern Beach, is open daily (8am–4pm) and sells coffee, muffins and ice-cream, basic groceries (frozen bread, meat packs, UHT milk, tinned tomatoes) and essentials (ice, bait, mozzie repellent). You can also hire beach equipment (snorkels, beach towels and umbrellas).

Take a walk from the long white sandy stretches of Eastern Beach to Western Beach at low tide, timing your run for sunset when the magnificent red colour spectrum is in full play.

EAT IT

At Raugi's Restaurant you can delve into some of the local native ingredients foraged in the surrounding bushland. This well-regarded place with a deck overlooking Western Beach offers a culinary experience where modern techniques are applied to local ingredients, such as illarr (berries) and gubinge (Kakadu plum), to create dishes favouring gels, foams and glazes with a distinctively local flavour. Treat yourself!

FIRST PEOPLES KNOW-HOW

Kooljaman is part of the Bardi Jawi People's land, and is owned under Native Title by the local communities of Djarindjin and Ardyaloon (One Arm Point). The running of the place is underscored by the land practices, cultural values and philosophy of the Bardi Jawi. Getting involved with tours and activities that tap into the wildlife and wondrous scenery through the eyes of the Bardi Jawi people is all part of the experience.

There are three recommended tour operators working out of Kooljaman's office with fascinating cultural immersions that could keep you here for weeks. Kooljaman's own tours range from a one-hour Bardi Jawi ranger chat about local history, languages and heritage (Wednesday 11am) to full-day adventure cruises and scenic flights. Bundy's Cultural Tours is run by Bundy, a Bardi Elder and Traditional Owner, who puts a personal spin on bush-tucker walks and fishing adventures where guests can learn traditional spear-fishing and cook their catch afterwards. Hunters Creek Tagalong Tours is run by Brian Lee who takes guests along a nearby waterway on a 4WD adventure to find mudcrabs and hear ancient stories around a campfire.

WILDLIFE WATCH

Birds, frogs and monitor lizards are a constant. Out to sea, keep a lookout for pods of dolphins and whales breaching just beyond the shoreline in season (July and Oct). Take a Bardi Jawi tour to really scratch the surface.

AND ANOTHER THING

Bookings are essential.

Roads are suitable for 4WD vehicles and camper-trailers only – no caravans allowed.

ALTERNATIVES

At the other end of the budget spectrum, there are dreamy stilted safari tents suited to couples ('deluxe') and families ('family') wanting creature comforts. They are set in lovely private locations in both the bushy interior and overlooking Eastern Beach (family), and on the cliffs overlooking Western Beach (deluxe). Facilities include:

- King-sized bed (deluxe)
- Queen bed and two singles (family)
- Linen and towels
- Ensuite
- Kitchen facilities (fridge/freezer, cooking equipment, cutlery, crockery)
- Solar power with generator back-up
- Gas barbecue
- Sofa (deluxe only)
- Fan
- Bore water

The views from the north-facing balconies of the deluxe tents is particularly mesmerising, a tri-colour of red soil across the bottom, deep blue ocean in the middle, and the cloudless pale blue sky above. Don't get me started on the sunsets!

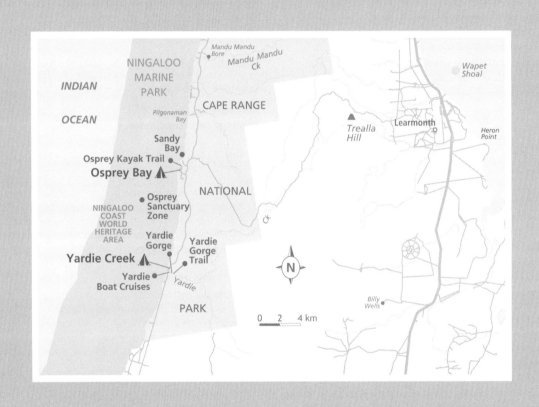

Wild, barren, basic camping between a national park and marine wonderland.

Yardie Creek

Cape Range National Park, WA

ACTIVITIES

FACILITIES

Ningaloo Reef gets a lot of attention on this peninsula, but Cape Range National Park is just as breathtaking for its rare and magnificent wildlife, ancient rock formations, Indigenous history and stunning flora. That the crystal-clear turquoise marine world of the former meets the rugged red escarpment of the latter right here at Yardie Creek makes this campground irresistible.

Visitors who aren't snorkelling with whale sharks or swimming with humpback whales turn up here to explore Yardie Gorge, a beautiful sweep of cliff-face that looks like somebody has swiped a big brushstroke of red and brown oil paint across the land.

There's a cruise up the gorge in a flat-bottomed aluminium boat (*see* p. 140) but my friends and I chose to walk the Yardie Gorge Trail (*see* p. 140), instead. Along the trail, rock wallabies with distinctive facial markings, textured feet for gripping the rocks and a long tail for keeping balance, hop among the foliage. A green, diamond-patterned snake wriggles across our dirt-pink path. The trail is lined with bush lemongrass and warty applebush that has a fruity aroma. When small hardy bush fig trees blossom with plump yellow figs, the local Jinigudera people know that new emu eggs are ready to harvest. Rock surfaces are patterned with recognisable brain coral fossils and shell imprints from a million years ago.

The campground is right next to this nature-fest in the sandy oceanfront vegetation. It has 10 unpowered sites neatly spaced along an unsealed road and demarcated by pine-log fencing. Tent site 8 sits next to the path to Yardie Creek and sites 3 and 4 sit either side of a path leading 50 metres down to a beach where the water is so clear you can spot fish from the shore. Snorkelling is a must. If you're lucky you'll nab the sites under the she-oak trees, for much-needed shade. These same sites are also close to two picnic tables that have views looking out across the water – perfect sundowner spots. Use the pit-toilet in the campground or walk to the upgraded bathroom block in the visitor parking which has a rock wall façade.

Yardie Creek is the southernmost point in the national park. Cross the blonde sandy unsealed road here and you're on a straight 4WD track down the Coral Coast with nothing much in between.

CATEGORIES

Young Travellers, Free, Family, Nature, Wi-Fi-Free, No Dogs, Nomads

GO DO IT

WHO   Milyering Discovery Centre and WA Parks and Wildlife Service; (08) 9949 2808; parks.dpaw.wa.gov.au

WHERE   Cape Range National Park, which is 90km south of Exmouth and 1200km north of Perth, WA.

ACCESS   88km south of Exmouth via Murat Rd for 12km, left onto Yardie Creek Rd for 76km. The campground is at the end of the sealed section of this road.

WHAT ELSE?

There's a picnic area near the start of the Yardie Gorge walks. It has more tree cover than the picnic tables in the campground.

The Yardie Gorge Trail is a 2-kilometre return walk, graded moderate, with some steeper inclines and a bit of tricky footwork, but it's worth the effort for the flora and fauna on show.

Yardie Nature Walk is a shorter 1.2 kilometre version (allow 40 minutes) of the Yardie Gorge Trail. It's equally rewarding with gorge and Ningaloo Reef views.

Yardie Boat Cruises can be booked at the on-site jetty or at the Exmouth Visitor Centre.

FIRST PEOPLES KNOW-HOW

The limestone spinifex that can be seen growing in circles was used by the local Jinigudera people, as both a flour to make damper bread and a glue used to make spear heads and fishing nets. The word 'Ningaloo' is a Jinigudera word that means a 'promontory' and today extends to adjacent Cape Range National Park and surrounding areas.

WILDLIFE WATCH

Look closely at the Yardie Gorge walls to see rock figs, swallow's nests, and large roosting nests of sea eagle and osprey that can reach two metres in diameter. The water ecology is similarly intriguing: the creek's water table has a layer of fresh water sitting atop a thicker layer of salt water. When the sand bar between the creek and the reef is open,

the water is permanently fluctuating, with rainfall and tides allowing rays, marine fish, reef sharks and turtles to enter the creek. When closed, these sea creatures can remain trapped for years at a time.

The rock wallaby population was nearly depleted with the introduction of foxes. The Western Shield Wildlife Recovery Program works to bring them back from extinction with the use of Yardie morning glory – an endemic plant used to make 1080 fox bait that local fauna has a tolerance for.

AND ANOTHER THING

Cape Range is known for its extreme heat. Temperatures can exceed 50°C from November to March. The cooler months are recommended and the usual rules apply: bring a tarpaulin or awning for shade, carry adequate water, wear sunscreen and a hat.

ALTERNATIVES

Osprey Bay (see p. 141) is a bigger campground with a focus on the coast and coral reef, which you can access straight off the beach.

Self-sufficient beachfront camping with snorkelling and kayaking.

Osprey Bay

Cape Range National Park, WA

MAP ON PAGE 138

ACTIVITIES

FACILITIES

Hands down, one of the most magical experiences I've ever had was snorkelling with whale sharks along this coastline. For a full 15 minutes, I trailed one of these majestic gods – the biggest fish in the sea, taking in the slow side-to-side of its massive tail, admiring its intricate body constellation – and being so immersed I felt like I was breathing underwater without the aid of goggles and flippers.

To see whale sharks you need to head about 15 kilometres off-shore on a daytrip boat tour and it's highly recommended, but the other amazing thing about this coastline is that a boat is not essential to see the marine life. With the largest fringing reef in Australia, stretching 300 kilometres from North West Cape to Red Bluff, you can experience the unfathomable marine beauty and biology simply by walking from the beach into the water.

If this sounds like fun, then a few nights at Osprey will be, too. The campground has 46 sites that are essentially gravel carparks generously spaced along two unsealed loop roads that create a figure of eight. Loop one (sites 30–46) at the northern end is smaller, but generators are allowed so it could be noisier. Loop two at the southern end (sites 1–29) has the spots closest to the water (7, 9, 11, 13, 16, 17), some with their own little tracks to the beach. They book out earliest. Both loops have toilet blocks and picnic tables.

The campground has recently been updated. Facilities include:

• Lovely curved limestone rock walls around the picnic tables
• Sheltered picnic tables with ocean views
• Functional and well-kept pit-toilet blocks
• Excellent storyboard info about the reef

Along the coast, crumbling red rock shelves kiss the blue turquoise water (this is known as Turquoise Bay), but in the gaps are lovely tan-coloured sand beaches, creating places for sunbakers and kids building sand castles. Spend the day idling here or don a pair of goggles and flippers to explore the local marine life. Alongside the myriad fish and soft and hard coral, look out for intriguing reef creatures, such as nudibranchs (colourful sea slugs), startling sea stars, sea cucumbers, sea urchins (that look like spiky balls), hermit crabs and colourful clams. A good day will get you a reef shark, a green turtle and even a sting ray, especially if you consider the kayak trail (*see* p. 142).

At the northern end of the campground there's a 630-metre walk to Sandy Bay. Swim, snorkel or picnic along the water's edge here. It's also the place for kite- and windsurfing.

Osprey Bay

CATEGORIES

Young Travellers, Family, Nature, Wi-Fi-Free, No Dogs, Boomers, Nomads

GO DO IT

WHO Milyering Discovery Centre and WA Parks and Wildlife Service; (08) 9949 2808; parks.dpaw.wa.gov.au

WHERE Cape Range National Park, on the north-west cape, 90km south of Exmouth and 1200km north of Perth, WA.

ACCESS 80km south of Exmouth via Murat Rd for 12km, left onto Yardie Creek Rd for 66km. Follow signs for left turn towards campground, then third turn right.

WHAT ELSE?

There's a rip on this beach that can get swimmers into trouble. Follow guidelines on beach signs for avoiding it.

Osprey Bay is a shore-based recreational fishing zone, which allows recreational fishers to fish from the shore only, not from boats.

For an up-close encounter with a whale shark I can highly recommend Live Ningaloo (liveningaloo.com.au). The company might be a bit more expensive than the competition, but you pay for quality boats and equipment, knowledgeable staff and small groups with a maximum of 10 people.

WILDLIFE WATCH

Ningaloo Marine Park covers an area of 264,343 hectares and is included in Ningaloo Coast World Heritage Area. Its protected biodiversity includes astonishing marine life. According to the Department of Parks and Wildlife there are approximately 500 species of fin fish, 300 species of coral, 600 species of mollusc and 90 species of echinoderm, with tropical species at the southernmost point of its range and temperate species at the northernmost point of its range.

STEP IT UP

Kayak moorings – black buoys with white tops – have been fixed at several sites along Ningaloo's World Heritage–listed Marine Park to enable day-use kayaking and snorkelling. These sites include Bundegi, Tantabiddi and Osprey sanctuary zones in the north and Maud Sanctuary Zone in the south at Coral Bay.

The Osprey Kayak Trail is a 3 kilometre return paddle that leaves on a loop from the beach south-west for 1.1 kilometres to the first mooring known as 'the blue lagoon'. At a depth of 3–7 metres (depending on tide), you can tie your kayak up and snorkel to see giant clams, anemone, big reef sharks (5–6m, so I hear), lion fish, ornate crayfish and several species of coral. Then paddle south for 500 metres to 'Bungle Bungles' the second mooring, where it's shallower at 3–4 metres with schools of smaller fish and coral, including bombies and staghorn. Paddle north-east back to the launch site. Allow three hours, including snorkelling time.

AND ANOTHER THING

The ground is rock hard here and tough on tent pegs. Come prepared with a hammer or weights.

The landscape is sandy with coastal ground vegetation and not a tree in sight, so come prepared with a tarpauline or similar shade covering.

ALTERNATIVES

Yardie Creek campground (see p. 139) is smaller with a focus on the Yardie Creek Gorge and the remarkable Cape Range National Park, but t's also beachside.

Opposite Sandy beaches and turquoise waters make Osprey Bay a swimmer's (and fisher's) paradise

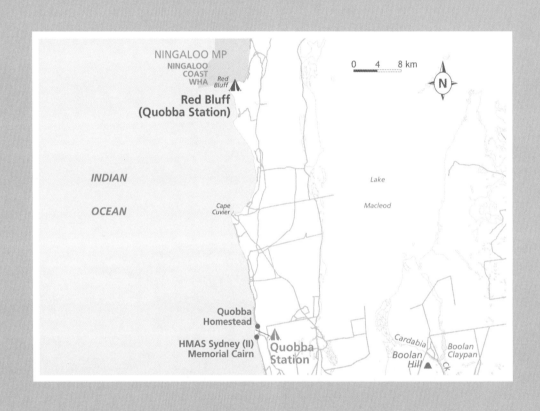

Desert meets ocean with humpback whales and world-class waves.

Red Bluff (Quobba Station)

Carnarvon, WA

ACTIVITIES

FACILITIES

When people talk of camping at Red Bluff they talk of wild crashing surf, big blue horizons, a rugged coastline of red battered cliffs, breaching whales and black nights awash with stars. But they also talk of the soul and spirit here, of nature's calming ways, of respite from the digital world and of being at one with the elements. The combination is what makes this place, on Western Australia's spectacular Quobba coast, so special.

In recent times a couple of mega celebs spent time at Red Bluff campground. Their social media clips about it have since reached millions. For die-hard surfers and adventurous travellers, this kind of exposure fuels the fear of the place being overrun with less hardy tourists. But for now, at least, its isolation, 900 kilometres away – or a 10-hour drive – from the nearest city of Perth, should help maintain the status quo.

Red Bluff campground is part of Quobba Station, a 75,676-hectare sheep station stretching along 80 kilometres of exasperatingly beautiful Indian Ocean coastline between Point Quobba north to Red Bluff, which is on the southernmost tip of the UNESCO World Heritage–listed Ningaloo Marine Park.

The landscape is desolate, unpredictable and vast but incredibly beautiful. The red rocky headland for which the campground is named, turns a rusty red when the rising and setting sun washes over it. The surf is absolutely world-class, with a huge left-hand reef break producing waves that tip 2.5 metres. Surfers from around the globe beeline it here, especially from May through to August when the surf is at its finest.

The campground is basic at best, but this is part of the joy. Unpowered caravan and camping sites are spread along the gravel road adjacent to the ocean and sport sensational water views. The sites higher up on the dunes are awesome when whales breach close to shore, but pitching your tent metres from the beach also has its advantages. The sites are spaced far enough apart for peace and privacy and all of them are within easy reach of the string of amenities blocks (with drop-toilets that share the amazing views).

Each campsite has its own fire-pit but you'll need to BYO firewood (or buy it at Quobba Homestead shop). The campground has a site manager and a shop/cafe which is open from April to October. It sells toasties and drinks, including coffee and mango smoothies that everybody raves about. Saturday night is pizza night. North of the campground, tables with (albeit flimsy) shelters are dotted along the waterfront, offering a smidgeon of shade.

Stepping it up a notch, there are stilted canvas safari tents known as 'retreats' (for two people) and 'bungalows' (for up to six people). They sit in a splendid elevated position on Red Bluff cliffs and have meditative decks that overlook the ocean's breaching whales, dolphin pods and surfers. They were built in 2004 and have the wear and tear to show for it, but they are neatly kitted out with: a queen bed, bunks (in the bungalows), a small kitchen (with fridge/freezer, microwave, gas cooker), solar power, an ensuite and a barbecue.

For a real surfer-vibe, the campground's handful of basic 'shacks' are flat-roofed huts made from palm fronds, canvas and cement. They have old springy beds but are also perfect for rolling out a swag. Some of them have been upgraded. Ask when booking. If you're staying in the safari tents and shacks you still need to BYO linen, towels, pillows, cooking utensils and equipment and water. Also, it's a two-night minimum stay.

CATEGORIES

Young Travellers, Dog-Lovers, Nature, Nomads

GO DO IT

WHO   Quobba Station; (08) 9948 5001; quobba.com.au

WHERE   Red Bluff campground is part of Quobba Station,
           in Macleod. It is about 140km north of Carnarvon,
           about 900km north of Perth and 1550km south-
           west of Broome, WA.

ACCESS   From Carnarvon, follow North West Coastal Hwy
           for 30km. Turn left at the Quobba Station sign
           onto Blowholes Rd and drive for about 50km to
           the 'King Waves Kill' sign. Turn right onto the
           unsealed road for the last 6km to Quobba Station.
           The 60km road from Quobba Station to Red Bluff
           is dirt and gravel and can get sandy and pot-
           holed in parts. It's graded several times a year, so
           conditions vary. People with 2WDs report getting
           through no problems, people with SUV 4WDs
           report wishing they had a bigger vehicle. If you're
           towing a caravan or you're concerned about the
           drive, Quobba Station recommends pulling up at
           the homestead campground (see below) for a night
           and making a daytrip out to Red Bluff to check
           the conditions.

WHAT ELSE?

Quobba Homestead, about 60 kilometres south of Red Bluff
campground, was established along with the station in 1898.
It has been owned by the Meecham family for more than
40 years and the family run both the tourism side of the
business and about 10,000 head of sheep. The homestead sits
alongside some of the original buildings and infrastructure,
including the blacksmith's workshop and stables. It has a
store (open daily 10am–4pm), selling bread and milk, ice,
bait, basic camp supplies and drinks (non-alcoholic). You
can hire snorkelling gear and borrow life-jackets. Eftpos
is available but there's no fuel. Fill up in Carnarvon,
80 kilometres south. There's camping at Quobba Homestead,
too (see p. 147).

Dogs are welcome at Red Bluff campground (but not at
Quobba Homestead) by previous arrangement only. Part
of the deal is they must be kept on a lead and they're only
allowed on certain parts of the beach. They're not allowed
in the shacks and safari tents or at the cafe. Owners need
to respect fellow campers and the natural environment by
cleaning up dog poo. You might be asked to pay a $50 deposit.

Quobba Station has been described as having some of
the best land-based game fishing in the world. Check out
Quobba's website for tips on where to catch pink snapper,
Spanish mackerel, trevally etc.

Near Quobba Point, 60 kilometres north of Red Bluff, take
a pit-stop at Quobba Blow Holes to watch water spouting
20 metres high through holes in the rock when conditions
are right. Pull off the road nearby for a selfie next to the
iconic 'King Waves Kill' sign. There's also decent surfing at
Blow Holes and at Seventeen Mile Well, 20 kilometres south.

CULTURE VULTURE

A fierce battle between the German ship *HSK Kormoran*
and *HMAS Sydney* in November 1941 ended in the sinking
of both ships. The 645 crew on *HMAS Sydney* were all lost,
as were 80 of the Kormoran's crew. Of the 316 survivors,
103 landed at Quobba Station, 46 at Seventeen Mile Well
and 57 in a steel lifeboat at the beach at Red Bluff. (The
others were presumably pulled from the water to safety.)
The plot thickens: in 2007 a surfer discovered the remains
of a 1934 model Mauser handgun in the water at Red
Bluff. The following year, the wrecks of both ships were
discovered approximately 150 kilometres from Shark Bay on
Dirk Hartog Island. A memorial cairn commemorating the

HMAS Sydney, which was erected near Quobba Homestead back in 2003, is in an uncannily accurate position along the coast.

WILDLIFE WATCH

Humpback whales make their annual pilgrimage past Red Bluff from late May to October. Surfers report seeing them up close near the reef. Keep your eyes peeled for dolphins and turtles and, at low tide, reef sharks in the rockpools. Kangaroos and monitor lizards roam the campground, too.

AND ANOTHER THING

Campsites cannot be booked but even in the busiest times it's possible to get a site. If in doubt, ring ahead.

Bring lots of water, plenty of food and a shade annex or similar.

ALTERNATIVES

The only other camping allowed on the station is at Quobba Homestead. It has powered and unpowered sites, toilet facilities and hot showers. It is close to a beach, with excellent rock pools, shells and whale watching. It's an ideal pit-stop before heading to Red Bluff.

The Quobba Homestead Long Cottage - originally the station garage, and the Cottage, the old overseer's residence, are today used for visitor accommodation.

Opposite Quobba Station and sunset *Below* Aerial view of the campground

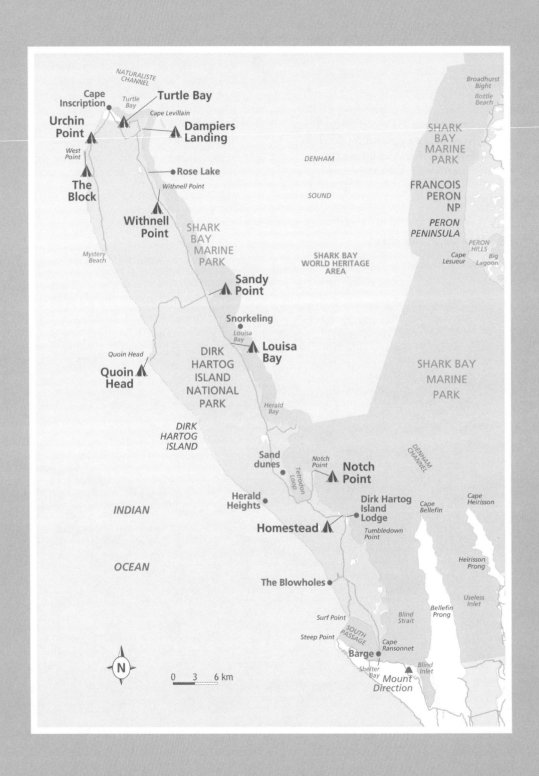

Dirk Hartog Island

Remote island camping on a wilderness 'ark' with beaches, blowholes and lingering sunsets.

Dirk Hartog Island

Dirk Hartog Island National Park, WA

ACTIVITIES

FACILITIES

Dirk Hartog Island lies in the mesmeric Shark Bay, Western Australia's first UNESCO World Heritage–listed site. It is the most western point of Australia: all that lies between this land mass and the east coast of Madagascar are the island blips of Mauritius and Réunion, and the expanse of the Indian Ocean. The seclusion and isolation of this locale, accessible via plane, boat charter or 4WD barge (*see* p. 150), means that few people have been privileged enough to tread here.

Stretching 80 kilometres north–south and between 3 and 15 kilometres wide, Dirk Hartog Island has become known as an 'ark' for its endangered wildlife, an environment where loggerhead turtles, lemon sharks and white-breasted sea eagles, to name a few, can exist in their natural environment without fear of introduced predators. For campers, it is an opportunity to set up tent in one of the most truly remote natural wilderness areas on the planet.

There are nine national park campgrounds spread around the island, as well as private camping at Homestead Camping Grounds (*see* p. 150). The national park campgrounds have no facilities, so you need to be prepared to self-cater.

The east coast campgrounds (Turtle Bay, Dampiers Landing, Withnell Point, Sandy Point, Louisa Bay and Notch Point) are sheltered with family friendly beaches ripe for swimming, beachcombing, snorkelling and stand-up paddleboarding. Of these, Turtle Bay and Louisa Bay are, I think, the picks. Turtle Bay is larger than Louisa Bay, with an elevated position making it a hot spot for seeing whales. Access from the camping area to the greeny-blue beach is via a short downhill stroll. Louisa Bay sits on a shallow beach with a coral garden about 200 metres from shore. You can snorkel here to see coral trout and scribbled angelfish nibbling around staghorn and cabbage corals. Sandy Point is more of an overnight campground on the way to sites closer to the water's edge.

The west coast sites (Urchin Point, The Block and Quoin Head) are boltholes for groups of fisherpersons attracted to rugged cliff-faces, wind-lashed landscapes and spectacular sunsets.

The private camping at Homestead Camping Grounds is located 20 kilometres north of the Cape Ransonnet barge landing area, on the east of the island. It's part of

Above Dirk Hartog Island Homestead

Dirk Hartog Island Lodge. It includes: Salty's Campground, which has 18 unpowered campsites scattered throughout the coastal greenery only 50 metres from the shallow shore; Buddy's Beach Camp and Jed's Beach Camp are similarly unpowered and close to the beach, but they're exclusive sites suited to pre-booked families and groups. Facilities at the Homestead Camping Grounds include:

• Camp kitchens
• Tables and chairs
• Gas barbecue and gas stove burner
• Flushing toilets
• Hot water showers
• Drinking water
• Campfires

All of the Homestead Campground sites can be booked as a package, including 4WD barge transfers from the WA mainland (*see* Go do it). Petrol (book ahead two weeks in advance), firewood and ice (pre-booked) are available from the Homestead Bay office.

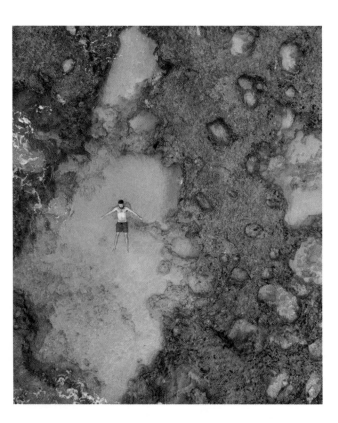

CATEGORIES

Young Travellers, Family, Nature, Wi-Fi-Free, No Dogs, Boomers, Nomads

GO DO IT

WHO   Dirk Hartog Island; (08) 9948 1211; dirkhartog.com.au

WHERE   Off the Gascoyne coast of WA, about 850km north of Perth and 1800km south-west of Broome.

ACCESS   The 4WD barge *Hartog Explorer* operates seven days a week from Shelter Bay, on the mainland at Steep Point. The barge is a purpose-built landing craft designed with capacity to carry a 4WD vehicle with off-road camper-trailer, and passengers. The access road to the Steep Point barge on the mainland is long and rough (140km unsealed track – about three hours driving) and recommended for those with previous 4WDing experience. You're best to arrive at Steep Point the day before the journey across to Dirk Hartog Island and stay the night at Shelter Bay, near the barge departure point. Book your campsite here with Steep Point Rangers (parks.dpaw.wa.gov.au/site/steep-point).

WHAT ELSE?

When not luxuriating on Dirk Hartog's breathlessly beautiful beaches, there are plenty of natural wonders to tick off your bucket-list. When the swell is nearing 3 metres or more, the Blowholes, on the island's south-west side, rocket into the air and can be seen from 20 kilometres away.

Between August and May, Rose Lake on the island's north-east blushes an otherworldly pink.

The sand dunes are another fun outing, particularly if you have a bodyboard handy.

The 600 feet high cliffs of Herald Heights are the best vantage point to see the last glimpse of Australian sunlight before it dips below the westerly horizon.

Dirk Hartog Island Lodge will soon be opening Wirruwana – a social hub with a visitor centre, bar and cafe. Dirk Hartog Island manager Kieran Wardle said the hub will provide a central meeting place for all campers, visitors and tour operators. 'They'll be able to access information about the island, purchase merchandise, check-in to their

accommodation and enjoy barista-made coffee,' he said. During peak periods, Wirruwana will host pizza nights and sunset drinks and, for the first time, campers will be able to join tours, including whale watching (Sept/Oct) and a sunset tour. It will be open from Easter through to October each year.

CULTURE VULTURE

Cape Inscription, on the northern tip of the island, was the landing site of Captain Dirk Hartog in 1616, Vlaming in 1697, Baudin in 1801 and de Freycinet in 1818. Read all about it on the storyboards here.

Dampiers Landing, named for Englishman William Dampier, sits on the north-east side of the island. The navigator and explorer who voyaged to what was then New Holland in 1699, spent a few days on the island where he coined the name for Shark's Bay. Equally significantly, he made extensive botanical and geographical observations of the plants and wildlife. His detailed musings on the plant life in particular became one of the first recorded collections of botanicals in Australia. A plaque commemorates his visit.

WILDLIFE WATCH

There's always something to see on this island. On the south-west of the island, Surf Point is a marine sanctuary where hundreds of Nervous Sharks can be spotted (July to Oct).

At Cape Inscription and Turtle Bay, watch as the humpback whales swim through (July to Nov).

The island's nesting (Dec to Feb) and hatching (Feb to Apr) loggerhead turtles can also be seen at Turtle Bay.

Throughout the year, keep an eye out for nesting sea eagles and ospreys.

AND ANOTHER THING

The national park has a Leave No Trace policy, which means depositing solid human waste in holes dug 15–20cm deep at least 70 steps away from water, campsites and trails.

ALTERNATIVES

Dirk Hartog Island Lodge is eco-accommodation that sits 30 metres from the jade-blue water. Guests use it as a base to kayak and stand-up paddleboard and revel in the night-time fires, sunset drinks and freshly caught fish barbecues. There's also a stone villa for hire. It is self-contained and sleeps seven guests in three rooms.

Opposite Floating in the rock pools *Above* The campsite at sunset

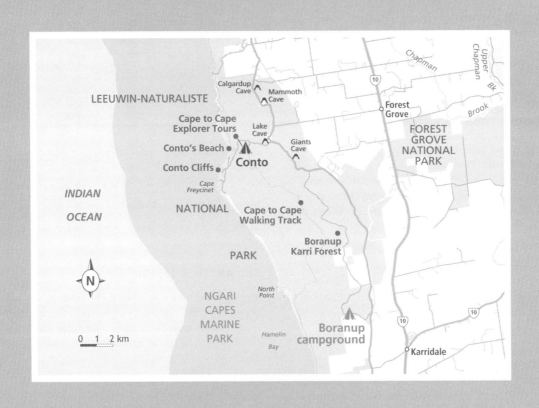

A sprawling campground with top-notch amenities close to Conto's Beach.

Conto

Leeuwin-Naturaliste National Park, WA

ACTIVITIES

FACILITIES

Leeuwin-Naturaliste National Park is a dynamic and rugged slice of wilderness extending 120 kilometres north–south from the lighthouses of Cape Naturaliste to Cape Leeuwin. It's a showcase of white limestone cliffs and waters that are so turquoise they look like somebody has added a dash of blue curaçao to the Indian Ocean. But it's also a treasure trove of other landscapes, including a honeycomb of caves embedded in the cliffs and the incredible Boranup Karri Forest (*see* p. 154).

Conto Campground (or Conto's as it's known) is the most popular in Western Australia. It sits in the thick of this natural world, a kilometre or two as the crow flies (4 kilometres by road) from Conto's Beach, a superb arc of white sand backed by cliffs and coastal greenery, where swimming, snorkelling, fishing and surfing are de rigueur. In addition, the famed Cape to Cape Walking Track cuts through the campground, making walks and hikes through white sand dunes and wildflowers to coastal cliff-tops a hard-to-resist option.

Numbering 116 campsites, Conto's also has reams of space. The sprawling tract of sandy bottomed bushland, alive with peppermint gums, sheoaks and coastal pandanus, stretches about 1 kilometre in diameter. It is laid out like a well-planned housing estate, so it's easily navigable with a wide main entry road branching off into seven well-signed main loops: Isaacs, Whalers, Chuditch, Davies, Hamelin, Whistlers and Quenda, and one small loop: Wanil.

Each loop has between seven (Wanil) and twenty-one (Hamelin) campsites that are spread along both sides of the access loop roads. Chuditch and Quenda have hard surfaces and are suitable for caravan and camper-trailers only. Wanil and Davies, which are smaller sites immersed in thicker bushland, are for tents only. The other loops are mixed-use combinations of tent, campervan, caravan and camper-trailer sites. The bigger sites are clearly delineated with pine-log stumps, while the smaller tent sites are spread along lovely grassy areas with nearby picnic tables and plenty of shade.

Conto's is a well-equipped campground. A recent $1.1 million funding from the State Government's Royalties for Regions program saw the campground upgraded with 29 new campsites, as well as new fire-rings, picnic tables, toilets and landscaped barbecue areas. The roads, signage and paths were also improved, making access between the camping loops easier. Facilities at each loop include:

- Water (not for drinking)
- Sheltered barbecue areas (except Davies, Isaacs, Whalers and Whistlers)
- Picnic tables
- Fire-pits (except Isaacs)
- Toilet blocks (except Wanil)

Expect to see Western grey Kangaroos hopping around the wooded areas. If you hear something shaking the trees branches at night it is likely to be possums.

CATEGORIES

Family, Nature, Wi-Fi-Free, No Dogs, Boomers, Nomads

GO DO IT

WHO   WA Parks and Wildlife Service; (08) 9219 9000; parks.dpaw.wa.gov.au

WHERE   Conto Rd, Boranup in Leeuwin-Naturaliste National Park which extends 120km along Margaret River's western coastline in WA's South West region. The campground is 300km south of Perth and 18km south of Margaret River.

ACCESS   From Margaret River head south-east towards John Archibald Dr. Exit the roundabout onto Boodjidup Rd for 7km, then turn left onto Caves Rd for 9km, before turning right onto Conto Rd for 2km. The campground is at the end.

WHAT ELSE?

From Conto's take a 10-minute drive south along Caves Rd to beautiful Boranup Karri Forest, a sanctuary of towering karri trees: one of the world's tallest tree species and native to this part of Western Australia.

Campers can follow short sections of the Cape to Cape Track (see Step it up) to explore the area immediately around the campground, including a route through sandy trails to Conto Cliffs looking over the beach.

EAT IT

For an Indian Ocean sunset with style, Cape to Cape Explorer Tours (capetocapetours.com.au) hosts a 3-kilometre walk from Conto campground along sandy trails, through karri forest and past gardens of wildflowers to Conto Cliffs. You'll watch the sun setting on rolling waves as passionate host Janita Cottman pours sparkling and hands around local nibbles, including camembert from Yallingup Cheese and biscuits from Margaret River Crackers.

Margaret River's 14-year-old farmers' market (margaretriverfarmersmarket.com.au) draws a crowd to the Education Campus on the town's main street every Saturday morning. About 50 local stall operators sell a feast of produce, including Uralba marmalade, Cape Farm olive oil and Bettenay's nougat.

FIRST PEOPLES KNOW-HOW

The Wadandi and Bibbulman people, traditional owners of the Busselton, Dunsborough and Margaret River areas, are part of Noongar First Peoples group of south-west Western Australia. About 55 kilometres north of the campground, Koomal Dreaming's Ngilgi Cave Tour (bookings are essential: koomaldreaming.com.au) offers a chance to explore some of the world's most intriguing limestone caves, while tapping into the rich and beautiful Noongar culture. Alongside soft-spoken Noongar host Josh Whiteland, you'll descend into caves of stalactites and stalagmites and be treated to a didgeridoo rendition in the cavernous amphitheatre and, afterwards, a bush-tucker walk and fire-lighting demonstration. It's highly recommended.

STEP IT UP

Accessible directly from the campground, the Cape to Cape Track (capetocapetrack.com.au) is a spectacular 135 kilometre long nature immersion in a coastal escarpment of cliffs and rock formations, wildflowers and native grasses, dolphins and humpbacks.

AND ANOTHER THING

When making a booking, you need to choose a loop rather than a specific site. The campsites within that loop are on a first-come, first-served basis.

The campground has strict rules: alcohol is banned, excessive noise is not tolerated and any noise needs to cease at 9pm.

Don't forget to BYO drinking water.

ALTERNATIVES

About 17 kilometres south of Conto, Boranup Campground is small with just seven sites for tents and campervans only. It's near the stunning Boranup Karri Forest.

Previous Nearby Injidup Beach, along the Cape to Cape Track
Opposite Driving through Boranup Karri Forest

Conto

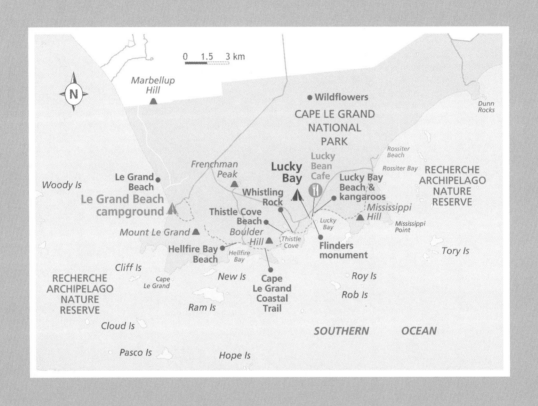

Coastal camping with friendly kangaroos, white sand and azure water.

Lucky Bay

Cape Le Grand National Park, WA

ACTIVITIES

FACILITIES

On Australian best beach bucket-lists, Lucky Bay rivals Queensland's Whitehaven Beach (*see* p. 230) for its drifts of floury white sand and rolling bluest-of-blue water. Indeed, seeing Western grey kangaroos lazing on the wet sands at sun-up and sun-down might just tip the scales in Lucky Bay's favour.

The long curve of beach and campground are located in Western Australia's Cape Le Grand National Park, the land of the Njunga people. This remote 31,801 hectares of country is known for its rolling coastal heath, teetering ocean-facing cliffs and stunning beaches. Looking offshore across the Southern Ocean is a scattering of more than 100 islands, part of the Recherche Archipelago.

It might be remote, but such is its picture-postcard beauty that Lucky Bay is extremely popular. Visitors to Esperance think nothing of the 45-minute drive south-east for a chance to photograph sun-baking kangaroos and to 4WD on the sandy tracts (an activity that attracts the ire of those beach-goers who prefer sandy footprints to tyre tread). Swimming, snorkelling, surfing and fishing are all part of the package here.

The campground is at the western end of the bay, next to the day-use carpark, on a stretch of land covered in knee-high coastal bush and spinifex grass. It is slightly elevated so that even those campers furthest from the beach can pour their morning coffee while spying shards of cobalt blue sea between the vegetation, caravans, amenities blocks and facilities.

The 56 unpowered campsites have same-size bays that cater to all codes – tents, swags, campervans, camper-trailers and caravans, and are neatly spaced along a sealed figure of eight (of sorts) access road. There's also a central area for tour-operator camping. Sites are on a first-come, first served basis, with the row of nine sites closest to the beach filling first. Facilities include:

- Sheltered picnic tables
- Pit-toilets and flush toilets
- Sheltered gas barbecue area
- Solar powered hot showers (not guaranteed)
- Washing up area
- Generators permitted (8am–1pm and 5–9pm)

The neighbouring day-use carpark does increase the number of visitors on the beach near the camping area, but it also has its benefits. The numbers help support an awesome coffee caravan called Lucky Bean Cafe, right on the beach – complete with a barista machine, deckchairs and the all-important 'decent latte'. Muffins, toasties and ice-cream are also available or ask for a 'kangacino'. You'll see the caravan's flags fluttering.

CATEGORIES

Young Travellers, Family, Nature, Wi-Fi-Free, No Dogs, Boomers, Nomads

GO DO IT

WHO   WA Parks and Wildlife Service; (08) 9083 2102; parks.dpaw.wa.gov.au

WHERE Cape Le Grand National Park, 631 km south-east of Perth and 56 km east of Esperance (50 minutes on a sealed road), WA.

ACCESS 62km from Esperance via Fisheries Rd, Merivale Rd, Cape Le Grand Rd and Lucky Bay Rd.

WHAT ELSE?

Over the headland from the campground, take the well-signed 2.8 kilometre easy walk from Lucky Bay to Thistle Cove through the dunes and coastal heath, with superb views of the Southern Ocean coastline along the way. Thistle Cove matches Lucky Bay for sheer beauty and there's a 'whistling' rock to check out. This is a small section of the Cape Le Grand Coastal Trail (see Step it up). Allow 45 minutes one-way.

Kangaroos like to beeline to the fresh water rivulets running over the sand into the ocean. On days when there are fewer roos around, you've a good chance to see one at close quarters if you head to the beach spot just below the rocky Flinders monument. The monument is to explorer Matthew Flinders, who, in 1802, when surrounded by the hazardous islands of the Recherche Archipelago, managed to sail his *HMS Investigator* into this area of refuge that he then named 'Lucky Bay'.

On a busy day, check out Cape Le Grand's other similarly breathtaking white-sand beaches, including Thistle Cove (2km south-west), Hellfire Bay (19km west) and Le Grand (12km west). They're often less crowded than Lucky Bay.

The water is freezing – bring a wetsuit or thermal rashie.

Rock-climbing is popular 9 kilometres north-west at Frenchman Peak and 15 kilometres west at Mount Le Grand.

Western Australia is renowned for its incredible wildflowers, with over 12,000 species blooming in spring (mid-Aug to Nov in this region). At Cape Le Grand National Park you'll see groves of *banksia speciose* and *banksia puchella*, among others. There's a wildflower trail from Perth to Esperance which includes the national park. See: australiasgoldenoutback.com

WILDLIFE WATCH

Western grey kangaroos are the stars of this campground, and keep an eye out for pygmy honey possums and bandicoots. At the western end of the bay, pods of dolphins can be seen playing in the water and look further out over the Southern Ocean to spot humpback whales in season (June to Oct).

STEP IT UP

Cape Le Grand Coastal Trail (trailswa.com.au) is a 15 kilometre long bay-to-bay hike from Le Grand Beach to Rossiter Bay via Hellfire Bay, Thistle Cove and Lucky Bay. It is for experienced walkers but it can be broken into four sections. Le Grand Beach to Hellfire Bay, and Hellfire Bay to Thistle Cove are graded difficult. Thistle Cove to Lucky Bay is moderately easy, and Lucky Bay to Rossiter Bay is moderately difficult. The entire walk will take about eight or nine hours one-way.

AND ANOTHER THING

If you drive your 4WD onto the beach, normal road rules apply: beware of pedestrians, drive slowly and know your vehicle.

ALTERNATIVES

Le Grand Beach Campground, 12 kilometres west of Lucky Bay, is similarly beautiful and located within earshot of the waves. It has 14 sandy bottomed campsites strung along cleared coastal heath, toilets and an indoor kitchen and picnic area.

Opposite Surf, sniffs, snaps and snacks are all part of the Lucky Bay experience

Northern Territory

From Outback desert landscapes to northern tropical savannah, Northern Territory's beauty and rich Indigenous culture can be explored in the stunning national parks of Uluṟu-Kata Tjuṯa, Kakadu and Nitmiluk

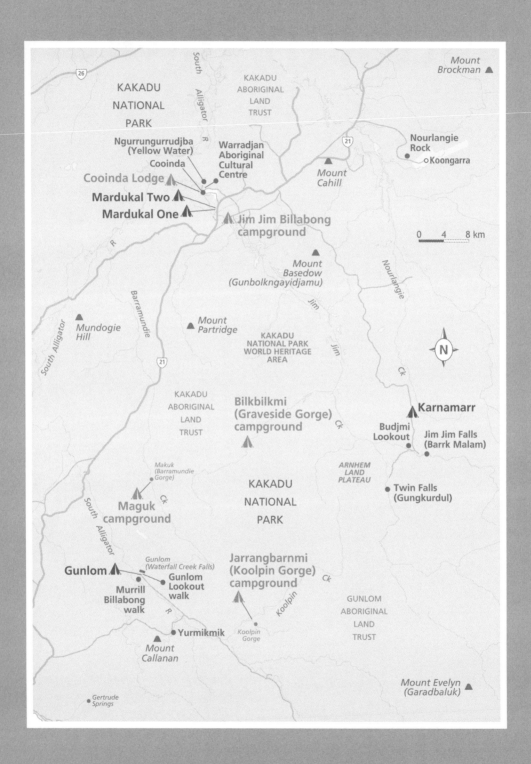

Mardukal

KAKADU NATIONAL PARK

South Alligator R

26

Mount Brockman ▲

KAKADU ABORIGINAL LAND TRUST

21

Ngurrungurrudjba (Yellow Water)
Cooinda
Cooinda Lodge ▲
Mardukal Two ▲
Mardukal One ▲

Warradjan Aboriginal Cultural Centre

Mount Cahill ▲

Nourlangie Rock ●
○ **Koongarra**

▲ **Jim Jim Billabong campground**

0   4   8 km

Mount Basedow (Gunbolkngayidjamu)

Nourlangie

R

Jim

Jim

Barramundie

South Alligator

Mundogie Hill ▲

Mount Partridge ▲

KAKADU NATIONAL PARK WORLD HERITAGE AREA

N

21

KAKADU ABORIGINAL LAND TRUST

Bilkbilkmi (Graveside Gorge) campground ⛺

Ck

Makuk (Barramundie Gorge) ●

Karnamarr ▲
Budjmi Lookout ▲
Jim Jim Falls (Barrk Malam) ●

ARNHEM LAND PLATEAU

Twin Falls (Gungkurdul) ●

KAKADU NATIONAL PARK

Maguk campground ⛺

Ck

South Alligator

R

Gunlom (Waterfall Creek Falls)
Gunlom ▲
Murrill Billabong walk
Gunlom Lookout walk

Jarrangbarnmi (Koolpin Gorge) campground ⛺

Koolpin

Ck

GUNLOM ABORIGINAL LAND TRUST

▲ ● **Yurmikmik**
Mount Callanan ▲

Koolpin Gorge ●

Gertrude Springs ●

Mount Evelyn (Garadbaluk) ▲

A billabong locale close to fuel, food and daytrip departures.

Mardukal
Kakadu National Park, NT

ACTIVITIES

FACILITIES

As a standalone campground Mardukal (formerly Mardugal) wouldn't rate on aesthetic alone, but put into context – as an accessible 2WD nature-based campground in the heart of Kakadu – it stands its ground. The campground sits right next to Mardukal Billabong in a typical Kakadu landscape of ochre reds and vibrant greens. Cooinda hub campground is just 6 kilometres away, granting you easy access to national park passes, fuel, bistro food, barista coffee and an alternative campground (*see* p. 164). At Cooinda you can also book daytrips and tours, most of which depart locally. Ngurrungurrudjba (Yellow Water Billabong, *see* p. 164) is also a short drive away from Mardukal, and is a small taster of the exquisite natural beauty – and exceptional sunsets – to be encountered throughout the national park. Ideally, campers in Kakadu would spend a couple of nights at Mardukal to make plans for the rest of their adventure.

Maradukal campground is loosely divided into Mardukal One and Mardukal Two. Mardukal One, otherwise known as the top campground, is the bigger option suitable for caravans and bigger vehicles. A bitumen driveway loops through it, revealing flat leaf-scattered earth and the occasional green grass, with leafy eucalyptus trees granting slices of shade. Mardukal Two, the lower campground, is the smaller area for tents only and has more bushy coverage. Bags one of the individual tent sites here for a bit more privacy and closer encounters with the local agile wallabies. That said, Mardukal Two is closed during the wet season (Nov to Mar) because it floods, while Mardukal One is open year-round.

Facilities include:

- Large toilet and shower blocks located on spacious grassy knolls
- Tank rainwater suitable for drinking
- Concrete picnic tables
- Fire-pits dotted around
- Mardukal One also has a generator zone

Both sites have scenic billabong views, framed by old thick-trunked gums, paperbark trees and water pandanus. The frog song and bird sounds generated by this natural oasis make for morning and evening soundtracks that would do well on a meditation app – such is the serenity.

In your downtime, follow the campground signs to the Billabong walk, a tranquil 1 kilometre easy trail leading to a picnic area on the water where you can hang out with blue-winged kookaburras. This is a popular spot to drop a line (and there's a boat ramp at the campground), but keep to the high bank away from the water – large saltwater crocs lurk here and going anywhere near the water's edge is a big fat no no.

Previous Ellery Big Hole, near Glen Helen Gorge, Tjoritja (West MacDonnell) National Park

CATEGORIES

Young Travellers, Family, Nature, Wi-Fi-Free, No Dogs, Boomers, Nomads

GO DO IT

WHO   Bowali Visitor Centre; (08) 8938 1120; parksaustralia.gov.au

WHERE   Kakadu Hwy, Kakadu National Park, approximately 300km or a 3-hour drive east of Darwin, NT.

ACCESS   From Bowali Visitor Centre at Jabiru in the north of the national park, it's about 50km south-west on the Kakadu Hwy.

WHAT ELSE?

Kungarden walk is a mini-immersion in the environment. The easy 2-kilometre trail loops from the campground through a lush woodland of bloodwood eucalyptus and liniment trees (scrunch the leaves for a lovely native wood aroma).

As one of the more accessible sites in Kakadu, Ngurrungurrudjba (Yellow Water Billabong) is busy with tourists but its popularity doesn't outweigh its beauty. Get here for a river cruise and a pink-clouded sundown with the chance to spot crocs and birds among the lily pads. Book ahead at Cooinda hub.

CULTURE VULTURE

The stunning 2006 film *10 Canoes*, directed by Rolf de Heer and Peter Djigirr, is set in the Arafura wetlands of neighbouring Arnhem Land in the time before European colonisation. Narrated by David Gulpilil and starring his son Jamie Gulpilil, it is a magnificent insight into Indigenous culture and a feast for the eyes for anyone who loves this part of the world. Spoken in Ganalbingu language, and subtitled English, it was the first film in an Australian Indigenous language.

EAT IT

Taste of Kakadu festival (northernterritory.com/kakadu-and-surrounds/events) is a 10-day food exploration, with pop-up degustation dinners, campfire stories, traditional cooking demonstrations with local Bininj and Mungguy people and guided bush-tucker walks.

FIRST PEOPLES KNOW-HOW

Warradjan Aboriginal Cultural Centre, 6 kilometres away from the Mardukal campground, is a great introduction to the culture of the Bininj (north of the park) and Mungguy (south) Indigenous groups, of which there are 19 clans. It dives deep into the importance of the kinship system, which defines how people relate to each other.

Get local on the wildlife lingo: in the language of the Liyagawumirr and Manyarrngu clans, kaldurrk are blue-winged kookaburras, rakul are partridge pigeons, kornobolo are agile wallabies and dalkken are dingos. They can all be spotted at the Mardukal campground.

STEP IT UP

About 90 kilometres from the campground, Ubirr rock art site is a natural-world gallery of exceptional Indigenous rock art, including excellent examples of long-neck turtles and brim fish, painted in the X-ray style. A pleasant walk to the nearby lookout reveals views across the floodplains. It's a contemplative and memorable place to see the sunset.

AND ANOTHER THING

I visited this national park during dry season (May to Oct). In the wet season (Sept to Apr), it's a different place again. Check the park website and visitor centre for conditions and road closures and plan ahead – the heat and long-distance hard-yakka driving can kill the vibe if you're not prepared.

Camping fees can be paid onsite during the dry season, but head to Bowali Visitor Centre (50km north-east on Kakadu Hwy) during the wet.

ALTERNATIVES

If you're in a 4WD, Jim Jim Billabong bush campground is a quieter, smaller, more basic option with a fire-pit, pit toilets and a boat ramp. It's 8.3 kilometres from Mardukal.

There's a commercial campground at the Cooinda hub with 100 powered sites and 200 unpowered grassed sites. Also in Kakadu, sensational Karnamarr (formerly Garnamarr, see p. 165) and Gunlom (see p. 168).

A well-kept campground close to two Kakadu must-do waterfalls.

Karnamarr
Kakadu National Park, NT

MAP ON PAGE 162

ACTIVITIES

FACILITIES

To make the most of two of Kakadu National Park's most iconic and jaw-dropping attractions – Jim Jim Falls (Barrk Malam) and Twin Falls (Gungkurdul) – campers should park themselves at Karnamarr (formerly Garnamarr) for a night or three. You won't feel hard-done by. Twin Falls was closed on my visit (as is often the case, due to boat access issues), but Jim Jim Falls is reliably open in the dry season.

It's only 5 kilometres from the campground to Jim Jim (and a further 5km to Twin Falls) but driving at 10km/h and slowing to 3km/h when crossing rocky patches and trickling creek beds means it takes half an hour to get to the carpark. Once there it's a challenging 1-kilometre walk through monsoonal rainforest that requires rock-hopping along a creek bed and navigating oversized boulders. It takes a couple of hours and is not for the faint-hearted, but it's sure worth the effort. Even without water (in the dry season), the base of the would-be falls is spectacular, with a huge waterhole or plunge pool surrounded by 200 metre high red cliffs that reverberate with the echoes of excitable visitors. The swimming hole's inky black depths and bone-chilling cold can be overcome with the deceptively long but rewarding swim to the other side. There's also a pretty sandy beach area with clear shallow waters. It is signed off the main track or you can swim to it from the main waterhole. The Barrk Marlam walk to the plateau above Jim Jim Falls branches off the main walk and is best for fit and experienced climbers.

The well-kept, unpowered campground with a red-dirt road, swathes of grass and skinny bright green gum trees is on the edge of the serene Arnhem Land escarpment. You can see the red-rock cliff-faces rising from the flat-treed landscape into the blue sky while lying in your tent.

The campground caters to 200 campers (though on my visit in August there were only a handful of people around), with tour groups at one end and campers at the other. Facilities in both areas include:

• Modern amenities blocks with attractive pitched corrugate rooves
• Flushing toilets and hot showers (powered by solar panels)
• Water tanks on tall stands providing drinking water

You'll need to BYO firewood (buy from petrol stations) to use the concrete fire-rings, but gas stoves are preferred.

A gate on the falls side of Karnamarr Campground is locked between 8.30pm and 6.30am for visitor safety. Campers need to leave the falls areas in time to be at Karnamarr before gates are locked.

There is no booking system. Camping fees are collected by the park manager. You'll need correct change (there are no eftpos facilities). Check campsite availability at Bowali Visitor Centre.

CATEGORIES

Young Travellers, Family, Nature, Wi-Fi-Free, No Dogs

GO DO IT

WHO   Bowali Visitor Centre; (08) 8938 1120;
parksaustralia.gov.au

WHERE   Jim Jim Falls Rd, Kakadu National Park,
approximately 340km or a 4-hour-drive east of
Darwin, NT.

ACCESS   From Kakadu Hwy, turn south-east onto Jim Jim
Falls Rd and follow the dirt road for 47km.

WHAT ELSE?

Park managers and rangers present regular free slide shows
and talks about the local flora and fauna, and Indigenous
culture and traditions. Ask for details on arrival.

From the picnic area at Jim Jim Creek Crossing, the
moderate grade 1 kilometre return walk to Budjmi Lookout
reveals a green-kissed woodland landscape with escarpment
cliffs rising up behind. Allow 45 minutes.

FIRST PEOPLES KNOW-HOW

Karnamarr means 'red-tailed black cockatoo' in the
Kunwinjku language and you have a fair chance to see
these marvellous winged creatures flying through the
Arnhem Land escarpment. The name Jim Jim comes from
the Kundjeyhmi word for water pandanus – anjimjim.
Kundjeyhmi and Kunwinjku are dialects of the same
language – their speakers can understand one another.

WILDLIFE WATCH

On my visit, park manager Richard Perry, a khaki-clad guy
sporting a well-loved Akubra hat, had caught a death adder –
one of the world's top five deadliest snakes, in his kitchen
the night before. With it now sleeping restfully in a big metal
bin, he showed it around to the campers so we would know
what to look for – and keep away from – in the bush. This
one had muted black and pinky brown stripes but according
to Perry they can be striped gold, and so like tinsel 'you
could put them on a Christmas tree'. He reckoned this was
the same one he had caught two months back because it had
a bung eye, the change of colour possibly due to it shedding
its skin.

AND ANOTHER THING

The campground is accessible in dry season (Apr to Oct) by
4WD vehicles only – caravans are not recommended and
camper-trailers will need to be unhooked and left in the
designated parking area before continuing onto the falls.
The dirt road in is narrow, corrugated in parts with humps,
mounds and ditches that could tear the bottom out of a
non-terrain vehicle never mind rattling the brain out of
your skull.

ALTERNATIVES

The closest is Jim Jim Billabong campground, a basic
bush option with a fire-pit, pit toilets and boat ramp.

Near Kakadu Highway, Cooinda hub campground has
100 powered sites and 200 unpowered grassy sites.
Also in Kakadu, Mardukal (formerly Mardugal, *see*
p. 163) and Gunlom (*see* p. 168).

Opposite It's a bit of a trek to get to nearby Jim Jim Falls, but it's
worth the effort. Just watch out for unwanted visitors

A grassy campsite neighbouring Kakadu's showcase infinity plunge pool.

Gunlom

Kakadu National Park, NT

MAP ON PAGE 162

ACTIVITIES

FACILITIES

To describe Gunlom, or Waterfall Creek, as breathtaking is not to overstate it. When you arrive and see the heavenly scene – of a plunge pool spilling over the infinity edge of a cliff with green savannah floodlands sprawling out beneath it – it does indeed require an extra intake of oxygen. And that's on top of the steep goat track that leads up to this string of swimming holes, which is quite a workout.

Gunlom is one of the major tributaries of the upper South Alligator River, the only large tropical river system in the world to be entirely protected within a UNESCO World Heritage national park. This is one of the most photographed places in Kakadu, and probably the most iconic, but once you've snapped the obligatory 'bathing on the edge of the escarpment shot', there are other equally beautiful pools to explore above and behind the main one. My friend and I took a cheeky right-turn on arrival and found ourselves a private clear-water pool, with its own waterfalls cascading through red rocks formed like little mini gorges.

A new grade-two gravel track, with a steady rather than steep gradient, and a set of stairs at the end, had shortened the walk to about 20 minutes, but it has attracted controversy. Parks Australia has been charged with failing to get an authority certificate for the construction and at time of print this new walking track and the upper pools were closed at the request of the Traditional Owners until further notice. Check ahead.

A full day or even two at Gunlom's upper pools is the main attraction, but it is not essential to loving this place. Next to the carpark and a sprawling grassy picnic area, you can follow a 200-metre boardwalk to Gunlom plunge pool, the catchment for the 85-metre falls above. This oasis of calm – sandy-bottomed and fringed by pandanas trees – is majorly overlooked, given the competition, but it's worthy in its own right. The simplicity of spending time here can essentially extend your stay.

The campground is about 150 metres or so from the main carpark, with unmarked and unpowered sites sprawled amid red-trunked savannah trees on patches of (mostly) struggling grass. With plenty of space you can really spread out here. Facilities include:

• A toilet block with flushing toilets
• Solar-powered hot water showers
• A tank for drinking water
• Concrete picnic tables dotted around the space
• A little sectioned-off car-free space to pitch tents

If it's really dry and dusty (like it was in August on my visit), campers might like to hang in the day-use picnic area, which has lovely thick grass and healthy shade trees fed by sprinklers.

CATEGORIES

Young Travellers, Family, Nature, Wi-Fi-Free, No Dogs, Boomers, Nomads

GO DO IT

WHO   Bowali Visitor Centre; (08) 8938 1120; parksaustralia.gov.au

WHERE   Gunlom Falls, Kakadu National Park, 330km or a 4-hour drive from Darwin, NT.

ACCESS   From Wirnwirnmila Mary River Roadhouse, take the Kakadu Hwy north-east for 12km, then turn right onto Gimbat for 26km, before making a slight left onto Gunlom (road) for 10km.

WHAT ELSE?

Gunlom day-use area is a hub for ranger guided walks and activities (free with your parks pass), including a walk reflecting on creation and history (Friday 5–6.30pm) a slideshow (Friday 7.30–8.30pm) exploring 'southern Kakadu stories', and a walk (Saturday 8–9.30pm) to the plunge pools. Confirm activities with the park manager on arrival.

Climb to the top of the escarpment on the Gunlom Lookout Walk for views of South Alligator River Valley and Marrawal Plateau. It's a steep 1-kilometre trail for hardy walkers and takes about an hour.

Try the 2.5 kilometre flat and easy return walk leading to Murrill Billabong and the South Alligator River. It's bird-happy, with honey eaters, galahs and kookaburras keeping you company.

Yurmikmik, on the road to Gunlom, has a series of walks through monsoon forests, open woodland and creek country between the Marrawalk Plateau and the South Alligator River. All walks start from the carpark and include the 2-kilometre, 45-minute return Boulder Creek walk, which has a rewarding swimming hole and the two-hour Yurmikmik Lookout walk, with clear views over incredible Jawoyn land.

FIRST PEOPLES KNOW-HOW

The Mary River region is Jawoyn land, and there are strong cultural ties between this part of Kakadu and its southern neighbour Nitmiluk (Katherine) National Park (*see* pp. 171, 173). It is home of Bula, the Rainbow Serpent, and a veritable story book of Indigenous cultural sites and traditions.

STEP IT UP

Maguk plunge pool (about a 2.5-hour drive via Gimbat road and Kakadu Highway) rivals Gunlom for its beauty. After a flat 2-kilometre bushwalk through monsoon forest and paperbark swamps, the foliage clears to reveal a big circular waterhole, with splendid cascading falls on its far side. You can waterplay here with goggles and snorkel (to see turtles, fish and watersnakes, like we did) or go the extra 1 kilometre on the signed walk above the falls to a series of rock pools that overlook the main waterhole. There's a basic bush campsite nearby, if you decide to make a night of it.

AND ANOTHER THING

Camper-trailers and caravans are welcome but the road in is heavily corrugated and 4WD vehicles are recommended, depending on the weather conditions.

The nearest hub for fuel and food is Mary River Roadhouse, about 48 kilometres or a 2-hour drive from Gunlom Campground.

ALTERNATIVES

There are wilderness campsites at Jarrangbarnmi (Koolpin) gorge and Bilkbilkmi (Graveside) gorge. They have their own plunge pools but can be difficult to get to and require permits (environment.gov.au/node/33435) that take seven days to process.

Mary River Roadhouse campground has powered van sites, toilet amenities, a bar, fuel and local information. It serves as a decent pit-stop on the way to more nature-based campsites. Also in Kakadu, Mardukal (formerly Mardugal, *see* p. 163) and Karnamarr (formerly Garnamarr, *see* p. 165).

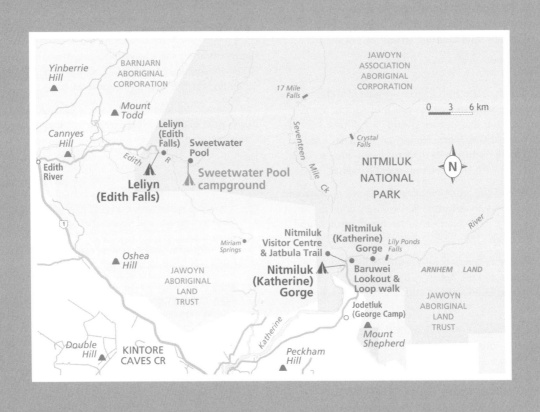

Comfortable camping with swimming holes on the doorstep.

Leliyn (Edith Falls)
Nitmiluk National Park, NT

ACTIVITIES

FACILITIES

If you were contemplating choosing between camping at either Leliyn (Edith Falls) *or* Nitmiluk (Katherine) Gorge (*see* p. 173), think again. Nitmiluk National Park's two main campgrounds battle it out for bucket-list natural immersions, and both deserve your time. Like Nitmiluk Gorge, Leliyn campground is lauded for its short-walk proximity to breathtaking natural beauty.

A few metres from the tent sites, a huge freshwater swimming hole, stretching 150 metres across, has Garden of Eden appeal, with a plunging waterfall on the far side, lush pandanus and young eucalyptus trees around its edge and grassy knolls, where bikini-clad backpackers laze about. Bring your goggles and flippers. The waterhole is the size of a lake and ripe for spotting red-tailed rainbow fish, archerfish and northern snapping turtles. At the entry point closest to the campsite, there's a shallow swimming area suited to amateur swimmers and a small island that young families like to explore. On my stay, there were amateur free-climbers scaling the red rock walls that fringe one side of the pool. Freshwater crocodiles (goymarr) live in this swimming hole but they're mostly harmless unless you disturb their nesting (which is why the pool is out of bounds between 7pm and 7am).

The campsite itself is a sprawling well-maintained space, with 40 non-powered sites, concrete paths and bright green grass hiding what would otherwise be yellow dirt. Some of the best spots are in the dappled shade under the campsite's leafy native trees away from the spray of road dust.

Facilities include:

- Free gas barbecues
- Drinking water taps
- Tables dotted around the site
- Super-clean bathroom facilities
- High-pressure hot showers

Another big plus at Leliyn campground is the kiosk, with its colourful bunting, metal chairs and smattering of greenery. It operates as a gift shop, cafe, pizza shop and general go-to for all things outdoors. You pay your camp fees here, then tuck into bacon and eggs, salad wraps or barramundi burgers before browsing the shop for essentials (toothpaste, Vegemite, pancake mix, sunscreen) and non-essentials (Kakadu Blue massage oil, Roogenic native teas, real crocodile skulls). You can exchange swimming hole stories with fellow nomads at 'pizza and live music' nights on Mondays and Thursdays.

The series of storyboards under a sheltered area at the campground is a great source of information about the area's Jawoyn people, who own Nitmiluk National Park, and about the abundant local wildlife, including ghost bats, rock ringtail possums and wallabies, all of which you've a good chance to see while camping.

CATEGORIES

Young Travellers, Family, Nature, Wi-Fi-Free, No Dogs, Boomers, Nomads

GO DO IT

WHO   Leliyn kiosk; (08) 8972 2884; nt.gov.au

WHERE   Nitmiluk National Park is about 244kms south-east of Darwin and 60km north of Katherine, in the NT.

ACCESS Leliyn (Edith Falls) can be reached by following the Stuart Hwy north from Katherine for 40km, then following a sealed road for another 20km.

WHAT ELSE?

You could spend all day waterplaying here but it would be blasphemy not to explore further. The Leliyn Trail is a pleasant (albeit a little steep and exposed in places) 2.6 kilometre two-hour loop on a dirt bush trail, replete with pretty native flowers and darting birdlife. It features an excellent lookout but the main feature is the Upper Pool, a smaller, quieter and equally bountiful croc-free swimming hole, with amphitheatre rock walls, a waterfall you can soak under, and little gullies of water and smooth rock slides that keep kids entertained. Pack a picnic and spend the day here.

Sweetwater Pool walk is an 8.6 kilometre return walk from the campground to a relaxing waterhole on the Edith River. It is graded moderate to difficult and takes about 4 hours.

CULTURE VULTURE

Nitmiluk Festival (nitmilukfestival.com.au) in mid-September, is an annual Katherine community celebration, with markets, foodie experiences and cultural events held at both Nitmiluk (Katherine) Gorge (*see* p. 173) and at Leliyn.

EAT IT

Fifty minutes away, Marksie's Stockman's Camp Tucker Night (marksiescamptucker.com.au) is a quintessential Aussie dining experience, with Marksie cooking a traditional camp-oven damper and bush stew made great with partner Penny's home-grown native ingredients.

There are plenty of scenic swimming spots here, including Leliyn (Edith Falls)

AND ANOTHER THING

There are no bookings and Leliyn is usually full in peak tourist season (June–Sept). Try getting to the kiosk at 8.30am to book a 'first come, first served' site, then hang by the pool until 10am check-out when you can nab a spot. Leliyn is often closed during wet season.

ALTERNATIVES

Nitmiluk (Katherine) Gorge (*see* p. 173) is another hot-spot locale.

There are also year-round campsites at Wangi and Florence Falls in Litchfield National Park. Wangi is the most talked-about, with picturesque falls, swimming holes and boardwalks, but keep in mind Litchfield is the closest to Darwin so it draws the bigger crowds.

Poolside camping alongside gorgeous gorge activities.

Nitmiluk (Katherine) Gorge

Nitmiluk National Park, NT

MAP ON PAGE 170

ACTIVITIES

FACILITIES

Whether you're following its meanderings overhead on a scenic helicopter ride, dipping a canoe paddle into its calm waters, or traipsing along its sandstone banks, the wild beauty of famed Nitmiluk (Katherine) Gorge can leave even the most intrepid traveller's jaw ajar. That you can comfortably camp in the heart of the action, is just another wow factor.

Located 29 kilometres north-east of Katherine and 320 kilometres south-east of Darwin in Nitmiluk National Park, Nitmiluk is a geological spectacle featuring a trail of 13 gorges carved by the rain-fed waters of the Katherine River flowing from the red and rugged sandstone of the Arnhem Land Plateau. In the dry season (Apr to Oct), the gorges are separated by rock gullies, creating tranquil waters suited to swimming and canoeing and exploring in flat-bottom tourist boats. In the wet season, the surge of rain and deluge of water that flows down the plateau from Kakadu sees it transform into a heaving river, navigable only from the air.

The national park is the traditional land of the Jawoyn people and the visitor centre and tours are managed on a 99-year lease by the NT Parks and Wildlife Commission. With many employees hailing from the Jawoyn community's 17 tribes, Nitmiluk is as much a geographical marvel as it is an Indigenous heritage and cultural wonder (*see* p. 174).

At the end of an activity-filled day, the campsite is a well-spaced flat expanse that would be dust-blown in the dry season if it weren't for sprinkler-fed green grass, paperbarks and other leafy native flora that make it feel like parkland. Facilities include:

• Unpowered and powered sites
• A small permanent 'tent village'
• A huddle of self-contained cabins
• Picnic tables and chairs
• An amenities block
• Barbecue, sinks and refrigerators

The green lagoon-shaped Jatti Pool is for campers only, and is a little oasis surrounded by palms and shade-cover. There is also a restaurant and from 4.30pm it serves snacks, dinner and drinks; it's a good place to talk animal sightings and such with fellow travellers.

Overleaf Campgrounds are the perfect base to explore nearby Nitmiluk Gorge by land and water

CATEGORIES

Young Travellers, Family, Nature, No Dogs, Boomers, Nomads

GO DO IT

WHO   Nitmiluktours; 1300 146 743; nitmiluktours.com.au
WHERE   Nitmiluk National Park is about 240kms south-east of Darwin, NT.
ACCESS   The Nitmiluk Gorge Visitor Centre is sign-posted off Stuart Hwy, 29km north-east of Katherine.

WHAT ELSE?

The Nitmiluk Visitor Centre is within easy walking distance of the campground. It's a wealth of information on tours, activities and walks. Book tours in person or online (nitmiluktours.com.au).

The 4.8 kilometre return Baruwei Lookout and Loop walk, with views of the gorge, is accessible from the campground. It connects with the longer medium-to-difficult Southern walks that reward with their bush campsites, picnic spots and swimming holes away from the crowds.

To fully experience Nitmiluk Gorge, take a helicopter ride and opt for a remote landing near one of the swimming holes. Even better than a helicopter ride, canoe to the fourth, sixth and ninth gorges to camp overnight.

I did a half-day Malappar Traveller canoe adventure tour (nitmiluktours.com.au), which starts with a scenic boat ride along gorge one, then a paddle through gorge two and three. This self-guided option gets you away from the crowds and up-close to the towering red cliffs and riverbanks where freshwater mangroves and river pandanus are home to cormorant and darter birds and snake-necked turtles. Little signs on some beaches warn canoeists away from freshwater croc nesting sites (it is free of salties in the dry season), but there are plenty of places to park up for an essential dip.

CULTURE VULTURE

Nitmiluk Festival (nitmilukfestival.com.au), in mid-September, is an annual Katherine community celebration, with markets, foodie experiences and cultural events held at both Nitmiluk (Katherine) Gorge and Leliyn (Edith Falls, see p. 171).

EAT IT

The Nabilil Dreaming Sunset Tour (nitmiluktours.com.au) is a treat-to-self. It's a 3.5-hour dining experience on board a boat. Watch the sun set on the red cliffs of two gorges while sipping on sparkling wine and indulging in a three-course meal.

A 20-minute drive away from the Nitmiluk campsite, Marksie's Stockman's Camp Tucker Night (marksiescamptucker.com.au) is a quintessential Aussie dining experience, with Marksie cooking a traditional camp oven damper and bush stew made great with partner Penny's home-grown native ingredients.

FIRST PEOPLES KNOW-HOW

The cliff-faces that cast vertiginous shadows on the water are home to stunning Nitmiluk rock art sites and the year-round daily tours – with names like the Timeless Land 3-Gorge Tour and the NitNit Dream 2-Gorge Tour – and all have a cultural angle. The Ancient Garlaar River Safari tour is a 2.5-hour exploration of gorge one, with a personal cultural guide at the helm. It includes a stop at one of the Nitmiluk rock art sites and a cultural deep-dive into the stories of the Jawoyn people. See nitmiluktours.com.au to book tours.

STEP IT UP

Departing from Nitmiluk Gorge, the famed Jatbula Trail is a 62 kilometre one-way walk to Leliyn (Edith Falls, see p. 171). It follows the trail walked by generations of Jawoyn people along the western edge of the Arnhem Land escarpment, with overnight camping at some of the region's most beautiful waterfalls.

AND ANOTHER THING

The campsite is open year-round, but check ahead with Nitmiluk Tours as to which activities are subject to seasonal conditions.

ALTERNATIVES

Leliyn (Edith Falls, see p. 171) is another hot-spot locale within Nitmiluk National Park.

There are also year-round campsites at Wangi and Florence Falls in Litchfield National Park. Wangi is the most talked-about with picturesque falls, swimming holes and boardwalks, but keep in mind Litchfield is the closest to Darwin so it draws the bigger crowds.

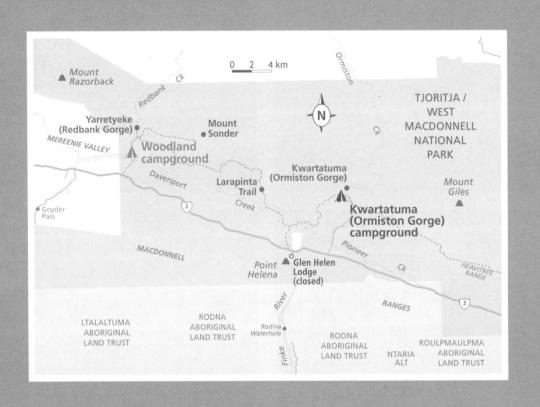

A camping landscape that channels the paintings of Albert Namatjira, with a waterhole, hot showers and gorge walks.

Kwartatuma (Ormiston Gorge)

Tjoritja (West MacDonnell) National Park, NT

ACTIVITIES

FACILITIES

A swimming hole in the desert is like a magnet to weary travellers, and sensational Kwartatuma (Ormiston Gorge) doesn't disappoint. This permanent year-round watery oasis is an outback beauty, with sandy banks and red rock cliffs shaded by she-oaks and the region's iconic ghost gums. The southern end is deep – almost 14 metres – and the (very) cool waters provide relief for hardy walkers, repose for campers and a sanctuary for the kingfishers, dunnarts, rock rats and dingoes that share the escarpment.

The red rock gorge is part of the mammoth slab of red quartzite running through the middle of Tjoritja (West MacDonnell Ranges), endowing the region with its fascinating geological character. Roughly 12 kilometres wide, it has withstood millions of years of erosion and now stands out boldly against the flat landscape.

On one hand, the red desert environment is dirty, dusty and arid with flies and heat that can drive even the hardiest to distraction, but on the other, its harsh beauty is one of its addictive qualities. You can get a feel for it in the works of Western Arrernte artist Albert Namatjira (*see* p. 179) whose landscape paintings are referenced at every turn: the crimson orange of the gorge walls when hit with afternoon sun, the blues formed when rock falls into shadow, the hazy green of eucalyptus leaves against golden desert sands.

Set up your tent, have a cold dip (or, blessedly, a hot shower) and soak it all in.

Kwartatuma (Ormiston Gorge) is the main hub for park rangers at Tjoritja (West MacDonnell Ranges) and campers reap the benefits. There's a visitor centre, ranger station, plenty of seats and storyboards, and a walks information shelter. Taarna Kiosk, serving real espresso iced coffee, might just seal the deal.

The campground has a dozen or so designated campsites that are suitable for caravans, campervans, camper-trailers and tents on a first-come, first-served basis. Facilities include:

- An amenities block with toilets and hot showers (the only Tjoritja (West MacDonnell) National Park campsite with hot showers)
- Free gas barbecues
- Picnic tables

The sites are quite squishy in what is essentially a dusty carpark, but the waterhole (500m away) makes up for it, as do the incredible walks – both short and long, that are part of the Kwartatuma (Ormiston Gorge) experience.

Above Kwartatuma (Ormiston Gorge) campground has facilities including an info centre, hot showers, gas barbecues and sheltered picnic areas

CATEGORIES

Young Travellers, Dog-Lovers, Family, Nature, Wi-Fi Free, No Dogs, Boomers, Nomads

GO DO IT

WHO   Kwartatuma (Ormiston Gorge); (08) 8956 7799; nt.gov.au/leisure/parks-reserves/find-a-park/find-a-park-to-visit/ormiston-gorge

WHERE   135km west of Alice Springs and 243km east of Kings Canyon in Tjoritja (West MacDonnell) National Park, NT.

ACCESS   From Alice Springs, follow sealed Larapinta Dr 46km, turn right onto Namatjira Dr for 81km, and follow the signposts right onto Ormiston Gorge Access road for 7.5km.

WHAT ELSE?

There are several walks direct from the campground and visitor centre. Start with the 5-minute (300m, one-way) amble to the waterhole along a paved path. Build up to the Ghost Gum Lookout walk (1.2km, 45-minute return) with its superlative views of the gorge. Continuing from the lookout, complete the Ghost Gum walk, which loops around the western side of the gorge back to the waterhole. Then conquer the Ormiston Pound circuit walk (8.5km, 3- to 4-hour loop) over the flat expanse of the pound and back along the gorge by the main waterhole.

Taarna Kiosk is open daily and serves toasties, focaccias, sausage rolls and scones alongside fruit smoothies and ice creams. Indigenous art, artefacts and crafts are also on sale.

Territory Parks Alive is a program of free guided walks, talks, slideshows and spotlight activities run by the rangers from May to August. Inquire at the visitor centre.

Campers note: the ground is hard – bring a hammer or similar to get those tent pegs in.

Most waterholes are extremely cold, even during summer. Prolonged exposure can result in hypothermia.

Keep all food and clothing, including shoes, securely stored away from dingoes at this campground.

Yarretyeke (Redbank Gorge), 35km west of the campground, has a 90 minute return walk from the carpark which follows a pretty creek to a swimming hole within the gorge of dazzling coloured rock.

FIRST PEOPLES KNOW-HOW

This landscape has been home to the Western Arrernte (Western Aranda) people for tens of thousands of years. They are part of the Arrernte group who are the Traditional Owners of the land, thought to cover 120,000 square kilometres of Central Australia.

The most famous Western Arrernte man was contemporary artist Albert Namatjira (1902–59), whose famed watercolour paintings brought the light play and vivid colour of Tjoritja (West MacDonnell Ranges) to life. Namatjira's *Quarritana, Finke River (Organ Pipes)* and his signature Rwetypeme (Mt Sonder) paintings hang in the National Gallery of Australia in Canberra. According to the gallery: 'Namatjira was aware of the physical presence of ancestral beings embodied in the towering ghost gums and geological forms of the surrounding mountains and gorges ... Namatjira did not simple render the Central Australian landscape through a European gaze ... As an Indigenous artist, Namatjira was able to subvert and question the possessive function of the landscape genre. These images were not an example of assimilation, they were a display of reclamation.'

Namatjira's works can also be seen locally at Araluen Arts Centre in Alice Springs, alongside an intriguing collection of other Indigenous works depicting this region. If you're coming from Alice Springs, you'll pass it on the way to the campground.

WILDLIFE WATCH

Birdwatchers keep your peepers open to see spinifexbirds, dusky grasswrens, sacred kingfishers and grey honeyeaters.

The park is also an important fauna refuge, with the rediscovery the long-tailed dunnart and the central rock rat in the nineties. Keep an eye out for them.

STEP IT UP

The 231-kilometre Larapinta Trail stretches through Tjoritja (West MacDonnell) National Park and offers extended and overnight bushwalks for experienced and well-prepped walkers. Walk the whole trail or bite off one or two of the 12 sections. Ormiston Gorge is the trailhead for sections nine and ten. Section nine (graded hard) is a rough and narrow track with some steep, long climbs. Section ten (graded medium) is a rough and narrow steeply undulating track. The final section of the Larapinta – the 16 kilometre return walk from the Yarretyeke (Redbank Gorge) carpark (35km west) up Rwetypeme (Mt Sonder), rewards with astonishing views of a red landscape that sprawls out below. It's challenging and uphill. Give yourself a fighting chance by leaving early, getting there for sunrise and returning before the full heat of the day. (Allow six hours return).

AND ANOTHER THING

Tank water (which needs to be boiled) is available but limited so bring your own. Camping fees (cash only, no change available) can be paid onsite. Rangers check daily. The park is accessible all year round but the cooler months, from April to September, are the loveliest.

ALTERNATIVES

Udepata (Ellery Creek Big Hole) Campground (49km east) and Woodland Campground at Yarretyeke (Redbank Gorge, 34km west) are similarly located near fantastic swimming holes and scenery. They're smaller basic campgrounds, but quieter too. At time of publication Glen Helen Lodge and campground (12km south) had ceased operating.

Opposite Kwartatuma (Ormiston Gorge) waterhole, 500 metres from the campground, offers cool reprieve from the desert heat

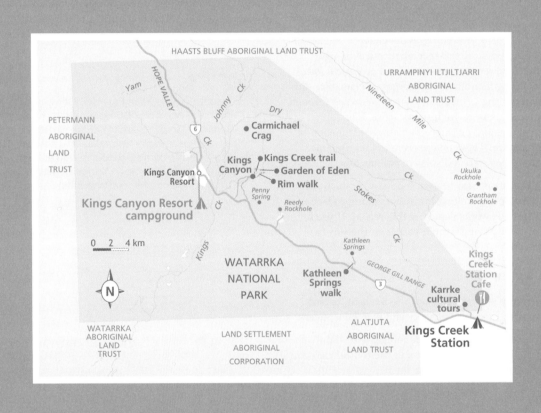

HAASTS BLUFF ABORIGINAL LAND TRUST

URRAMPINYI ILTJILTJARRI
ABORIGINAL
LAND TRUST

PETERMANN
ABORIGINAL
LAND
TRUST

Yam

HOPE VALLEY

Johnny

Ck

Dry

Nineteen

Mile

Ck

Carmichael
Crag

Kings Creek trail

Kings
Canyon

Garden of Eden

Rim walk

Ukulka
Rockhole

Kings Canyon
Resort

Penny
Spring

Grantham
Rockhole

Stokes

Reedy
Rockhole

Kings Canyon Resort
campground

Ck

0   2   4 km

Kings

WATARRKA
NATIONAL
PARK

Kathleen
Springs

Ck

Kings
Creek
Station
Cafe

N

Kathleen
Springs
walk

GEORGE GILL RANGE

3

Karrke
cultural
tours

WATARRKA
ABORIGINAL
LAND
TRUST

LAND SETTLEMENT
ABORIGINAL
CORPORATION

ALATJUTA
ABORIGINAL
LAND TRUST

Kings Creek
Station

Red-dirt outback camping near spectacular Kings Canyon.

Kings Creek Station

Petermann, NT

ACTIVITIES

FACILITIES

Kings Canyon in Watarrka National Park is the main reason travellers would find themselves immersed, so far from anywhere, in the wild red desert landscapes of outback Northern Territory. This incredible gorge, with walls that reach 100 metres in parts, cuts through the sandstone, which is more than 400 million years ago. Today it feels like a million stones, boulders and domes of all different shapes and sizes have been rounded and worn, roughed and smoothed, battered and bruised, by geological whims that are so ancient the timeframe is almost meaningless.

Happily, Kings Creek Station campground is an easy 35 kilometres – or a 20-minute drive away. This 1800 square-kilometre property sits just outside the boundary of the south-east corner of Watarrka National Park in a landscape of desert oaks, red dirt, spinifex-dotted desert scrub and big skies. The beautiful George Gill Range, home to Kings Canyon, takes up a sizeable strip of the horizon.

It's a tourist hub, for sure, but it's also a working cattle and camel farm, operated by owners Lyn and Ian Conway, whose family has been in the region for more than a century, so it feels like a genuine Aussie Outback immersion. The campground is set up with large powered and unpowered sites for tents, swags, caravans and camper-trailers. You can choose the site to suit your needs, but I suggest that you steer clear of the sites close to the Roadhouse, which gets noisy early with tour bus departures. There are some great grassy areas,

especially near the playground, but red dirt and a bit of grit in your teeth is the expectation in these parts. Facilities include:

- Toilet block
- Shower and laundry facilities
- Camp kitchen
- Fire-pits
- Playground
- Grassy picnic area
- Swimming pool (it's not exactly flash but it is blessedly shaded by trees in the heat of the day)

The property also has safari tents. They're permanent canvas cabins constructed of steel frames, with shared bathrooms and mod-cons, such as electricity and linen. The luxury glamping tents are a step-up again. They have all the trimmings, including king-sized beds, bathrooms, bathrobes and a bush-inspired barbecue dinner.

When you're not escaping the heat there's plenty to do at the campground: pet the donkeys and camels, talk to the cockatoo in reception, walk to the sunset lookout, and take a quad-bike or buggy tour to see the property's Indigenous art sites.

Stargazing and lazy evenings around the fire are all part of the experience at this campground.

CATEGORIES

Family, Nature, Wi-Fi-Free, No Dogs, Boomers, Nomads

GO DO IT

WHO   Kings Creek Station; (08) 8956 7474;
kingscreekstation.com.au

WHERE Kings Creek Caravan Rd off Luritja Rd,
Petermann, Kings Canyon, near Watarrka
National Park, about 1316km south of Darwin
and 323km south-west of Alice Springs, NT.

ACCESS From Alice Springs head south on Stuart Hwy
for 130km, then onto Ernest Giles Rd for 100km
before turning right onto Luritja Rd for 60km,
and left onto unsealed Kings Creek Caravan Rd
for 2km. The property is at the end.

WHAT ELSE?

The spectacular Rim walk is the one to do. It's a 6 kilometre one-way route that takes about three hours. The path climbs to the edge of the gorge on one side, dips down into the Garden of Eden at its centre (an oasis within the gorge where cycads gather around a waterhole), then re-emerges on the other side

Along the way you'll climb steep marbled rock steps, brush past the branches of stunted mulga trees, clamber between great walls of ancient red rock, sit amid a landscape similar to that of the Bungle Bungles and stand on the precipice of breathtaking views, including one stretching, as the crow flies, 144 kilometres over a red landscape all the way to Kata Tjuṯa near Uluṟu. It is very special indeed. It's a good idea to start the climb early (the carpark was empty when I eagerly started at 6.45am, but having the place to myself was a bonus).

Helicopter flights along the top of the range to the breathtaking Carmichael Crag can be arranged, so too Indigenous cultural tours (*see* below).

EAT IT

The station has a cafe selling decent coffee, and comforts such as homemade stews with damper. The Kings Creek camel burger is the novelty speciality here. You can also put in an order for a gourmet picnic hamper, which can be eaten at one of the station's serene outback locations.

FIRST PEOPLES KNOW-HOW

Traditional Owner and Luritja woman, Christine Breaden, and her partner Peter Abbott, run Karrke Cultural Tours (karrke.com.au) from their ancestral home at Wanmarra, adjacent to Kings Creek Station on the Luritja Highway near the edge of Watarrka National Park. They share stories and information about the Luritja and Pertame (Southern Aranda) people, with a focus on survival in desert landscapes.

WILDLIFE WATCH

Most people wouldn't know that Australia has the world's biggest feral camel population, with more than 1.2 million roaming the desert. Their existence here hails from the 19th century, when exploring Australia's unknowable interior was a pioneering pursuit. In the 50 years from 1870, an estimated 20,000 camels were imported into Australia alongside their handlers from the Arabian Peninsula, India and Afghanistan. (The stories from these immigrants have only recently been given their rightful place in history.) By the 1930s, trains and motorised transport made short-shrift of camels used as pack animals and they were released into the wild. Since then, their numbers have grown in pest proportions. Part of Kings Creek Station business involves selling camels for live export, live domestic sales and meat.

STEP IT UP

For an easy approach to Kings Canyon, the Kings Creek trail is a gentle 2.6-kilometre walk from the Kings Canyon carpark. It follows the creek between the canyon walls. Seeing the stunning iron-red canyon walls from below is a highlight.

Also from Kings Canyon carpark, the 2.6-kilometre walk to Kathleen Springs is another walking option with a pastoral history angle.

AND ANOTHER THING

From September to March, when temperatures are 36ºC or higher, access to Watarrka National Park is limited. Visitors must start the Kings Canyon Rim walk before 9am.

ALTERNATIVES

About 40 kilometres north-west, Kings Canyon Resort (kingscanyonresort.com.au) has a campground similarly located in the outback landscape. It's owned by a large property group so it's a more polished version of Kings Creek Station, with a little less of the salt-of-the-earth quality. For example, fires are allowed at Kings Creek Station, but not at Kings Canyon Resort.

Camping is not permitted in the national park.

Opposite Hiking along Kings Canyon is a bucket list experience

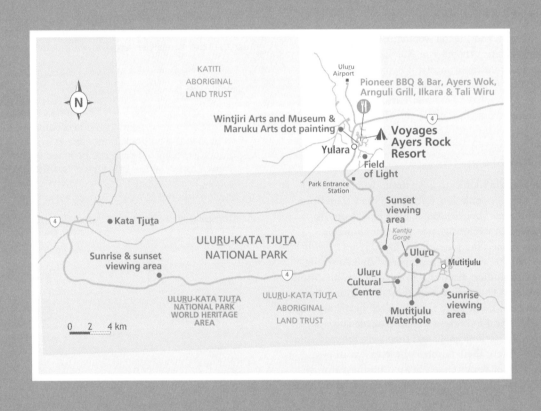

KATITI
ABORIGINAL
LAND TRUST

Uluru
Airport

Pioneer BBQ & Bar, Ayers Wok,
Arnguli Grill, Ilkara & Tali Wiru

Wintjiri Arts and Museum &
Maruku Arts dot painting

4

Yulara

**Voyages
Ayers Rock
Resort**

**Field
of Light**

Park Entrance
Station

Kata Tjuṯa

**ULURU-KATA TJUṮA
NATIONAL PARK**

Sunset
viewing
area

Kantju
Gorge

Uluru

Mutitjulu

Sunrise & sunset
viewing area

4

Uluru
Cultural
Centre

ULURU-KATA TJUTA
NATIONAL PARK
WORLD HERITAGE
AREA

ULURU-KATA TJUṮA
ABORIGINAL
LAND TRUST

Mutitjulu
Waterhole

Sunrise
viewing
area

0 2 4 km

Spacious camping with all the facilities and a pool near iconic Uluṟu.

Ayers Rock Resort

Uluṟu-Kata Tjuṯa National Park, NT

ACTIVITIES

FACILITIES

Ayers Rock Resort campground's marvellous proximity to Uluṟu is its most outstanding feature. The enigmatic 348 metre high sandstone monolith, with a circumference of 9.4 kilometres, can be seen erupting from the flat landscape within minutes of the campground. You can't climb the rock any more – on 26 October 2019 (to coincide with the 34th anniversary of the return of Uluṟu to its Traditional Owners), the steep, 800-metre climb to the top was closed for good. The focus now is on exploring from a respectful distance – approach it on the back of a camel, view it from a sand dune at sunset or walk around the base to see where the Mala (rufous hare-wallaby) people camped when they first arrived at Uluṟu, the Mutitjulu Waterhole and nearby rock art cave.

Before 1983 campers and caravanners could actually drive through the spinifex grass and stunted trees to park their rigs right at the base of Uluṟu. I can imagine it now, a festival of that era's mullet haircuts, stubbie shorts and Life Be In It T-shirts, setting up canvas tents and mosquito nets against the sacred site, before kicking back on a camp chair with a beer in hand. Happily, Australia has progressed and the populace is becoming more educated about the cultural traditions and sensitivities of the local Aṉangu people. Campers are now relegated, like everyone else, to accommodation within Voyages Ayers Rock Resort.

Located 15 kilometres from Uluṟu, the resort has eight accommodation options to suit different tastes and budgets – from five-star rooms at Sails in the Desert to dorm beds at the Outback Pioneer Lodge and cabins and campsites at Ayers Rock Campground.

The Ayers Rock Campground space – some of it grassy, most of it red dirt – is part-shaded by clumps of gums and sheoak trees. The best camp spots are on the boundary fence-line where there are more trees and a tad more privacy. Facilities include:

- Air conditioned cabins
- Powered caravan sites
- Space for campervans, motor homes and camper-trailers
- Powered (numbering 198) and unpowered (numbering 220) tent sites
- A swimming pool
- Playground
- Volleyball court
- Outdoor kitchen and barbecue areas
- Bathrooms with hot showers and laundry facilities

Being part of the resort has its advantages, with a free shuttle bus that accesses the local IGA supermarket and town square, Wintjiri Arts and Museum, a medical centre and various dining and drinking options. Depending on your mood and budget, there's the Pioneer BBQ & Bar at Outback Pioneer (where you can cook your own meat), Ayers Wok noodle bar in the town square, Arnguli Grill at Desert Gardens Hotel and Ilkari upmarket buffet restaurant at Sails in the Desert.

The freebie activities are another bonus of being part of the resort. Knowledgeable local Aṉangu guides host bush food experiences, ecology and museum tours and guided garden walks on a daily basis.

CATEGORIES

Young Travellers, Dog-Lovers, Family, Nature, Boomers, Nomads

GO DO IT

WHO   Voyages Ayers Rock Resort, Ayers Rock
          Campground; (08) 8957 7001;
          ayersrockresort.com.au
WHERE   Yulara Dr, Yulara, near Uluṟu-Kata Tjuṯa
          National Park in the south of the NT, about
          450km from Alice Springs.
ACCESS   Well-signed off the Lasseter Hwy.

WHAT ELSE?

Kata Tjuṯa, a nearby series of 36 large rock domes is equally as beautiful as Uluṟu for its natural beauty and cultural significance. Experience the wonder and awe of the Red Centre's spiritual heart on walks, including Kata Tjuṯa National Park's 7.5 kilometre Valley of the Winds walk and Uluṟu's 12-kilometre base walk (parksaustralia.gov.au/uluru/do/walks).

For an outback adventure, the Sunset Camel Experience (ulurucameltours.com.au/tours) will have you riding high through the desert on a camel. Time your run to see the sun setting on Uluṟu. End the tour with champagne and outback bush foods, including fresh-baked damper.

Enjoy a sunrise breakfast, followed by a 12-kilometre Uluṟu Sunrise and Segway tour with an informative guide (ayersrockresort.com.au/experiences/detail/uluru-segway-tours) around the base of Uluṟu.

CULTURE VULTURE

As darkness falls, Field of Light (ayersrockresort.com.au/events/detail/field-of-light-uluru), an exhibition by celebrated British artist Bruce Munro, illuminates the desert. Walk through a garden of 50,000 spindles of light in a spectrum of wildflower colours.

EAT IT

With Uluṟu as the special guest, Tali Wiru (ayersrockresort.com.au) is a fine-dining dinner on a desert dune, with a menu that weaves native bush tucker into the menu. Start with spinifex-baked beetroot with goat cheese, buttery grilled scallop with pickled emu apple (a cousin of the blueberry or muntri) and kangaroo jerky with crispbread and quandong (a desert peach). A didgeridoo performance, open-fire and star-gaze are all part of the experience. It operates seasonally from late March to mid-October. If you miss the Tali Wiru season opt instead for Sounds of Silence, a similarly memorable if not quite as flash desert dining experience in full view of Uluṟu.

FIRST PEOPLES KNOW-HOW

Maruku Arts dot painting (maruku.com.au) provides an intriguing introduction to Aṉangu art. Join a workshop or take a tour with one of the local artists. Book ahead.

AND ANOTHER THING

This campground consistently sells out, especially during school holiday periods, so book ahead.

ALTERNATIVES

The closest campsite is 40 kilometres east on the Lasseter Highway at Curtin Springs or 300 kilometres north at Kings Creek Station (*see p. 181*).

Opposite top left Camel tours are one popular option for viewing Uluru *Opposite top right* Maruka Arts dot painting offers an introduction to Aṉangu art

Queensland

Island hop the Whitsundays, camp on some of the most beautiful beaches in the world, see where the Daintree Rainforest meets the Great Barrier Reef and adventure up north to the rugged Cape York Peninsula

Eliot and Twin Falls

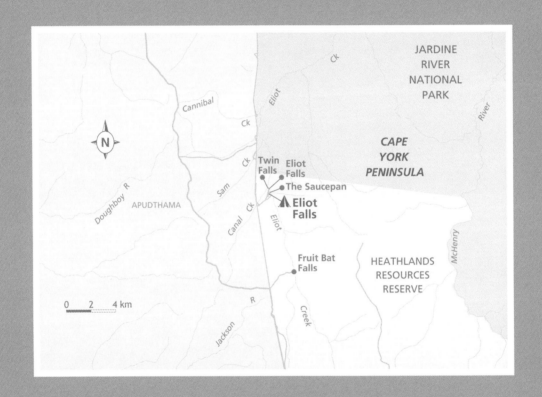

Previous Waterside camping at remote Chilli Beach in Kutini-Payamu (Iron Range) National Park, Cape York Peninsula

A hard-to-access campground with beautiful swimming holes that make it worth the journey.

Eliot and Twin Falls

Cape York Peninsula, Qld

ACTIVITIES

FACILITIES

The corrugated dirt roads on Cape York Peninsula can be bone-numbingly bumpy, teeth-grittingly unpredictable and eye-wateringly dusty. You need to be self-sufficient and an experienced driver of a 4WD, as there is also a water crossing (*see* p. 192). But all is forgiven within minutes of arriving at Eliot and Twin Falls. Located on the northern boundary of Heathland Conservation area adjoining Jardine River National Park, the campground is nestled in a pretty triangle of woodland wedged between two fantastically beautiful and swimmable creeks.

On the northern side, Eliot Creek, a scrawny green tree-fringed waterway, has two unique swimming spots. The Saucepan, accessed by a short bush trail, has wide shallow waters that flow over plates of sandstone into deep pools that are, given the whitish rock bottom, almost turquoise in colour and crystal clear, so that you can see little fish darting around. Further downstream, Eliot Falls has deeper and more dramatic pools with red-rock walls that create a mini gorge system. On the southern side of the campground (a 2-minute walk away), Twin Falls has a more tranquil flow, with little sandstone rockpools alive with tadpoles, and burbling waterfalls that cascade from one swimming hole to the next before emptying into Eliot Creek.

My family and I spent two joyous days exploring all three swimming spots – jumping off the whitewash into deep underwater holes (we checked the depth with goggles beforehand), finding little caves and hidey holes on the banks, floating downstream past rock walls alive with little fly-eating pitcher plants and following fish on underwater adventures. All three sites are within minutes of the campground and easily navigable via a mix of dirt tracks, concrete paths and boardwalks.

The campground itself has 25 campsites in varying sizes that cater up to four vehicles (eight people), including off-road campervans and camper-trailers. Campsites 20–31 are closest to the dirt tracks leading to the Saucepan, but sites 7–19 are slightly bigger and closer to the toilet facilities. Some sites have fire-rings and picnic tables (and a couple even have those characteristic termite mounds). There are fresh water taps dotted along the circular road for everyone to access.

Keep in mind there's also a large camping area for commercial operators and a day-use parking area, so this place does get busy in high season, despite the tricky access road. When we visited in October during the lead-up to the wet season, there were only a handful of sites occupied and we had the swimming holes mostly to ourselves.

CATEGORIES

Young Travellers, Family, Nature, Wi-Fi-Free, No Dogs, Boomers, Nomads

GO DO IT

WHO   Queensland Parks & Wildlife Service; 13 7468; parks.des.qld.gov.au

WHERE   Heathland Conservation area, adjoining Jardine River National Park, is 900km north-west of Cairns and 100km south of Bamaga, on the tip of Cape York Peninsula in Tropical North Queensland.

ACCESS   To access Eliot Falls from Bramwell Junction, follow the Southern Bypass Rd for 119km and turn right onto Telegraph Rd, from where it is 7km to Eliot Falls. An alternative (rougher) route follows Telegraph Rd from Bramwell Junction.

WHAT ELSE?

Easy walking tracks around Eliot Falls makes exploring lots of fun. One right-turning timber walkway on the path to Twin Falls descends to a viewing platform overlooking Eliot Creek and a natural sandstone platform above the falls.

Fruit Bat Falls, 4 kilometres away, is equally resplendent in natural beauty. It has a day-use area, with picnic tables, toilets and a timber walkway that leads to a swim spot.

FIRST PEOPLES KNOW-HOW

This is the traditional country of several groups, including people from the Atambaya, Angkamuthi, Yadhaykenu, Gudang and Wuthathi language and social groups. It is their living cultural landscape, with places of significance throughout, and the Traditional Owners are involved in the protection and management of the area.

WILDLIFE WATCH

The northern Australian brush turkey (with a purple instead of yellow throat wattle) is a popular sight scratching around in the dirt. The green ants nests that look like homemade Aussie rules footballs are an intriguing vision as they sway on the branches of skinny trees, also home to rainbow lorikeets and Sulphur-crested cockatoos. Get the torch out at night to see possums and spy spiny knob-tailed geckos. Keep an eye out for a native grevillea tree, which has shiny round woody seed pods that split in the heat, earning them the name bushman's clothes pegs.

STEP IT UP

In 1887, a dead-straight north–south telegraph line was completed to provide communications with remote Cape York Peninsula. Known today as the Old Telegraph Track, the untamed dirt road forms the western boundary of the park and reserve. While hire vehicles aren't insured on it, 4WD die-hards consider it something of a rite of passage.

AND ANOTHER THING

This place is remote and the 7-kilometre road into Eliot Falls is rough, with a significant water crossing. Visitors should take heed and be self-sufficient when venturing here. Queensland Parks advises travelling with another vehicle and carrying adequate fuel, basic spare parts, 4WD recovery gear, food, water and first-aid equipment.

Come the wet season (Dec to May) heavy rains prevent access.

ALTERNATIVES

There is camping 32 kilometres north of Eliot and Twin Falls campground at South Jardine River, on the Old Telegraph Track (allow 3.5 hours).

About 85 kilometres south-east of Eliot and Twin Falls campground, also on the Old Telegraph Track (allow 4.5 hours), Captain Billy Landing is right on the beach and has basic facilities, including toilets.

Opposite top left One of the campground's intriguing termite mounds *Opposite top right* Family time at Eliot Falls *Opposite bottom left* Eliot Creek just below the falls

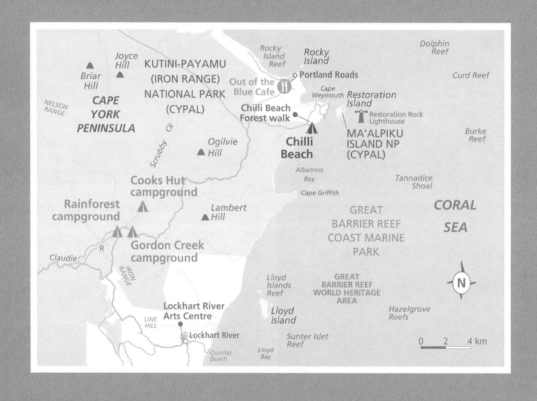

Remote, tropical beachfront camping in white sand dunes.

Chilli Beach

Kutini-Payamu (Iron Range) National Park, Qld

ACTIVITIES

FACILITIES

Flocks of metallic starlings swoop and swirl through the pink-hued evening sky before landing to nest on a tiny island just offshore at Chilli Beach. The vision splendid, which occurs between September and April, is David Attenborough-esque in its wild beauty and another feather in the nature cap of this stunningly remote campground.

Chilli Beach is located in Kutini-Payamu (Ironbark) National Park, a 53,160-hectare wonderland that feels doubly remote given it is only accessible by 4WD. The journey through the park, with views of the shrub and heath-covered Mt Tozer Range, standing 543 metres above sea level, is part of its beauty. So too its claim to having the largest tract of lowland tropical rainforest in Australia – a home for endemic wildlife, with many species found only on the northern Cape York Peninsula and in New Guinea. Keep an eye out for the big four: green python, colourful eclectus parrots, spotted cuscus and black and red palm cockatoos.

The campground is another tent-pitching plus. It takes up 1 kilometre of white quartz-sand on a beach stretching 7 kilometres and is striped with the shadow of lazy coconut palms. There are 25 marked campsites that are nicely spaced and wedged between tide and tropical greenery so you'll barely notice your neighbours (if indeed there are any). In October when I visited it was blissfully empty but, word is, it is popular in peak season. The sites have either beach frontage or short tracks through the greenery to the shoreline. Sites 13 and 14 are postcard-perfect beachfront spots but when the wind picks up sites 19 and 20 are set off the beach and more protected.

Four new toilet blocks have composting toilets and are handy to all sites, except 1, 2 and 3 at the northern end. The picnic tables need an upgrade, so it's better to rely on the shaded day-visitor tables.

Estuarine crocodiles can be seen in the waters here so waterplay is out of the question, but beachcombing rewards with fresh-fallen coconuts (which we managed to tap into and drink for breakfast). There's also a nice stroll to the northern end of the beach (best at low tide) to spy Ma'alpiku Island National Park (*see* p. 196) just off the coast.

CATEGORIES

Young Travellers, Family, Nature, Wi-Fi-Free, No Dogs, Boomers, Nomads

GO DO IT

WHO   Queensland Parks & Wildlife Service; 13 7468; parks.des.qld.gov.au

WHERE   Kutini-Payamu (Iron Range) National Park, Cape York Peninsula approximately 614km (or an 8-hour drive) north of Cooktown, Qld.

ACCESS Turn off the Peninsula Development Rd onto Portland Roads Rd, 35km north of the Archer River Roadhouse. On the gravel road, drive 97km to Lockhart River Rd junction. Continue along Portland Roads Rd 17.4 km to the turn-off to Chilli Beach camping area, which is 6km away.

WHAT ELSE?

There's a short and easy 720-metre, 10-minute walk through coastal dunes and vegetation from the entrance to Chilli Beach to the northern end of the campsite.

CULTURE VULTURE

The Lockhart River Art Centre (lockhartriverart.com.au) has exhibitions of paintings, sculptures and artefacts created in the distinctive Lockhart River Gang style. Community Elders play a role in the centre and funds raised are used to provide artists with canvas, brushes, paints and exhibition-related travel.

EAT IT

This could be Australia's most remote restaurant – and what a find. On tiny Portland Roads Road, Out of the Blue cafe (actually the front balcony of the owners' house) dishes up prawn rolls and calamari salads for lunch and, with a booking, garlic prawn linguini and sirloin steak for dinner. For campers living on baked beans it's the stuff dreams are made of. It's open Thursday to Tuesday, 10am–2pm and book for dinner.

FIRST PEOPLES KNOW-HOW

Ma'alpiku Island National Park is where Captain Bligh landed after the well-documented mutiny on his ship the *Bounty*, in 1789. The subsequent European colonisation of the region saw the Traditional Owners, the Kuuku Ya'u (including the Kungkay people and Kanthanampu people) displaced and removed from their traditional lands. It was handed back in 2011 and retains its rich cultural significance, with known ceremonial sites and story places.

Kutini means cassowary and Payamu means rainbow serpent – names that are related to important stories for the Kuuku Ya'u people.

WILDLIFE WATCH

Sadly, ocean currents deposit debris and rubbish on the northern end of Chilli Beach from as far away as Vanuatu and the Philippines and more than 5 tonnes of marine debris is removed from the beach every year. Help by collecting a little extra rubbish – see tangaroablue.org for more ways to help.

Spotlighting at night reveals nocturnal birds, such as owlet-nightjars, along with striped possums and sugar gliders. You might hear the rustle of melomys, a small native mouse-like rodent that gets busy at night, the quacking call of the Australian woodfrog and the flapping wings of bare-backed fruit bats.

STEP IT UP

From Mt Tozer carpark (about 35km from the campground), take an easy 10-minute, 40 metre return walk to the viewing platform for scenic views of this volcanic landmark.

AND ANOTHER THING

Alternative access to Chilli Beach via the Frenchmans Track is a challenging unmaintained and unpredictable route. It is not recommended.

ALTERNATIVES

There are three other small camping areas in the national park: Rainforest and Cooks Hut are shady rainforest campsites on the Claudie River and Gordon Creek campsite sits on a creek replete with birdlife. Cooks Hut is the only one with toilet facilities.

Chuulangun Campgrounds (kaanjungaachi.com.au) by the Wenlock River on the homelands of the Kuuku I'yu Northern Kaanju people is a pet-friendly bush campsite with hot showers.

Gritty outback riverside camping Croc Dundee-style.

Kalpowar Crossing

Rinyirru (Lakefield) National Park, Cape York Peninsula, Qld

MAP ON PAGE 198

ACTIVITIES

FACILITIES

My English partner particularly loved this campsite. He reckoned it was the kind of Aussie outback campground that you imagine yourself in when you dream about travelling in Oz from afar. I have to agree it's very Croc Dundee.

Rinyirru (Lakefield) National Park is huge. At 5370 square-kilometres it is the second largest national park in Queensland, a vast landscape of croc-inhabited waterholes, lily-padded lagoons, ant-hilled grasslands and red-dirt roads that criss-cross rivers fringed with enormous mango trees and gnarled paper-bark gums. One main unsealed road (Lakefield Rd) dissects the park from north to south, offering ease of navigation and access to 24 designated campgrounds. Most of them are small and secluded and either sit riverside or by a waterhole. Many of them are hardly discernible from the surrounding landscape, save for a patch of flattened grass or a rectangle of dirt. We checked out a couple of sites just off the main road, but with very few tourists around in October, choosing Kalpowar Crossing was a no-brainer. It's the biggest and best-equipped of two main river-crossing campgrounds (the other is Han Crossing).

This sprawling dirt and leaf-littered campground, with 19 sites, sits on the western bank of the Normanby River just short of the concrete causeway crossing. Its gangly roadside eucalypt trees offer sporadic shade but it's hot here especially with the midday sun sitting high overhead, so opt for the shadier spots along the riverbank (sites 7–15). Facilities include:

- Fire-rings
- Picnic tables and water taps shared between the sites
- Well-maintained toilet blocks located at each end of the campground
- A separate cold shower block

It's a wild old immersion here. Crocs patrol these waters and it's only the steep, wide bank between the tent sites and the water that allows campers to sleep at night without fear of a wandering predator. Our site (number 9) was next to a welcoming set of stairs leading down to the muddy riverside – we braved it to the halfway mark to watch ducks and cormorants swimming amid weeping paperbark branches in the current.

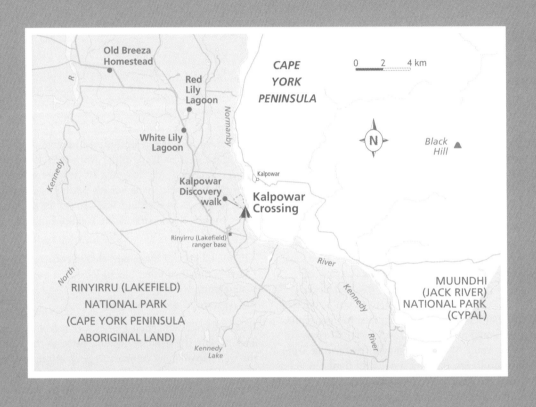

CATEGORIES

Young Travellers, Family, Nature, Wi-Fi-Free, No Dogs, Boomers, Nomads

GO DO IT

WHO   Queensland Parks & Wildlife Service; 13 7468; parks.des.qld.gov.au

WHERE   Rinyirru (Lakefield) is a national park in Lakefield, 1700km north-west of Brisbane and 340km north-west of Cairns on Cape York Peninsula, Qld.

ACCESS   Via Lakefield Rd in the centre of the park near Kalpowar Crossing.

WHAT ELSE?

The flora at Kalpowar really stands out. What look like standard natives from a distance, are resplendent close-up with buds, blooms, stamens and seedpods. They're unlike anything you're likely to see in other parts of Australia.

Check out the campground's river height sign to see where the water rises to in the wet season. You'd have been camping up to your waist in water in 2006.

The 4 kilometre return Kalpowar Discovery walk starts from near the day-use carpark and meanders along the riverbank woodlands. With dappled shade, it's an easy and serene immersion in the sights and sounds of the bush. Listen for hopping wallabies, spy crocs and spot birdlife. It should take about 90 minutes.

CULTURE VULTURE

Pastoral leases were granted on Cape York Peninsula in the late 1800s. Standing in the empty grounds of the Old Laura Homestead in the dry heat of the day gives you a sense of the hardship of bygone days. The corrugated-iron homestead, its teetering verandah shaded by pink frangipani trees, is what remains of the old cattle station. Owned by an Irishman and worked by the local Indigenous people, it had 8000 head of cattle in its heyday at the end of the 1800s. It's located 60 kilometres south of Kalpowar on Lakefield Road.

North of Kalpowar, just off Lakefield Road, the Old Breeza Homestead is marked by a fantastically old and outsized mango tree (you can't miss it), its branches bountifully laden with green fruit. Old cattle yards and a couple of outbuildings are all that remain of this horse and cattle station, abandoned in 1890.

FIRST PEOPLES KNOW-HOW

This is the land of the Lama Lama and Kuku Thaypan peoples, the Bagaarrmugu, Mbarimakarranma, Muunydyiwarra, Magarrmagarrwarra, Balnggarrwarra and Gunduurwarra clans and their related families. There are still living memories of the Elders' hard lives working on the old station homesteads in what is now the national park. These days, Traditional Owner families are involved in the protection and management of the area.

WILDLIFE WATCH

The birds are particularly abundant here: singing in the morning (lorikeets), squawking in the afternoon (cockatoos) and circling at dusk (Brahminy kites). They join crickets and frogs (which you can hear jumping around in the leaves) and wallabies (thumping in the surrounding bush) in a natural-world orchestra that makes this campground really special.

Detour off Lakefield Road (it's signed) to Red Lily Lagoon to see an oasis of water covered in huge green lily leaves and pink-flowering lotus lilies. Across the road, White Lily Lagoon is similarly picturesque with small white lilies. Look for brolgas, egrets, ibis and comb-crested jacanas to name a few.

AND ANOTHER THING

Book before you come. There is no internet or mobile coverage within the national park and the touchscreen booking facility at Rinyirru (Lakefield) ranger base is unreliable.

The park is closed throughout the wet season every year (1 Dec to 31 May).

ALTERNATIVES

There are around two dozen campsites in Rinyirru (Lakefield) National Park, many of them secluded and suited to only one or two vehicles. Their appeal and accessibility changes according to the seasons. Hann Crossing camping area looks brilliant in the wet, but when we drove through it was a dust bowl.

Top Colourful waterlilies bloom in a billabong in the park
Bottom Red-tailed cockatoos gather on a nearby tree. Birdlife is especially abundant in the park

Free beachside camping under the palm trees, Robinson Crusoe-style.

Archer Point

Cooktown, Qld

MAP ON PAGE 202

ACTIVITIES

FACILITIES

This campground makes you feel miles from anywhere, like you've opted out of the rat race and chosen wild nature and natural beauty over the chaos of modern life. Where if you hang around long enough, Robinson Crusoe might just stroll around the tip of the next headland and give you a wave.

Archer Point's word-of-mouth reputation as a free campsite plays a part in evoking this marooned feeling, as does its off-the-beaten track locale. The slither of public land is hemmed in by glistening Walsh Bay and the Coral Sea on one side, and by Annan River (Yuku Baja-Muliku) Conservation Area on the other. Beyond the conservation area, Annan River (Yuku Baja-Muliku) National Park, the traditional land of the Yuku Baja-Muliku people, covers 8700 hectares of wilderness with no facilities and no access.

To get to the campground, hardy travellers must take the unsealed but well-kept road off the Mulligan Highway through the conservation area. When you arrive, there are none of the usual toilet and barbecue facilities that give most campsites a sense of civilisation. Just a windswept treeless point with a lookout that has a small lighthouse and a picnic table where – if the wind isn't up – you can take in a blue and green pantone of land, sea and islands.

All this, of course, amps up its attractiveness. There are three or four open swathes of treeless land next to the water where caravans plant themselves, but tents are best pitched among the gently swaying coconut palms and silty sand mounds in the more sheltered south-facing area on the right as you enter. You'll likely switch into high 4WD to navigate the dunes – this is un-demarcated camping with very silty sand.

The views here stretch from the crocodile-inhabited mangroves on the eastern point, past the small island out at sea and across broad expanses of white sand beach strewn with black granite pebbles. Extensive shallow turquoise waters are perfect for knee-deep water play and throwing a line in, while keeping a watchful eye out for crocs. Further west along the beach there's a small creek trickling into the sea.

We stayed here in October and shared the dunes with just two other campers who joined us for sundowners on the beach in the fading light, and we shared their beach campfire when the stars came out.

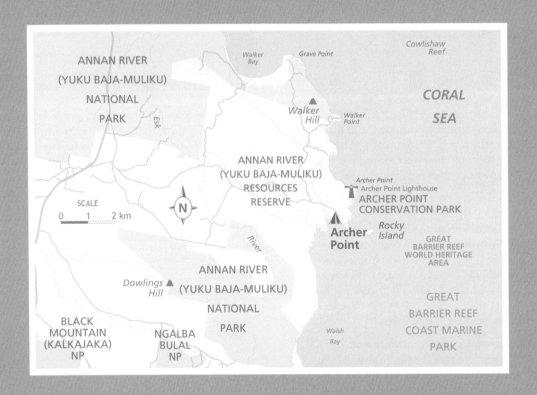

Opposite This off-the-beaten-path campsite with its leafy palm trees and isolated beaches feels like you've been marooned on your own private island

CATEGORIES

Free, Dog-Lovers, Family, Nature, Wi-Fi-Free, Nomads

GO DO IT

WHO   Free camping on public land; just turn up; archerpoint.com.au.

WHERE   Archer Point, Archer Point Rd, 15km south of Cooktown, Qld.

ACCESS Archer Point Rd is a 9.6km unsealed road signposted off Mulligan Hwy.

WHAT ELSE?

When the wind is up, you might find yourself with more company. Archers Point is well known as a kite-surfing spot among locals counting on regular strong trade winds. Best window is in the dry season (May to Sept).

CULTURE VULTURE

South on Mulligan Highway, Black Mountain viewing area in Black Mountain (Kalkajaka) National Park overlooks the eastern side of the curious other-worldly black granite boulder-strewn slopes. The boulders appear black because of the microscopic lichens and algae that grow on them. They are the source of many Indigenous legends.

EAT IT

In Cooktown, Driftwood Cafe serves tropical smoothies on a lovely sundeck overlooking the park and the bay. On most days, Nicko parks his van across the road, so you can buy prawns, coral trout and wild barramundi direct from the trawlers.

FIRST PEOPLES KNOW-HOW

From Cooktown, book a half-day Aboriginal Rock Art Experience at Normanby Station homelands. Join Traditional Balngarrawarra Owners (of Melsonby and Normanby land) amid the sandstone country and tropical flora exploring rock art rarely been seen by outsiders. See: cultureconnect.com.au

WILDLIFE WATCH

Keatings Lagoon Conservation Park, on the road to Cooktown, is for binocular-toting bird lovers. It's home to Wawu Balgal Bubu walk, a 1.4 kilometre return journey along a boardwalk that skirts the edge of a lily-pad-laden lagoon. At the end of it, a bird hide is the spot to spy on migratory waterbirds making the most of the fresh water.

STEP IT UP

Mount Cook summit walking track in Mount Cook National Park, near Cooktown, has an easy 800-metre walk to a picnic spot and lookout, and a longer, steeper climb through rainforest where you'll be rewarded with views of the Great Barrier Reef and northern Wet Tropics World Heritage areas.

Isabella Falls, 30 minutes' drive north of Cooktown, has a pristine swimming hole with a rope swing.

ALTERNATIVES

Various commercial camping sites are available in Cooktown. North of Cooktown, Endeavour Falls Tourist Park has a natural setting close to the falls.

A beachside and rainforest immersion where its magnetism also lies in its remoteness.

Cape Tribulation

Daintree National Park, Qld

MAP ON PAGE 206

ACTIVITIES

FACILITIES

There's a coconut spike at Cape Trib campground, which is to say that its proximity to a palm-shaded beach is such that the occasional crash and thud of a coconut hitting sand – and becoming breakfast – is all part of the paradisiacal experience. Cape Tribulation is a special place, a tiny town where the remarkable Daintree National Park – home to an ancient rainforest that is older than the Amazon – meets the impeccable Coral Sea coastline and the Great Barrier Reef. Cape Tribulation is not only accessible *only* via ferry, it marks the final stop for 2WD vehicles touring out of Cairns, and the end of the sealed road for 4WD travellers going north on the rugged Bloomfield Track. The town, much of which is hidden in the foothills and foliage of the fringing Daintree, is strung along the main road. The campground is a spacious, well-kept and grassy stretch of land between this road and Myall Beach, with the rainforest encroaching on its borders.

It's a commercial campground (there are only a handful in this book), but it is done right. It's set out in a figure-eight, with camper-trailer and caravan sites (all powered) at the southern end and smaller tent and campervan sites (mostly non-powered) on the northern end. All campsites are dotted around the edge of the figure-eight so that the central grassy area remains free even in peak season, amplifying privacy and sense of space. Unpowered sites tucked into the rainforest (37, 35, 33, 31, 29, 27, 25) are the most popular – they're shaded and have their own little sandy trails down to the

beach, but four main tracks put the beach in reach within minutes for all. Facilities include:

- Exceptionally well-kept cooking and barbecue facilities
- Two bathroom blocks (with hot showers) and laundries with coin-operated washing machines

And what a beach it is. This section has no public access (except for the occasional horseriders), so campers have the white sand and pockets of rainforest – complete with volleyball net, rope swings and rough-hewn log seats, to themselves. At low tide, tiny 'bubbler crabs' make art from little balls of sand, and the exposed craggy rocks are ideal for spying tiny fish. The reprieve from the heat as the sun disappears behind the hills, makes the beach a great place to be for sundown. Afterwards, you can head to The Sand Bar in the green corrugate building that also houses the reception. This is the campground's lively fairy-light-lit restaurant-cum-bar serving wood-fired pizzas and fish and chips at weekends. There's a happy hour with $10 fresh prawns and nachos, a kids menu and a fire-pit to tell stories around.

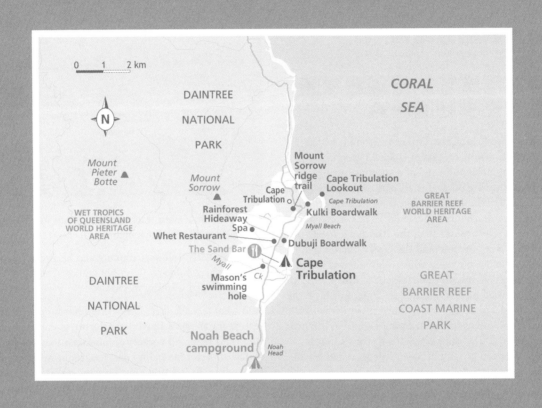

CATEGORIES

Young Travellers, Family, Nature, Wi-Fi-Free, No Dogs, Boomers, Nomads

GO DO IT

WHO   Cape Trib Camping; (07) 4098 0077; capetribcamping.com.au

WHERE   Lot 11 Cape Tribulation Rd, Cape Tribulation, approximately 83km or one hour and 45 minutes north of Port Douglas, Qld.

ACCESS   The campground is 45 minutes from the Daintree ferry on Cape Tribulation Rd. Look out for the big yellow sign just after Mason's Store. The 800m gravel driveway is suitable for 2WD vehicles.

WHAT ELSE?

An espresso coffee window opens from 7.30am, and the kiosk has essentials including pancake mix and maple syrup.

Kayaking tours, half-day Great Barrier Reef tours, jungle tours and horserides are all available in the area, with information and bookings able to be made from the campground.

About 2 kilometres north of the campground, Dubuji Boardwalk offers an easy stroll through the Daintree's mangrove swamps, lowland rainforest and beach, and Kulki Boardwalk, 3 kilometres north, takes you to the Cape Tribulation Lookout.

Mason's swimming hole, up behind Mason's Cafe is a 10-minute walk from the campground. Put a gold coin in the donation box (for maintenance) and swim among turtles in a pool shrouded in rainforest.

Sneak in a Thai massage at Rainforest Hideaway spa (capetribulationspa.com.au) and catch a yoga class at nearby Whet Restaurant every Wednesday at 6pm (premshanti.com)

WILDLIFE WATCH

Cape Tribulation Wilderness Cruises (capetribcruises.com) has the only boat permitted in the Cape Tribulation section of Daintree National Park. It runs a one-hour mangrove discovery tour and it's a chance to see estuarine crocodiles in their natural environment.

The Southern Cassowary, found in Cape Tribulation and the Daintree, is one of Australia's most unique and endangered birds. The flightless birds, some more than 2 metres tall, have a tall 'casque' or helmet on their heads, black plumage and brilliant red and blue neck wattles. They tend to be well camouflaged in their surroundings. If you do spot one, tell all. See: daintreecassowary.org.au

STEP IT UP

Ramp up the difficulty, on Mount Sorrow ridge trail, a steep 7-kilometre walk (allow six hours) through lush rainforest where you'll scramble over tree roots and rocks to be rewarded with views from an elevation of 680 metres that takes in both rainforest and reef. It starts at Kulki Boardwalk day-use area, 3 kilometres north of the campground.

AND ANOTHER THING

From the end of January to the start of April, the campground closes for the wet season – to book for the following camping season make contact after April.

ALTERNATIVES

Noah Beach, south of here, is a spectacular beachfront campground in the heart of Daintree National Park. The only amenity is a small toilet block, but it's the pristine natural immersion that draws adventurous campers here. With only 15 sites, it's difficult to get a site.

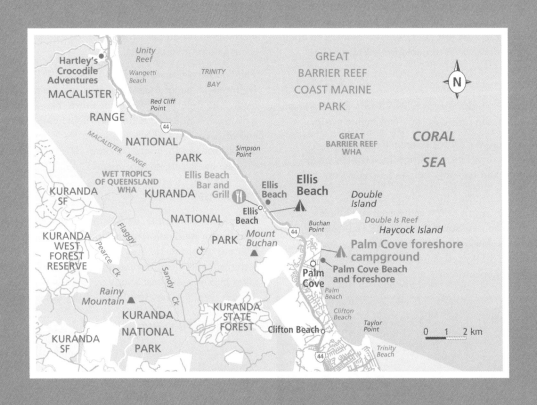

Tropical beachfront camping overlooking the Great Barrier Reef.

Ellis Beach

Cairns, Qld

ACTIVITIES

FACILITIES

As far as location goes, Ellis Beach is pretty special. And it's not just the beachfront view. Its position, on a curvaceous stretch of the road between Cairns and Port Douglas, sees the leafy tendrils of the coastal ranges behind touching the white sands and blue waters of the Coral Sea. What a combo!

It's a commercial campground (there are only a handful in this book) with all the bells and whistles that make for easy camping. Turn left at reception for a veritable village of ocean bungalows, budget holiday cabins and flats. Turn right to drive through the caravan site (with 47 powered sites) to the unpowered camping section at the quieter southern end. This small area has a tidy little circuit of about 20 sites squeezed together. The roadside spots can be noisy with traffic so get here as close as possible to 10am check-out time to snaffle the beachfront sites, where just a single log fence and a few seaward-leaning coconut trees separate tents and campers from the lapping waves. It's the perfect spot to pull up a couple of camp chairs and binoculars for views towards Double Island.

Central to the camping area is a sail-covered camp kitchen, with a barbecue, hot plates, fridge and a sink. (I left my Aeropress coffee-maker here if anyone finds it.) It's kept

exceptionally tidy and is a convivial spot to gather and chat with the mixed and friendly crowd of campers. Other facilities include:

- A commendably clean toilet block with hot showers
- A swimming pool
- In reception, an on-site tour desk, internet access and essentials such as mozzie repellent

Ellis Beach is considered one of the last spots on the coast travelling north where you would consider swimming (Four Mile in Port Douglas is another). There are croc warning signs near the public beach, but there's also a lifesaver patrolling so swimming is possible – but at your own risk. Certainly don't chance it between November and May, during stinger (and box jellyfish) season. Instead, stroll 200 metres north to the Ellis Beach Surf Lifesaving Club where they have stinger nets for safe swimming.

On my stay, in October, the waves were excellent for body-surfing, but the wind also churns up the silt, making the water turgid at this time of year. At other times, the sea can be picture-postcard turquoise blue.

CATEGORIES

Young Travellers, Family, Nature, No Dogs, Boomers, Nomads

GO DO IT

WHO   Ellis Beach Oceanfront Bungalows; 1800 637 036; ellisbeach.com

WHERE Captain Cook Hwy, Ellis Beach, approximately 30km (30 minutes' drive) north of Cairns, and 38km (35 minutes) south of Port Douglas, Qld.

ACCESS Via Captain Cook Hwy.

WHAT ELSE?

Walk north up the beach past the rope swings and mango trees to roadside Ellis Beach Bar and Grill. It is open for breakfast, lunch and dinner and promises good fun with $1 oysters on Sundays, buckets of prawns during happy hour and live bands every now and then.

Palm Cove Beach and foreshore, a 7-minute drive south, has a family friendly tropical beachfront with stinger nets, a jetty and restaurants aplenty.

Full- and half-day reef trips depart from marinas in both Cairns and Port Douglas. Slip on flippers and a snorkel to see the coral and marine life of the Great Barrier Reef.

EAT IT

Port Douglas Markets are on every Sunday 8am–2pm at Rex Smeal Park (next to St Mary's Chapel). Shop for fruit and vegetables, ripe coconuts, fresh juices and smoothies, plus locally made handicrafts, art and pottery.

FIRST PEOPLES KNOW-HOW

Mossman Gorge Centre (mossmangorge.com.au), 50 kilometres north, is an Indigenous eco-tourism development and gateway to beautiful walks, pristine waterfalls and swimming holes in the World Heritage-listed Daintree National Park. Take a Dreamtime walk to learn more about the culture and traditions of the Kuku Yalanji people.

Above This commercial campsite has the amenities that make for an easy camping experience

WILDLIFE WATCH

Hartley's Crocodile Adventures (crocodileadventures.com) 13 kilometres north, on a melaleuca wetland lagoon, offers the chance to see some of Tropical North Queensland's rare and exotic creatures in the flesh, and it's more tasteful than tacky. Take a 25-minute boat ride to spot crocodiles lurking in the murky waters and follow the Cassowary Walk for a look at these endangered fascinating birds, found only in these parts.

ALTERNATIVES

There is free camping at the foreshore reserve in nearby Palm Cove.

There are plenty of commercial campgrounds in Port Douglas, including Tropic Breeze Caravan Park (tropicbreeze.com.au), which has 54 powered sites for caravans and 17 tent sites. It's walking distance to Four Mile Beach and the main street.

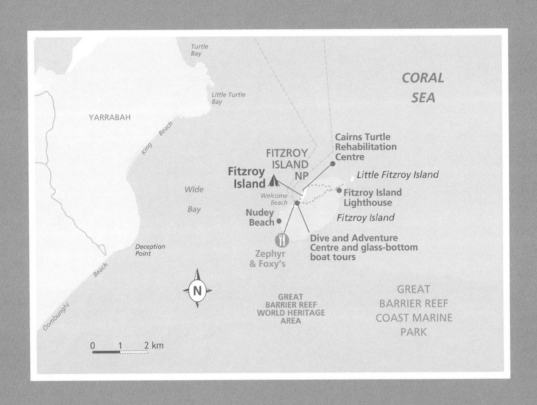

A Great Barrier Reef tropical island with rainforest, wildlife and palms.

Fitzroy Island

Cairns and the Great Barrier Reef, Qld

ACTIVITIES

FACILITIES

Camping on an island on the Great Barrier Reef – it doesn't get much better than that. Fitzroy Island is a 339-hectare tropical oasis located 29 kilometres south-east of Cairns – or 45 minutes by fast boat. It's truly tropical: covered in thick rainforest and woodlands, alive with lizards and birds, and fringed with mangroves, white beaches and coconut palms. With 97 per cent of the island classified as national park, it's its own little paradise.

The island has full public access and daytrips here make popular (and closer) land-based alternatives to the reef's offshore pontoon experiences. If you can stay a week, even better – you won't run out of things to do. The surrounding reef is a playground for snorkellers, divers, swimmers and boaters who have the benefit of pristinely clear water that sits on the same blue pantone spectrum as Chris Hemsworth's eyes. You can BYO your kit but if you're travelling light, you can sort flippers, masks and scuba gear from the dive centre and kayaks from the little flat-roofed hire hut on Welcome Beach.

Amid all this abundance, the campground is a simple affair, owned by council and run by Fitzroy Island Resort. It is located in a sheltered and grassy spot, next to the beach with hills rising behind and plenty of tree cover. It's only 5 minutes' stroll from the jetty so not too far to be lugging your gear. There are approximately 20 tent sites that are unmarked but require tents to be limited to a maximum of 3x3 metres, with two adults and two children per site. Campers reap the benefits of the resort, with access to all the tours, amenities and a great bar and restaurant (but the pool, sadly, is out of bounds). There's a modern toilet and shower block and barbecues on the waterfront. You'll need to bring all your supplies, including food. Emphasising the family friendly environment there's a no alcohol rule in the campground.

Walking and hiking are another drawcard. There are clearly signed and marked walking tracks that weave around the eastern side of the island, and a handy self-guide booklet (for a small fee for campers – less than $5) so you can navigate to the summit (269 metres), with its lovely views over Welcome Beach and to the historic lighthouse at the eastern end.

Located on the south-east side of the Island, Nudey Beach (*see* p. 215) is considered one of the Reef's most beautiful and it often stars in Tourism Queensland's promo material. The white beach has been formed by waves crashing and crushing the reef coral. The boulders at each end, smooth and polished by the elements, look like fat grey seals.

CATEGORIES

Young Travellers, Family, Nature, Wi-Fi-Free, No Dogs, Boomers, Nomads

GO DO IT

WHO   Fitzroy Island Resort; (07) 4044 6700; fitzroyisland.com

WHERE   On the Great Barrier Reef, 29km south-east – or 45 minutes by fast boat – from Cairns, Qld.

ACCESS   The 45-minute Fitzroy Flyer boat ride departs Cairns to Fitzroy Island and back daily. Departures are from Cairns Marlin Wharf, Berth 20.

WHAT ELSE?

Fitzroy Island Resort's glass-bottom boat tours explore the sheltered waters and the dazzling marine life around the island. Tours depart twice daily and bookings are essential.

The island's historical walk includes remnants from World War II military occupation and domestic objects from the families that once occupied the lighthouse.

CULTURE VULTURE

The first European to spot Fitzroy Island was Captain James Cook in 1770. He named it after Augustus Fitzroy, who was the British prime minister when Cook's ship, the *Endeavour*, set sail. The island has had various incarnations over the years as a quarantine zone (after an outbreak of smallpox in Asia), a mission for Indigenous Australians, a military base during World War II and a lighthouse station.

EAT IT

The resort's flashy a la carte restaurant, Zephyr, serves up dishes with an emphasis on Aussie produce, like fresh Tasmanian oysters and far-north Queensland lamb shank. A table on the balcony is a couple's treat but there's a kid's menu if the family tags along. Foxy's bar on the waterfront is a prime sundowner location with a fun casual atmosphere.

WILDLIFE WATCH

Geckos, lizard-like major skinks, non-venomous pythons, echidnas, bats, flying foxes and dozens of butterflies, birds and insects call this island home. And that's just on land. On the Reef, diverse marine life includes dozens of different coral species with visually suggestive names like staghorn, brain, spaghetti and elephant ear. Look out for parrotfish, clownfish and moon wrasse, blue-spotted stingrays, turtles and even whales (between July and Sept).

Fitzroy Island is home to a campus of the Cairns Turtle Rehabilitation Centre, a simple set-up in a shed with practical, above-ground circular swimming pools that are used for treating turtles that have had propellers run over them or ingested plastic bags. Daily tours reveal some heart-warming stories about turtle recovery and release back into the ocean.

STEP IT UP

I did an early morning walk to Nudey Beach, the island's geckos and major skinks skittering in the greenery at every footfall. This is actually not a nudie or nudist beach. 'It was named after a captain with an unfortunate last name,' according to my information sheet. And, for the record: 'Public nudity is illegal in Queensland'.

ALTERNATIVES

The closest campgrounds are in the Cairns region. See Ellis Beach (*see* p. 209) and Upper Davies Creek (*see* p. 217).

The island and surrounding reef is a playground for visitors

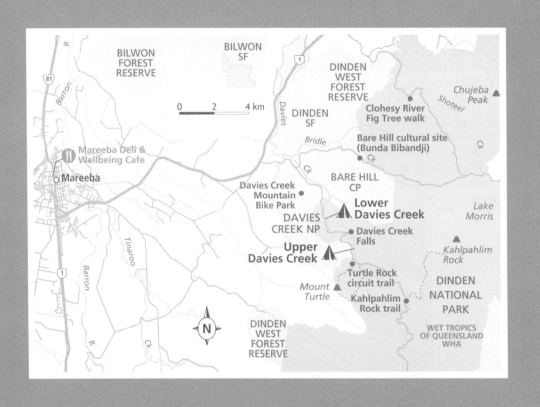

An idyllic creek-side camping spot for self-sufficient campers.

Upper Davies Creek

Dinden National Park, Qld

ACTIVITIES

FACILITIES

Some of the camp spots along Upper Davies Creek are so idyllic they remind me of paintings by Tom Roberts or Frederick McCubbin. All you need is a swagman filling his billy in the reflecting water and the picture would be complete.

Dinden National Park adjoins Davies Creek National Park, and is accessed via Davies Creek Road. All vehicles can travel the first six or so kilometres to Lower Davies Creek campground, but beyond this towards Upper Davies Creek, the gravel road gets rutted and steep and becomes suitable for 4WD and high-clearance vehicles only. The limited access teamed with the small number of campsites – just eight, make for peaceful and private camping, especially in the low season (outside of school holidays).

The sites are generously spaced along the creek with 'camp nodes' 1 and 2, camp nodes 3–6, and camp nodes 7 and 8 grouped together. Every two adjacent campsites have pitched-roof single toilet blocks and fire-rings.

We parked our tent-topped vehicle at camp node 2 in a sandy spot that stretches along the burbling sandy-bottomed creek. Sit on the banks here long enough and you'll soon see fish darting about, little turtles poking their noses into the air and dragonflies going about their business. A rock- and tree root-hopping path 10 metres upstream leads to a waterfall and private shoulder deep waterhole surrounded by smooth granite slopes and skinny eucalypts. Braving the frigid water (in October at least) for a dip is essential.

The crowd-pleaser here is the picnic area and swimming hole at Davies Creek Falls, a 5-minute drive from the campground back along Davies Creek Road. From the well-signed carpark, head left 200 metres along the downhill path to beautiful cascading falls that can be viewed from a fenced-off rock face. Alternatively head right on the 300-metre walk to the picnic spot. The swimming hole here is dreamy, with a beach, sandy bottom and chest-high clear water perfect for paddling in. You could spend a day here, no problem. If you do there's another track along the creek joining the picnic spot to the falls.

CATEGORIES

Young Travellers, Family, Nature, Wi-Fi-Free, No Dogs, Boomers, Nomads

GO DO IT

WHO   Queensland National Parks; 13 7468; parks.des.qld.gov.au

WHERE   Davies Creek Road, Dinden National Park, is in the Atherton Tablelands, approximately 60km or one hour from Cairns via Kuranda, Qld.

ACCESS   From Cairns, travel towards Kuranda on the Kennedy Hwy. After passing the Kuranda turn-off, travel a further 21km before turning left on to Davies Creek Rd. Travel 10km along Davies Creek Road (3.8km past Lower Davies Creek camping area).

WHAT ELSE?

Clohesy River Fig Tree walk is also within Dinden National Park (accessed from the Kennedy Hwy). The short 300-metre boardwalk skirts through a patch of wet tropical rainforest to a magnificent fig tree. Access is by 4WD with numerous creek crossings.

Davies Creek Mountain Bike Park is a network of trails traversing granite outcrops, sheoak and cycad forests and creeks in the Lamb Range between Mareeba and Kuranda. There are different lengths and grades to suit all rider levels. Walkers are welcome too.

EAT IT

On Mareeba's main street, Mareeba Deli & Wellbeing Cafe wouldn't look out of place in Melbourne's Lygon Street, with a glass counter filled with salami, cheese, pasta and bottles of fat olives for picnics or camping essentials. Coffee is barista-style and there's a dining area out the back for alfresco meals.

FIRST PEOPLES KNOW-HOW

The Buluwai clan have occupied the area including Davies Creek for more than 5000 years.

To get permission to visit rock art paintings along the Bare Hill cultural site (Bunda Bibandji, 4WD access-only), contact the Kuranda Mantaka Kowrowa Mona Mona Aboriginal Corporation, phone: (07) 4093 9296.

WILDLIFE WATCH

Davies Creek National Park and parts of Dinden National Park are home to the endangered northern bettong. These solitary possum-sized marsupials feed on truffles (underground fungi) found at the base of trees. They're nocturnal creatures so keep your eyes peeled at night as they hop about.

STEP IT UP

Further upstream between camp nodes 3 and 4, the Turtle Head Rock circuit trail is an 8-kilometre hike (difficult level) to a view-tastic summit topping 936 metres. It will take about three to four hours and you'll need to BYO water. Even higher, Kahlpahlim Rock trail formerly known as Lambs Head, is for hikers and runners keen to tackle a steep 1300-metre summit. It's an 11 kilometre return walk and takes about six hours. Both these walks reward with mesmerising Atherton Tableland vistas. Be sure to take supplies (water, food, first-aid kit), and start out early to beat the heat.

ALTERNATIVES

Lower Davies Creek camping area is another pretty creek-side spot amid granite boulders. Note you need to park and walk a short distance to the campsites.

Granite Gorge Nature Park (granitegorge.com.au), in Mareeba, has a huge commercial campground. Head to the rear of the site to chance one of the waterside spots with rope swings. There's a short gorge walk here, too.

Opposite Avid hikers should take the chance to explore Kahlpahlim Rock trail for some worthwhile views

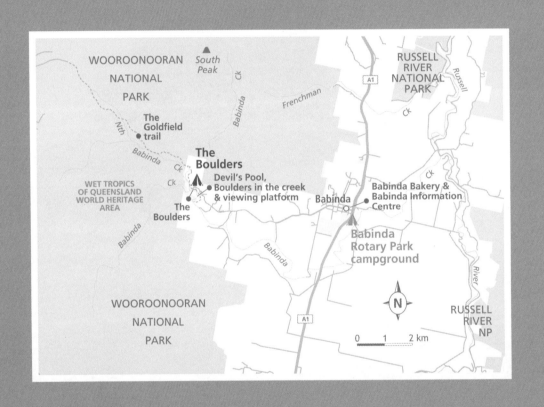

WOOROONOORAN
NATIONAL
PARK

▲ *South Peak*

Babinda Ck

Frenchman

RUSSELL
RIVER
NATIONAL
PARK

Russell

A1

Ck

The ● Goldfield
trail

Nth Babinda Ck

The Boulders

Ck

WET TROPICS
OF QUEENSLAND
WORLD HERITAGE
AREA

● Devil's Pool,
Boulders in the creek
& viewing platform

The ●
Boulders

Babinda

Ck

● Babinda Bakery &
Babinda Information
Centre

Babinda

Babinda
Rotary Park
campground

River

Babinda

WOOROONOORAN
NATIONAL
PARK

A1

N

RUSSELL
RIVER
NP

0   1   2 km

Free tropical camping, close to Babinda Boulders swimming hole.

The Boulders

Babinda, Qld

ACTIVITIES

FACILITIES

Thick, lush lime-green grass, lofty leaning palm trees, fluttering blue butterflies and hot and humid air: there's nothing quite like camping in far-north Queensland. Add a dripping wet rainforest full of ferns, a crystal-clear mountain creek and dramatic rock formations to the picture and the tropical canvas is complete.

This is the Boulders, a popular swimming spot and picnic area on the very edge of Wooroonooran National Park, in the foothills of the Bellenden Ker Range, which includes Queensland's highest mountain Bartle Frere. The gloriously clear and luminous green water in the creek and swimming areas here is reflected in the vine-tangled overhanging branches and dropping ferns of the surrounding rainforest. Take a dip in the bracing water of the first family friendly swimming hole and warm-up afterwards on the rocks, then head down the ravine on the short walk to Devil's Pool. Signs warn against swimming here. Near it is the viewing platform over the valley and so-called Boulders in the creek below, where centuries of wear and tear from deluges of water – the result of exceedingly high average rainfall – have smoothed a path through huge granite boulders that protrude from the creek bed like hippopotamus backs.

Easy concrete ramp accessibility and well-maintained sealed walking tracks make The Boulders an easy navigable pit-stop, so too the picnic areas, barbecues, playground and toilets near the carpark. The open grassy areas and tree shade continue next door in the campground, where 10 large unpowered green plots, suitable for tents, caravans, camper-trailers and bigger vehicles, are spaced around a central roundabout road.

The campground is basic, unpowered and nothing great aesthetically but its proximity to the wild beauty of The Boulders gives it a big thumbs-up. It is also one of the few in this book that is actually free, so there are no access fees, no parking fees and no national park fees. With this in mind enjoy it! Facilities include:

• Cold showers
• A toilet block (unceremoniously plonked in the middle of the roundabout)
• Picnic tables

CATEGORIES

Young Travellers, Free, Family, Nature, Wi-Fi-Free, No Dogs, Boomers, Nomads

GO DO IT

WHO   Babinda Information Centre; babindainfocentre. com.au; (07) 4067 1008
WHERE   Boulders Rd, Babinda, 65km south of Cairns, Qld.
ACCESS   From Cairns follow the Bruce Hwy north of Innisfail. At Babinda township follow signs to turn right onto Munro St/Boulders Rd for 6km.

WHAT ELSE?

Babinda is a cute town with characteristic Queenslander houses and an old railway station. There are a handful of shops including the excellent Babinda Bakery and an unmissable tourist information centre painted bright blue. It's on the corner of Bruce Highway and Munro Street.

About 20 kilometres south of the campground, in Wooroonooran National Park, Josephine Falls is one of Queensland's most beautiful waterfalls, fed by the clear mountain water from Bartle Frere, which you can see from the popular picnic area. Swim and jump into the green sandy-bottomed pools, slide down the natural slippery dips made from the smoothed granite rock and walk to the viewing platform overlooking the falls.

From Babinba Boulders you can follow the creek upstream for 1 kilometre to enter Wooroonooran National Park, where an easy walk takes you along the creek under king ferns and rainforest canopy. This is the southern end of the Goldfield trail. Retrace your footsteps to return at leisure (after 4km and ideally before the route starts to ascend) or *see* p. 223 for the longer trek.

CULTURE VULTURE

A storyboard at The Boulders tells of how in 1942 during World War II, a B25 Mitchell bomber, having approached heavy rain and cloud, crashed just below the peak of Bartle Frere. The seven crew were all killed, but their lives are still remembered, particularly in the township of Babinda.

FIRST PEOPLES KNOW-HOW

According to a legend of the Yirrganydji people, Devil's Pool is haunted by a young married woman named Oolana from the local Yidinji tribe who fell in love and ran away with Dyga from a visiting tribe. The lovers were captured near Devil's Pool by the Elders, at which point Oolana broke free and leapt into the creek waters. With that, the earth shook, and boulders tumbled into the creek crushing the woman. Her anguished cries can still be heard today and are the reason 17 lives have been lost at the waterhole since 1959.

STEP IT UP

The Goldfield trail follows a moderate 19-kilometre historic path through the rainforest of Wooroonooran National Park connecting Goldsborough Valley, 46 kilometres south of Cairns, with Babinda Boulders. It extends over babbling creeks and along trails with a soundtrack of bird calls and frog croaks. The highlight is a climb over a low saddle between Queensland's two highest peaks, Bartle Frere and Bellenden Ker. Allow 8–9 hours one-way.

AND ANOTHER THING

Cairns Regional Council does a decent job of maintaining the campground and The Boulders picnic area, but don't get too comfortable here. There's a 72-hour maximum stay. With no bookings possible, it's also first-come, first-served so you might face a bit of competition in July and during other peak times.

The rocks at The Boulders get very hot – wear footwear.

ALTERNATIVES

Rotary Park Campground is another free campground just across the highway at Babinda. It is dog friendly. Fires are not allowed.

Opposite and above Babinda Boulders is an iconic attraction and popular swimming spot

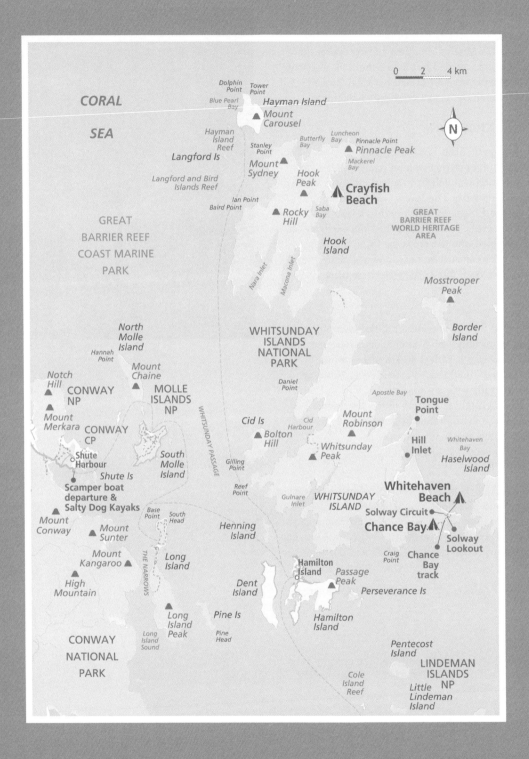

Crayfish Beach

CORAL

SEA

Dolphin Point
Tower Point
Blue Pearl Bay
Hayman Island
Mount Carousel
Hayman Island Reef
Stanley Point
Langford Is
Butterfly Bay
Luncheon Bay
Pinnacle Point
Pinnacle Peak
Mackerel Bay
Mount Sydney
Hook Peak
Langford and Bird Islands Reef
Crayfish Beach
Ian Point
Baird Point
Rocky Hill
Saba Bay
GREAT BARRIER REEF WORLD HERITAGE AREA

GREAT
BARRIER REEF
COAST MARINE
PARK

Hook Island
Nara Inlet
Macona Inlet

Mosstrooper Peak

North Molle Island
Hannah Point

Border Island

Notch Hill
CONWAY NP
Mount Chaine
MOLLE ISLANDS NP

WHITSUNDAY ISLANDS NATIONAL PARK

Daniel Point
Apostle Bay
Tongue Point

Mount Merkara
CONWAY CP
Cid Is
Bolton Hill
Cid Harbour
Mount Robinson
Hill Inlet
Whitehaven Bay

Shute Harbour
South Molle Island
Whitsunday Peak
Haselwood Island

Shute Is
Gilling Point
Reef Point

Scamper boat departure & Salty Dog Kayaks
Base Point
South Head
Gulnare Inlet
WHITSUNDAY ISLAND
Whitehaven Beach
Solway Circuit
Mount Conway
Mount Sunter
Henning Island
Chance Bay
Craig Point
Solway Lookout
Chance Bay track

Mount Kangaroo
THE NARROWS
Long Island
Hamilton Island
Passage Peak
Perseverance Is

High Mountain
Long Island Peak
Pine Is
Dent Island

Long Island Sound
Pine Head
Hamilton Island
Pentecost Island

CONWAY NATIONAL PARK
Cole Island Reef
LINDEMAN ISLANDS NP
Little Lindeman Island

WHITSUNDAY PASSAGE

Self-sufficient and blissfully remote island camping on the Great Barrier Reef.

Crayfish Beach

Whitsunday Islands National Park, Qld

ACTIVITIES

FACILITIES

When you've lugged your belongings between boat and beach and waved goodbye to the boatman, there's the sensation that any further communication with the outside world might be via a letter in a bottle. Such is the beautiful isolation of a place that you can only arrive at by boat (*see* p. 226).

Crayfish Beach campground sits metres from a smile of a beach in Mackeral Bay South on the eastern side of Hook Island, one of the bigger island in the Whitsundays, 25 kilometres from Airlie Beach. It is sheltered by a rocky headland on its eastern side and looks north and west towards hazy blue mountainous terrain on a similar piece of land jutting out further up the island.

Three campsites (a maximum of 12 people) are naturally demarcated by patches of sand and scrubby trees, and backed by a sandy creek inlet and impenetrable dry rainforest of casuarinas and towering hoop pines. The occasional pandanus adds a touch of bright green foliage. Shells scattered around the campsite are as big as baseball gloves, some with beautiful apricot spirals. There are no coconut trees in sight, so the coconut shells with husks still attached must have blown in on waves from distant shores.

I camped here (somewhat unbelievably in retrospect) with my adventurous 70-year-old mother. Tellingly, the sheer beauty of the place – white sand, achingly turquoise water, total seclusion – was enough to override the creature comforts lacking for a non-camper.

The campsite away from the (very basic) drop-toilet block and next to one of two picnic tables is the most desirable, but the heat of the day means following the shade. We moved our

simple two-man tent from beach to creek bed to tree shade, depending on the movement of the sun.

We shared the place with three Germans, a Belgian couple, and two Aussies who had set up their swags and fishing gear on the edge of the creek bed. They told us that roughly three years ago the reef, which you can access directly from the beach, was alive with colourful varieties of hard coral.

Today the coral has taken on a new form – at high tide its white patterned chunks and spheres look like decorative clay sculptures on the sea floor. On the beach at low tide, it chinks underfoot like broken glass. There's something beautiful about it, but there's no getting away from the fact this is a sign of a reef in decline, the result of both coral bleaching and Tropical Cyclone Debbie, which swept through the Whitsundays in March 2017 devastating marine ecosystems.

Happily, amid the cemetery of coral, there is plenty of marine life. Follow little fish when snorkelling off the beach, or take a dip from the rocky point for stingrays and turtles. A little further out, our camping friends spotted a one-metre blacktip reef shark and two-metre whitetip reef sharks (both harmless). There are also larger sharks in the Whitsundays (*see* p. 226).

CATEGORIES

Young Travellers, Nature, Families, Wi-Fi-Free, No Dogs, Nomads, Boomers

GO DO IT

WHO   Queensland Parks & Wildlife Service; 13 7468; parks.des.qld.gov.au

WHERE   Hook Island, Whitsunday Islands National Park, Qld.

ACCESS   Access is by private or commercial boat from Airlie Beach or Shute Harbour. Scampers (*see* Scamper island hopping) is the transfer company that drops off and collects campers.

WHAT ELSE?

There's a romantic wooden swing swaying over the sand at one end of the beach, adding a touch of whimsy to the isolation.

A 'coffee and wi-fi' sign on the beach is the remnants of a cheeky long-term camper and a reminder of what you're (not) missing out on.

Fancy a kayak? They can be hired before departure from Salty Dog Kayaks (saltydog.com.au), located next to Scampers office.

The Whitehaven Beach Ocean Swim (hamiltonisland.com.au) is a 2.75-kilometre open-swimming competition held on the beach in November each year as part of the Hamilton Island Triathlon.

WILDLIFE WATCH

High-profile shark attacks in the Whitsundays have prompted the development of a broader Sharkwise education campaign. Follow warning signs and be mindful that this is a natural habitat for sharks that are considered dangerous to humans.

AND ANOTHER THING

Camping permit tags must be displayed on tents so they can be clearly seen by QPWS rangers.

SCAMPER ISLAND HOPPING

Scamper (whitsundaycamping.com.au) is the boat company that connects campers to the campgrounds throughout the Whitsunday Islands. It's a well-run operation that also supplies camp kits – water, Eskys, sleeping mats, torches, cutlery, pots, detergent, camp stove, chairs, gas canisters and tents, as well as stinger suits, snorkels, flippers and kayaks. Owners Sandy and Wayne (who are lovely) have been in the business for 11 years and have set it up so that travellers can have the true-blue camping experience without needing to buy equipment. (This is what we did and it works a treat, but consider bringing your own blow-up mat – and substitute pillow, if you can't sleep on a yoga-style mat.)

Scamper, the boat, is a 10-metre aluminium high-speed barge. It can carry up to 34 passengers, plus gear, and has a shallow draft and drop-down front designed for walking gear direct from boat to beach. Part of Sandy and Wayne's job is logistics – getting campers on and off the different islands in time with the tides, which change with the seasons, is part of the challenge. Pricing is determined by the distance of the campground from Shute Harbour. Check the website for minimum numbers needed for some departures, non-swim campgrounds and possible site closures – it's a wealth of knowledge. The boat departs from the waterfront at Shute Harbour, approximately 9 kilometres south-east of Airlie Beach, where the office is located.

ALTERNATIVES

There are plenty of great campsites in Whitsunday Islands National Park. See Chance Bay (*see* p. 227) and Whitehaven Beach (*see* p. 230).

Off-grid and pristine white sand camping with snorkelling and walking thrown in.

Chance Bay

Whitsunday Islands National Park, Qld

MAP ON PAGE 224

ACTIVITIES

FACILITIES

Proximity to Whitehaven Beach is one of the attractions to Chance Bay campground, but it's a little piece of paradise in its own right. With white silica sand and warm, clear turquoise waters that turn sapphire blue as the water gets deeper – it's tourism brochure stuff. And with space for only 12 campers, it's quieter than its more popular neighbour, too.

Chance Bay is located on south-east Whitsunday Island, 27 kilometres east-south-east of Shute Harbour. The sands are almost as white as Whitehaven Beach (which you can access on a half-hour 3km walk through shady bush, and camp at, *see* p. 230) and the water is just as beautiful.

You can only arrive by boat (*see* p. 226) at mid- to high-tide. After off-loading gear from the boat, it's a bit of a trudge up a sandy path to a small elevated camping area with mesmeric views of the beach below and the distant wind-sculpted rocky crags of Pentecost Island. There are wooden picnic tables and, down a sandy path, a single drop-toilet, but the coastal growth is head-height at best so there's nothing by way of shade. Best to set your tent and sleeping gear up here and park your chairs and cooking amenities under the spindly sheoaks and barely-there shade trees down near the water. In the heat of the day, it's also a good idea to string some towels over branches for much-needed shade, but relief comes at the end of the day with shade from the western hills.

The water of Chance Bay glistens like diamonds and is so pristine you can spend hours watching the acrobatics of schools of whitebait and mackerel whose scales catch the sunlight as they dance around in the shallows. Dark ominous shadows that can give you a start while snorkelling turn out to be schools of bigger striped tropical fish – their colours luminescent against the pearlescent sand. Green, flatback and hawksbill sea turtles have all been spotted here. The one I saw looked like a rock until it ducked underwater at my intrusion. Fellow campers from France told me that while swimming further out they'd also seen stingrays wriggling out of the sandy bottom.

When the tide is low, another ecosystem is revealed: sea snails crawling the wet sand and crabs getting busy forming tiny little sand balls that make paisley patterns across the beach.

These sheltered waters are the safe haven for two-mast yachts, flashy catamarans and characteristic wood-hulled boats, whose inhabitants occasionally stop in for a walk on the beach. At night, the mast lights twinkle and cast stripes across the oily black water blending with the starlit sky above. Dreamy stuff.

CATEGORIES

Young Travellers, Families, Nature, Wi-Fi-Free, No Dogs, Boomers, Nomads

GO DO IT

WHO   Queensland Parks & Wildlife Service; 13 74 68; parks.des.qld.gov.au

WHERE   Whitsunday Island, Whitsunday Islands National Park, Qld.

ACCESS   Access is by private or commercial boat from Airlie Beach or Shute Harbour. Scampers (*see* p. 226) is the transfer company that drops off and collects campers.

WHAT ELSE?

The walk to Whitehaven Beach is well signposted from Chance Bay. It's a dirt and sand trail with some woodchip towards the Whitehaven Beach end. It's shaded most of the way by a mix of eucalypt, hoop pine and rainforest, with lizards and geckos rustling in the bushes as you walk along. Signs say it is 3.5 kilometres, but given the flat trail and the fact it took me 30 minutes, I'd put it closer to 3 kilometres. It ends near the very southern end of Whitehaven Beach.

At the Whitehaven end, turn right off the main trail to access the Solway Circuit which continues through cycads and rock ferns to Solway Lookout. From an elevation of about 50 metres, it has views across Solway Passage to Pentecost and Haslewood islands and Cape Conway. If you do both Whitehaven Beach and Solway Lookout, it's about 5 kilometres return.

The Whitehaven Beach Ocean Swim (hamiltonisland.com.au) is a 2.75-kilometre open-swimming competition held on the beach in November each year as part of the Hamilton Island Triathlon.

FIRST PEOPLES KNOW-HOW

The Ngaro people can trace their history in the Whitsundays islands and mainland back more than 9000 years.

WILDLIFE WATCH

High-profile shark attacks in the Whitsundays have prompted the development of a broader Sharkwise education campaign. Follow warning signs and be mindful that this is a natural habitat for sharks that are considered dangerous to humans.

Huge monitor lizards are a common sight trudging through the sand on the hunt for food. So too, enormous crows that have a penchant for attacking unguarded food bags with their beaks. Keep food packed away and don't feed animals – it's bad for them and they'll just keep annoying you (and every other camper thereafter).

STEP IT UP

Both the Solway Circuit and Whitehaven–Chance Bay tracks are part of the Whitsunday Ngaro Sea Trail, which blends seaways and walks across Whitsunday, South Molle and Hook islands. Traverse varying terrain, from rainforests and grasslands to rugged peaks, sandy-bottomed waters and remote tropical beaches. Salty Dog Kayaks (saltydog.com.au), located next to Scampers boat office (*see* p. 226), hosts tours and expeditions that follow the trail.

An adventurous marine biologist who I met in Cairns tipped me off about the amazing snorkelling in a sheltered reef area two bays west of Chance Bay. He said the marine life is exceptional, with stingers and reef sharks easy to spot. There's also a sand dune beyond the beach worth exploring. You'll need a kayak to get there (they can be hired from Salty Dog Kayaks).

AND ANOTHER THING

Camping permit tags must be displayed on tents so they can be seen clearly by QPWS rangers.

ALTERNATIVES

The Whitsundays has six island-based national parks with at least 29 campgrounds between them. All the sites are basic, with no drinking water or showers. See Crayfish Beach (*see* p. 225) and Whitehaven Beach (*see* p. 230).

Opposite You're never short of white sandy beaches at Chance Bay (with an occasional visitor or two)

Basic camping on a bucket-list beach fit for a marriage proposal.

Whitehaven Beach

Whitsunday Islands National Park, Qld

MAP ON PAGE 224

ACTIVITIES

FACILITIES

No list of ultimate Australian campsites would be complete without the inclusion of Whitehaven Beach. In fact, no list of ultimate *global* campsites would be complete without it. This eye-glaringly white beach – made from 98 per cent pure silica, a quartz derivative likely to have been washed here by sea currents over millions of years – stretches for 7 kilometres of uninterrupted dreaminess. When you cruise alongside it in a speed boat, the blurry blue-turquoise and white strip of beach backed by a hilly forest seems never-ending. Such perfection has made it the face of hundreds of ad campaigns, magazine covers and the backdrop to many a bended knee.

That you can camp here is one of life's little gifts. In 2018 the campground closed for implementation of a $3.9 million investment that included an upgrade of the camping area, a sheltered picnic area for daytrippers and a new long-distance walking track. The renovations and picnic area now complete and the new 29-kilometre track connecting Whitehaven Beach to Tongue Point via the Whitsunday Craig Trail was being constructed at time of this book's research.

Hidden in the trees about 10 metres from the southern end of the beach, the campground is in a purpose-built sandy and dirt clearing bordered by log fencing. The seven campsites with space enough for 20 campers are unmarked but the coastal bush creates little areas of privacy. Like all the campgrounds in the Whitsunday Islands, this one is basic but the facilities – picnic tables and a central drop-toilet – are new. As one of the more popular campgrounds, it sees more ranger visits so it is well-kept (but you still need to bring your own toilet paper).

You'll need a boat to get here (*see* p. 226). Boats are constantly dropping off tourists for daytrips and the sight of helicopters and sea planes, no doubt with honeymooners on board, are common, but the beach is big enough to withstand the traffic. What's more the tourists arrive after sunrise and leave before sunset, so chances are it'll be just you and a handful of fellow campers with a paradise all to yourselves.

Whitehaven Beach

CATEGORIES

Young Travellers, Family, Nature, Wi-Fi-Free, No Dogs, Boomers, Nomads

GO DO IT

WHO   Queensland Parks & Wildlife Service; 13 7468; parks.des.qld.gov.au

WHERE   Whitsunday Island, Whitsunday Islands National Park, Qld.

ACCESS Access is by private or commercial boat from Airlie Beach or Shute Harbour. Scamper (*see* p. 226) is the transfer company that drops off and collects campers.

WHAT ELSE?

Snorkelling is a must at Whitehaven, with turtle sightings almost guaranteed. The beach itself provides excellent exploratory terrain, with schools of tiny fish sparkling in the shallows and crabs scuttling on the wet sand at low tide. It's well worth packing a picnic lunch and venturing to the southern side of mesmerising Hill Inlet where gem-green waters wash over the sands creating brilliant bathing shallows for lazing about in. Don a mask to spot estuarine stingrays.

The Whitehaven Beach Ocean Swim (hamiltonisland.com.au) is a 2.75-kilometre open-swimming competition held on the beach in November each year as part of the Hamilton Island Triathlon.

WILDLIFE WATCH

High-profile shark attacks in the Whitsundays have prompted the development of a broader Sharkwise education campaign. Follow warning signs and be mindful that this is a natural habitat for sharks that are considered dangerous to humans.

Similar to Chance Bay (*see* p. 227), huge monitor lizards or goannas roam this campground. They can be an intimidating sight to the uninitiated but without food to rummage in, they'll soon look elsewhere. Whatever you do, don't feed them – it's bad for them and they'll just keep annoying you (and every other camper thereafter).

STEP IT UP

The walk to Chance Bay (*see* p. 227) from Whitehaven Beach is sensational. It is well signposted and accessed close to the campground. It starts off with woodchip but becomes dirt and sand closer to Chance Bay. It's mostly shaded with a mix of eucalypt, hoop pine and rainforest, with plenty of flora and fauna to take in as you walk along. Signs say it is 3.5 kilometres, but given the mostly flat trail and the fact it took me 30 minutes, I'd put it closer to 3 kilometres. Close to the Whitehaven end, turn off the main trail to access the Solway Circuit, which continues through cycads and rock ferns to Solway Lookout. With views across Solway Passage to Pentecost and Haslewood islands and Cape Conway, it's a spectacular place to see the sun come up and down. If you walk to both Chance Bay and Solway Lookout, it's about 5 kilometres return.

Both the Solway Circuit and Whitehaven–Chance Bay tracks are part of the Whitsunday Ngaro Sea Trail, which blends seaways and walks across Whitsunday, South Molle and Hook islands. Traverse varying terrain, from rainforests and grasslands to rugged peaks, sandy-bottomed waters and remote tropical beaches. Salty Dog Kayaks (*see* p. 226) hosts tours and expeditions that follow the trail.

AND ANOTHER THING

The soft white and powdery silica sand doesn't retain heat so it's perfect to walk barefoot on.

Camping permit tags must be displayed on tents so they can be seen clearly by QPWS rangers.

ALTERNATIVES

The Whitsundays has six island-based national parks with at least 29 campsites between them. All the sites are basic, with no drinking water or showers. See Crayfish Beach (*see* p. 225) and Chance Bay (*see* p. 227).

Opposite With 7 kilometres of pristine white sand beach and warm turquoise waters, there's a reason Whitehaven Beach remains such a popular camping destination

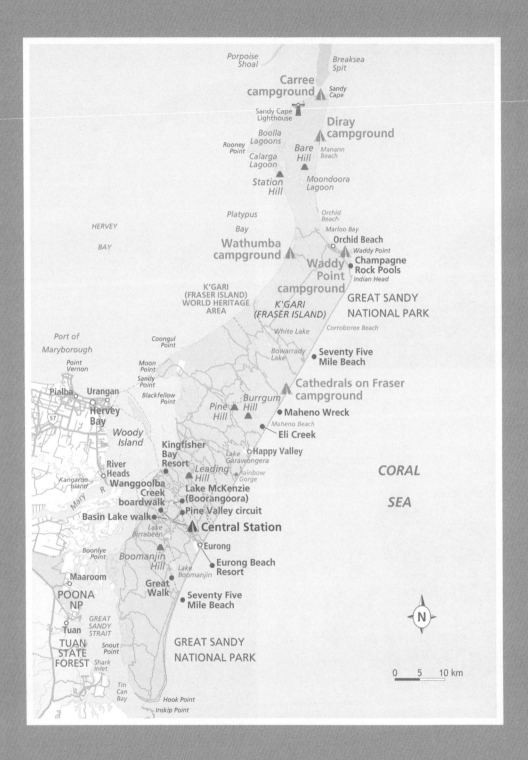

Porpoise
Shoal

Breaksea
Spit

Carree
campground

Sandy
Cape

Sandy Cape
Lighthouse

Diray
campground

Boolla
Lagoons

Manann
Beach

Rooney
Point

Bare
Hill

Calarga
Lagoon

Moondoora
Lagoon

Station
Hill

Platypus

Orchid
Beach

HERVEY

Bay

Marloo Bay

Orchid Beach

BAY

Wathumba
campground

Waddy Point

Champagne
Rock Pools

Waddy
Point
campground

Indian Head

GREAT SANDY

K'GARI
(FRASER ISLAND)
WORLD HERITAGE
AREA

K'GARI
(FRASER ISLAND)

NATIONAL PARK

White Lake

Corroboree Beach

Port of
Maryborough

Coongul
Point

Bowarrady
Lake

Seventy Five
Mile Beach

Point
Vernon

Moon
Point

Sandy
Point

Cathedrals on Fraser
campground

Blackfellow
Point

Pialba

Urangan

Burrgum
Hill

Pine
Hill

Maheno Wreck

Hervey
Bay

57

Maheno Beach

Eli Creek

Woody
Island

Lake
Garawongera

Happy Valley

River
Heads

Kingfisher
Bay
Resort

Rainbow
Gorge

CORAL

Kangaroo
Island

Wanggoolba
Creek
boardwalk

Leading
Hill

SEA

Lake McKenzie
(Boorangoora)

Basin Lake walk

Pine Valley circuit

Lake
Birrabeen

Central Station

Eurong

Boonlye
Point

Boomanjin
Hill

Eurong Beach
Resort

Lake
Boomanjin

Maaroom

Great
Walk

POONA
NP

Seventy Five
Mile Beach

Tuan

GREAT
SANDY
STRAIT

TUAN
STATE
FOREST

Snout
Point

GREAT SANDY
NATIONAL PARK

Shark
Inlet

Tin
Can
Bay

N

Hook Point

Inskip Point

0   5   10 km

Breathlessly beautiful rainforest camping on a UNESCO World Heritage island of sand.

Central Station, K'gari (Fraser Island)

Great Sandy National Park, Qld

ACTIVITIES

FACILITIES

Running north–south along the coast at Hervey Bay, K'gari (Fraser Island) is a golden slither of sand, stretching 123 kilometres in length and nearly 22 kilometres at its widest point. Its natural wonder claims to fame are almost too many to pen here. It is the largest sand island in the world, it has the purest strain of dingoes in the world, it is one of the few places on earth where rainforest grows in sand.

It is a landscape that shimmers with natural gems, with more than 100 lakes of varying biology, giant sand blows – or dune formations, reefs teeming with unique and native species, and a famed stretch of perfect beach that goes on, and on, and on ... for 75 miles and is appropriately named.

Exploring the terrain takes nous and some planning. With no roads per se, the sandy landscape is fit for 4WD vehicles only, so you'll need driving permits (*see* p. 237), 4WD know-how and general smarts – like knowing to get back to the ferry before the tide hems you in. With that sorted out, get ready for an off-map adventure.

Central Station campground is located inland from the tiny settlement of Eurong, right in the heart of a stunning emerald-green rainforest that somehow grips the sand beneath it. The large, formal camping area, bordered by a dingo fence, has 40 unpowered sites spread around two loops. A number of individual sites for tents and camper-trailers along with the sites for walk-ins have sandy white groundcover and are separated by little copses of pin-thin trunks for added privacy. Facilities include:

• Water taps
• Hot water showers ($2 coin-operated)
• Flushing toilets
• Barbecues
• Picnic tables
• A washing-up station

That the camping area was originally established as a forestry camp for the island's logging industry, is difficult to reckon with – given the surrounding beauty – but it's a story well told – among others – in the storyboards and the enormous tree stumps found near the neighbouring day-use area. Rubbish bins and a public phone can be found here too and it's where you can access Central Station's exceptional long and short walks.

CATEGORIES

Young Travellers, Family, Nature, Wi-Fi-Free, No Dogs, Boomers, Nomads

GO DO IT

WHO   Queensland Parks & Wildlife; 13 7468; parks.des.qld.gov.au

WHERE   Fraser Island, off the coast at Hervey Bay, approximately 300km north of Brisbane, Qld.

ACCESS   Fraser Island Barges (fraserislandferry.com.au) operate verges and ferries daily from River Heads, Hervey Bay, to Kingfisher Bay Resort, and Wanggoolba Creek.
Manta Ray (mantarayfraserislandbarge.com.au) operates a barge from Inskip Point, Rainbow Beach, to Hook Point on the south of Fraser Island.

WHAT ELSE?

The 950 metre circuit boardwalk around Wanggoolba Creek is the crowd-pleaser. It's an easy one-hour saunter past vine-strangled timbers, ferns, fungal-covered wood and giant staghorn plants. Look for catfish in the creek, too. This track continues to Pine Valley circuit: a 4.6 kilometre return route along an old logging track. In the other direction, Basin Lake is a 2.8 kilometre one-way walk. From here you can continue onto Lake McKenzie, and turn it into a 6.6 kilometre one-way walk or an 11.3-kilometre walk on a loop track.

The pure, chalky-soft white silica sand of Lake McKenzie makes it the perfect go-to for Central Station campers. It is a 'perched' lake, containing only pristine rainwater, rather than groundwater, in-flow or run-off, so it is jewel-like in its clarity. A scenic 2.2-kilometre drive from the campground will get you there in under ten minutes.

Fraser Island has two nature-immersed resorts: Kingfisher Bay Resort and Eurong Beach Resort that form the main infrastructure on the island. They're on opposite sides of the island and it takes about one hour of serious 4WD-ing to drive the 22 kilometres between them, with Lake Mackenzie on the way. They have rooms to suit all budgets and lagoon-shaped pools and campers can make use of the restaurants and guided tours and activities on offer.

Driving a 4WD along jaw-droppingly beautiful Seventy Five Mile Beach is the quintessential Fraser Island must-do. Marvel at sparkling waves in a rainbow of blue and green, sands criss-crossed with tyre tracks and an end-point that seemingly never arrives. The beach itself is known for dangerous currents and a large shark population but certain stops along the way are worth turning the engine off for. They include: the rusted remains of the *Maheno*, which has weathered the waves since 1935 when it was blown ashore during a cyclone; the Champagne Rock Pools naturally carved into the rock and accessed via a boardwalk; and Eli Creek where you can walk up to the bridge at the end of the boardwalk and float back down in pristine waters.

Between mainland Queensland and Fraser Island, the Great Sandy Strait is a 540,000 hectare marine park stretching about 70 kilometres. You can explore these dreamy clear waters and shallow sandy flats by hiring a boat – be it a yacht or a tinny – from Hervey Bay.

FIRST PEOPLES KNOW-HOW

The Butchulla people are the Traditional Owners of K'gari (Fraser Island) and by most accounts, the adjacent mainland, from Double Island Point in the south to the mouth of the Burrum River in the north, and west to Bauple Mountain. K'gari's shell middens, stone artefacts, traditional campsites and scarred trees are among the significant sacred and cultural sites located across the island. They ask that you leave only footprints.

WILDLIFE WATCH

Where do I start? Fraser Island's waterways are home to turtles, sharks, dugongs and humpback whales. The sand dunes are a habitat for kangaroos, wallabies, emus and dingoes. The trees and rainforests are home to approximately 300 different bird species. You'll share the campground with cheeky, bacon-loving kookaburras and shuffling monitor lizards, also known as goannas, who won't mind you if you don't mind them.

STEP IT UP

From near Central Station campground, serious hikers can access the 90 kilometre long Great Walk (or part of it) which takes 6–8 days to complete.

AND ANOTHER THING

Remember to obtain a QPWS camping permit and information pack before arriving (qld.gov.au/camping) or phone: 13 7468. You'll also need a vehicle access permit (parks.des.qld.gov.au) before driving on Fraser Island.

Central Station is accessible by high-clearance 4WD vehicles and off-road camper trailers.

ALTERNATIVES

There are numerous campgrounds on Fraser Island, each with different benefits.

Waddy Point beachfront campground, on the east coast near Waddy Point, is on the waterfront, plus it's the only place you can light fires at night.

Wathumba campground, on the western beach at Platypus Bay, is favoured by anglers and boasts pinky-orange sunsets. There's a boat ramp here.

Cathedrals on Fraser is a private campground (no permits needed), with powered and unpowered sites, cabins and a restaurant.

At Sandy Cape, on the most northern tip, Caree and Diray are remote sites with beach frontage but no facilities.

Above You can walk along the boardwalk or grab a tube and float down Eli Creek *Right* A short walk from Central Station has you exploring the lush emerald-green rainforest

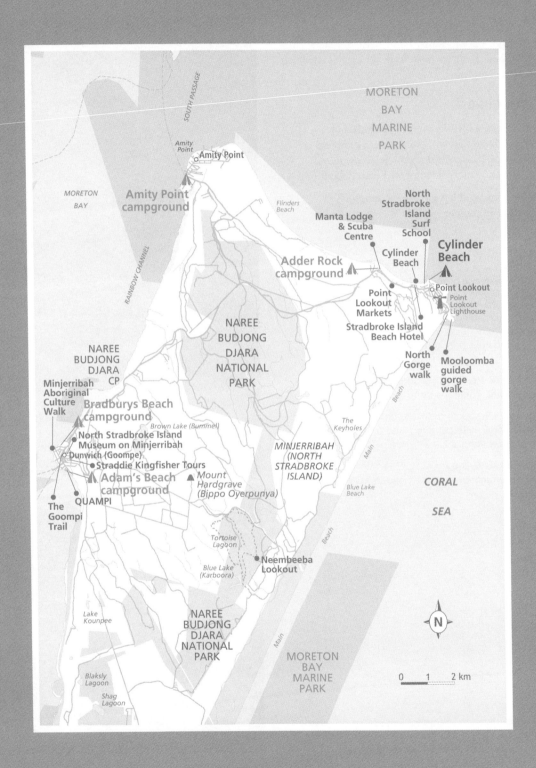

MORETON
BAY
MARINE
PARK

SOUTH PASSAGE

Amity
Point

○ Amity Point

MORETON
BAY

Amity Point
campground

Flinders
Beach

Manta Lodge
& Scuba
Centre

North
Stradbroke
Island
Surf
School

**Cylinder
Beach**

RAINBOW CHANNEL

Adder Rock
campground

Cylinder
Beach

Point Lookout
● Point
Lookout
Lighthouse

Point
Lookout
Markets

NAREE
BUDJONG
DJARA
NATIONAL
PARK

Stradbroke Island
Beach Hotel

North
Gorge
walk

Mooloomba
guided
gorge
walk

NAREE
BUDJONG
DJARA
CP

Minjerribah
Aboriginal
Culture
Walk

Bradburys Beach
campground

Brown Lake (Bummel)

North Stradbroke Island
Museum on Minjerribah
○ Dunwich (Goompe)

Straddie Kingfisher Tours

Adam's Beach
campground

▲ Mount
Hardgrave
(Bippo Oyerpunya)

MINJERRIBAH
(NORTH
STRADBROKE
ISLAND)

The
Keyholes

Main
Beach

Blue Lake
Beach

CORAL

SEA

QUAMPI

The
Goompi
Trail

Tortoise
Lagoon

Neembeeba
Lookout

Blue Lake
(Karboora)

Lake
Kounpee

NAREE
BUDJONG
DJARA
NATIONAL
PARK

Main
Beach

MORETON
BAY
MARINE
PARK

N

Blaksly
Lagoon

Shag
Lagoon

0   1   2 km

Family-friendly island camping close to a stunner beach with full amenities and watersports.

Cylinder Beach

Minjerribah (North Stradbroke Island), Qld

ACTIVITIES

FACILITIES

Some say, 'time warp', others say 'retro cool', but the general consensus is that laidback Minjerribah (North Stradbroke Island), colloquially known as 'Straddie' or 'North Straddie', is a little piece of Aussie paradise without the pretentions of similar beachy holiday hot-spots.

Minjerribah, at 275.2 square-kilometres, is the second-largest sand island in the world (the first is K'gari, Fraser Island, 400 kilometres north, *see* p. 235). It's located in beautiful Moreton Bay Marine Park, with long sand beaches and whales that literally jump out of the ocean for photo ops. Swimming, scuba-diving, snorkelling, surfing, kayaking and stand-up paddleboarding are all on the itinerary here. In addition, about half of the island is protected as Naree Budjong Djara National Park, home to curious kangaroos and birdlife, eucalypt-fringed lakes and woodlands with excellent walking tracks.

The campground, near the community of Point Lookout, at the northern end of the island, has pride of place right on Cylinder Beach. On first impressions, fine-white sand and views to Moreton Island are picture-postcard perfect. Stay a while and the beach's other attributes start to shine – it is sheltered from westerly winds and is north-facing, which makes for full-sun days and waves that are big enough to surf. There's a lifeguard stationed at this beach adding to the family friendly nature of the place.

Campers are so close to the beach that these rolling waves become the soundtrack to any stay. The campsites are packed quite close together and are reasonably small (6x6m). There are eight powered sites, towards the rear of the campground, suitable for caravans, tents, camper-trailers and motorhomes. Sixty unpowered tent sites take up the centre of the campground and 15 coveted (and pricier) unpowered tent sites have undisturbed views of the beach and more space. To nab one, book online before arriving. None of the unpowered sites have parking. Vehicles need to be parked in the carpark 20 metres away, which does cause chaos if your allocated space is taken by a day-use visitor or neighbouring camper. On the upside, it keeps the tent area marvellously free of cars, so that kids can run around on the grass under the shade trees. The campground has been upgraded in the past couple of years and facilities include:

- Toilets
- Hot showers (beware: a 3-minute time-limit before it goes cold, and you need to run out into an open area to press the button again)
- Laundry with washing machine combined with a washing-up area
- Barbecue facilities
- Picnic tables
- Playground
- Free wi-fi
- A coin-operated laundry and dryer facilities
- Powerboards for charging mobile phones (or plugging in a microwave!)

During weekends and school holidays, coffee, pizza and ice-cream vans pull up at the campground. A man in a van also pops by daily selling ice, milk and bread. Bless.

CATEGORIES

Family, Nature, No Dogs, Wi-Fi, Nomads

GO DO IT

WHO   Minjerribah Camping; (07) 3409 9668;
        minjerribahcamping.com.au

WHERE   Off the coast at Moreton Bay, 30km south-east of
        Brisbane, Qld.

ACCESS Stradbroke Ferries (stradbrokeferries.com.au)
        operates 45-minute vehicle ferries and 25-minute
        passenger ferries between Toondah Harbour in
        Cleveland and Dunwich on Minjerribah.

WHAT ELSE?

Pack a picnic and your swimsuit and head to Lake Bummiera (Brown Lake), 25 kilometres south-west of the campground. It is a natural 'perched' lake, containing only rainwater, rather than groundwater, in-flow or run-off. Its cola colouring comes from the tannins of the fringing teatree leaves. Both lakes are sacred to the Quandamooka people.

The Mooloomba guided gorge walk is a 90-minute exploration of the sacred Mooloomba (Point Lookout) Indigenous landmark accompanied by cultural stories of the Quandamooka people. Book with Quandamooka Coast (q-coast.com.au).

Check out Manta Lodge & Scuba Centre (mantalodge.com.au) for scuba-diving; Straddie Kingfisher Tours (straddiekingfishertours.com.au) for kayak tours; Straddie Stand Up Paddle (straddiestanduppaddle.com) for paddleboarding; and North Stradbroke Island Surf School (northstradbrokeislandsurfschool.com.au) for surfing.

Minjerribah has three towns. Historical Goompi (Dunwich), where the ferry comes in, has cafes, supermarkets, a couple of art galleries and North Stradbroke Island Museum on Minjerribah. Amity Point is the smallest town with striking sunsets and good seafood eateries. Point Lookout has accommodation options and a mix of casual eateries and shops, including a supermarket 500 metres east of the campground. The East Coast Road Market is held here every second Sunday (8am–12pm).

The well-loved Straddie pub (Stradbroke Island Beach Hotel) has a cracking sea-view beer garden. It's a 10-minute walk (700 metres) west of the campground.

FIRST PEOPLES KNOW-HOW

The Native Title rights of the Quandamooka people, consisting of the Noonuccal, Goenpul and Ngugi tribes, were recognised in 2011. Their people have an ongoing connection to Stradbroke and North Stradbroke Island going back more than 20,000 years. To honour and respect this, Straddie Camping was recently renamed Minjerribah Camping. It is one step on the path to becoming Minjerribah again. Minjerribah is the island's original Quandamooka identity.

The old Sibelco mining huts on Adam's Beach were demolished in 2018 to make way for a $3.35 million Minjerribah cultural centre, part of the transition of North Stradbroke Island back to Minjerribah. It is expected to be completed in 2021 and will bring together ancient artefacts, contemporary art, music, dance and performance on the land facing the waters of Moreton Bay with a boardwalk connecting Adam's Beach and Dunwich Harbour. The centre will be known as QUAMPI – the Quandamooka Art, Museum and Performance Institute, which also refers to the local pearl shell of oysters eaten by the Quandamooka for thousands of years.

Join two walks led by Quandamooka guides: Minjerribah Aboriginal Culture Walk is a 90-minute tour (and there's a similar one called the Goompi Trail, taking one hour), exploring the ancient stories of Minjerribah. It begins in Goompi (Dunwich) and includes a guided nature walk identifying bush-tucker plants and learning about medicinal bush plants, traditional ochres and an old rock fish-trap.

WILDLIFE WATCH

Turtles, dolphins, manta rays and the breaching acrobatics of seasonal (late May to early Nov) humpback whales can be seen from Point Lookout on the North Gorge walk (see Step it up). It's whale watching without the sea-sickness. Quandamooka Coast hosts whale-watching walking tours (q-coast.com.au) during school holidays.

Kangaroos, koalas, kookaburras and penguins live here too.

STEP IT UP

About 4 kilometres east of the campground, North Gorge walk is a Minjerribah must. It follows an undulating boardwalk that extends from one rocky headland to another, revealing a dramatic gorge pounded by Pacific Ocean waves, in between.

Further afield, two of the island's lakes make worthy outings. Head 30 kilometres south of the campground to walk the 5.2 kilometre return route through woodlands and wildflowers to Karboora (Blue Lake), which means 'deep silent pool'. Neembeeba Lookout is on the walk.

AND ANOTHER THING

Minjerribah has great 4WD bush and beach tracks. Essential Vehicle Access Permits are available at the campground office or online (minjerribahcamping.com.au/plan-your-stay/4wding/4wd-access).

ALTERNATIVES

There are seven other campgrounds on Minjerribah and literally hundreds of campsites. They include:

Amity Beach is big, family friendly and known for its resident pelicans, koalas, and excellent sunsets.

Bradbury's Beach is a grassy campground with shade trees on the water's edge. It's a hangout for boat-owners and anyone wanting to drop a line in.

Similarly, Adam's Beach is set up for fisherpersons. It's close to Dunwich.

Adder Rock is a big campground in the Point Lookout community. It has cabins and eco-tents.

Tasmania

Camp on beaches along the East Coast, ferry to small and large islands and sleep amid some of the oldest forests in the world

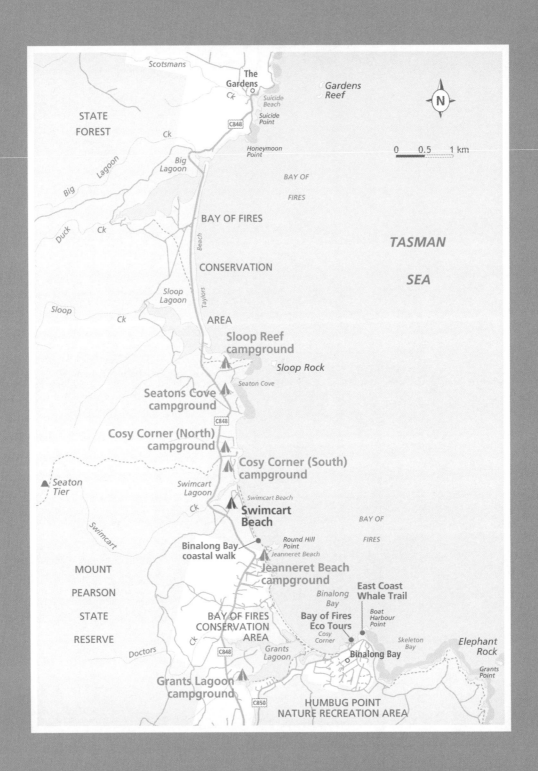

Free camping on a pristine stretch of coastline.

Swimcart Beach

Bay of Fires Conservation Area, Tas

ACTIVITIES

FACILITIES

Bay of Fires is so-called because early European explorers saw a string of fires lit by Indigenous people along its shores, but the name is equally relevant for the bright-orange lichen-covered granite boulders that decorate the water's edge. Their beauty is set off by beaches with sand as white and fine as table-salt and sparklingly topaz water – a match for any tropical beach.

Camping anywhere in this conservation area is a privilege, a chance to peek through boulders at a watery horizon, take emboldening dips in frigid waters, clamber among the rocks and caves and sink your toes into the dunes. Swimcart Beach is one of eight Bay of Fires areas in which to camp (*see* p. 246 for the others). Astoundingly, campsites here are free and you don't need to book ahead, and while you can only camp in designated campgrounds, it does feel like a throwback to the sepia-tinged days when pitching a tent on whatever beach you fancied was the done thing. With a four-week maximum stay, you could really take advantage of the barefoot luxury on offer, especially out of holiday season.

Camping in September, we were fortunate enough to be able to pick and choose our preferred campsite. We navigated to what felt like the most removed, one of two Swimcart Beach campground sites sidled up to the northern end of the beach in Binalong Bay at the end of Gardens Road. With the place all to ourselves, we pitched our tent in a prime position under the shelter of coastal sheoak trees, with a view between two orange boulders to the ocean. Grassy patches were perfect for our camp chairs and, next to us, a rough fireplace framed by rocks meant roasted marshmallows and billy tea were on the menu – this is real camping.

There are pit-toilets and, metres from the tent sites, a short path leading down to a private little beach cove framed by boulders on both sides. On day one we made this place our own – making mosaics from shells in the sand, following crabs, collecting (but not keeping, mind) mussel shells, snorkelling around the shallows and meditating. On day two we explored further around the foreshore to a water inlet, where the kids paddled, and a stretch of straight beach where they chased the waves in a game that started in squeals and ended in wet soggy shorts.

Apart from the wallabies, a few dog-walking locals, a kite-surfer, and the occasional glimpse of caravans making their way along a road in the distant hinterland, Swimcart Beach really feels remote and isolated. If you're all about getting away from it all, this place is brilliant.

Previous Loving the beach at Fortescue Bay campground, Tasman National Park (*see* p. 255)

CATEGORIES

Young Travellers, Free, Dog-Lovers, Family, Nature, Wi-Fi-Free, Boomers, Nomads

GO DO IT

WHO   Tasmanian Parks and Wildlife; (03) 6387 5510; parks.tas.gov.au

WHERE   Gardens Rd, Bay of Fires Conservation Area, 266km north-east of Hobart, Tas.

ACCESS From St Helens via the Binalong Bay Rd (C850), take the left turn-off onto sealed Gardens Rd, and follow the signs.

WHAT ELSE?

Binalong Bay coastal walk leads from Swimcart Beach campground south past Grants Lagoon to Binalong Bay.

North of Bay of Fires Conservation Area, Anson River is a good place to kayak. Kayaks can be hired at St Helens, which is 14 kilometres from the campground at the southern end of Bay of Fires.

St Helens is the largest town on Tasmania's north-east coast but in a laidback kind of way. Shops here sell all the essentials and there are cafes and eateries aplenty. It's a fishing town so expect to find restaurants serving fresh fish and crustaceans. To see the spectacular Peron Dunes, head to St Helen's Point Conservation Area, 15 kilometres north-east of the town.

Get out on the water with Bay of Fires Eco Tours (bayoffiresecotours.com.au). The Binalong Bay-based company hosts exploratory boat tours, such as its Bay of Fires Discovery Tour that takes in 28 kilometres of coastline, including Mount William National Park and the lighthouse at Eddystone Point.

WILDLIFE WATCH

The Bay of Fires is part of the East Coast Whale Trail. Signs at The Gardens and Binalong Bay provide information and stories about humpbacks, Southern-right whales, seals and pods of dolphins.

Vulnerable shorebirds, such as hooded plovers, pied oystercatchers, red-capped plovers and fairy terns live and breed along the beaches. Eggs and small chicks can be difficult to see so stay on the wet sand close to the water and keep dogs on a leash.

STEP IT UP

The luxe Bay of Fires Lodge Walk, run by Tasmanian Walking Company (taswalkingco.com.au), is a four-day 32 kilometre on-foot adventure that traverses sandy beaches, forests, rivers and coastline, with the luxury Bay of Fires Lodge as the home base. It's one of Tasmania's iconic walks along the lines of Three Capes Lodge Walk.

AND ANOTHER THING

You'll need to BYO food, petrol, water, firewood – and toilet paper. The price of a free campsite is fewer facilities and less maintenance.

ALTERNATIVES

There are seven other designated camping areas in the Bay of Fires Conservation Area. They are all found along Gardens Road, which runs parallel to the coast.

Policemans Point is in the middle section. Grants Lagoon, Jeanneret Beach (my pick), Cosy Corner South, Cosy Corner North, Sloop Reef and Seatons Cove are in the southern section.

All are suitable for tents, small caravans and campervans. All but two - Sloop Reef and Seatons Cove - have toilets.

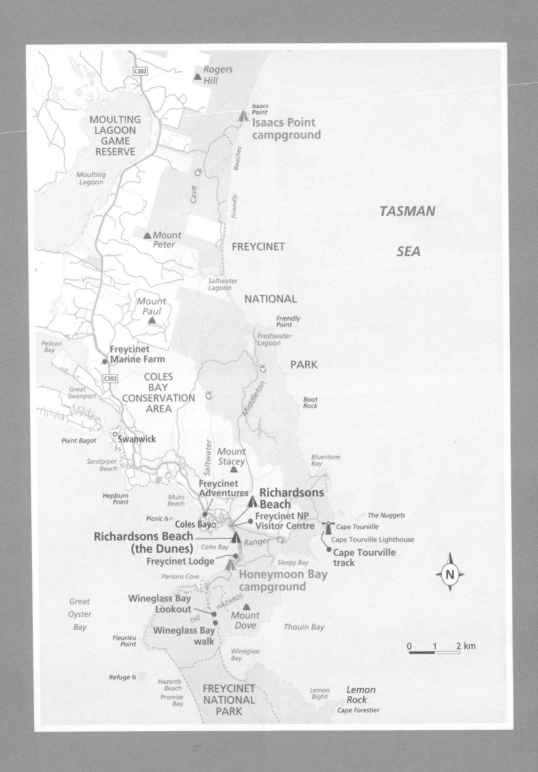

Guaranteed beachfront camping in an iconic Tasmanian landscape.

Richardsons Beach

Freycinet National Park, Tas

ACTIVITIES

FACILITIES

Mention Freycinet to any nature-lover and they'll likely get a dreamy look in their eyes about one of Tasmania's most iconic images – Wineglass Bay. This perfectly curved beach, with a lip of white sand, turquoise waves and deep blue sea is the main reason people visit the area, joining the throngs that tout it as one of the best beaches in the world.

Campers fortunate enough to score a campsite (there's a ballot, *see* p. 250) at this campground can walk the legendary trail to Wineglass Bay, but, on a shorter stay, you'd be forgiven for staying put. All tent sites here are beachfront, overlooking Coles Bay, but Richardsons Beach, especially on a still day, is beautiful in its own right. Its southern end is framed by national park, its northern end dotted with yachts, and its beaches scattered with oysters and clam shells.

The campground is located near to Freycinet National Park Visitor Centre, with staff quick to share reams of info about local walks, Indigenous culture and colonial history. It gives the campground a ship-shape, well-run feel. Sites 1–18 are closest to the visitor centre. They are powered and mostly set up for caravans, with tight-fit sites accessible to the amenities, including the coin-operated (hot) shower block and a recycle station. Sites 19–45 are the ones campers should make a beeline for. Accessed off a gravel road, they're generously spaced along the dunes backing onto Richardsons Beach, each with its own carpark, either next to the tent area or a few steps away. Each site is squared off by wood fencing, but it's the woody natives – wattles, sheoaks and gums that lend them real privacy. There's a basic toilet block with cold showers every 10 or so sites. (Note that sites 46–52 are located further south at Honeymoon Bay, perched on a granite knoll. They're only open over summer and at Easter).

You can (and we did) bend tent pegs trying to hammer into the ground at the 19–45 section but such complaints seem frivolous, given the waves are lapping a few metres from your tent down a private path. While we erected our tent, the kids were splashing in the shallows, chasing gulls and skimming oyster shells.

Towards the northern end of Richardsons Beach, a little dirt trail leads to a sheltered area with barbecues and picnic tables. There's a lagoon nearby and you can hear wallabies hopping through the bush. On the beach, abalone and mussel shells, oysters and seaweed are a nod to the rich marine life and a glimpse of what all beaches might have looked like before European settlement.

The calm waters make this a haven for kayakers and stand-up paddleboarders, whose rigs can be seen exploring the waters in the still or 'parked' in the campsites when the wind is up.

CATEGORIES

Young Travellers, Family, Nature, Wi-Fi-Free, No Dogs, Boomers, Nomads

GO DO IT

WHO   Freycinet Visitor Centre; (03) 6256 7004; parks.tas.gov.au

WHERE   Freycinet National Park, 194km north of Hobart, Tas.

ACCESS   From Tasman Hwy, turn into Coles Bay Rd for 28km, passing through the town of Coles Bay on your way, then turn right onto the sealed road to the visitor centre. A gravel road extends 500m to the campsites.

WHAT ELSE?

Freycinet Visitor Centre runs peak seasonal activities, including guided walks, presentations, films and slide shows at the outdoor cinema just behind the building.

Freycinet Adventures (freycinetadventures.com.au) rents kayaks and hosts tours. Spend an hour exploring the shallows, drifting with currents and playing spot the darting fish.

Freycinet Lodge is not far from the campground and, though a little demure in atmosphere, is good for a coffee with a view.

The hike to Wineglass Bay Lookout is a 3 kilometre return walk (90 minutes) from the visitor centre carpark. Take your bathers so you can take a dip at the other end.

There are plenty of short walks in the area, including the 500-metre Cape Tourville circuit, which begins 7 kilometres east of the campground from the carpark at the end of Cape Tourville Road. It's a family friendly, 20-minute stroll along a boardwalk where you've a chance to see whales, dolphins or seals in the beautiful bays that occupy every turn in the trail. You can also take a detour to the Cape Tourville Lighthouse, an unmanned lighthouse built in 1971. It's not a heritage lighthouse, nor is it open to the public, but it's an attractive milestone all the same.

Coles Bay, 9 kilometres north-west of the campground, is a small town with essential shops and a service station.

For more of a holiday vibe, head 44 kilometres south of the campground to the seaside town of Bicheno. It has beaches, a blowhole and East Coast Natureworld (natureworld.com.au), where you can see Tassie devils in their native environment. But its biggest drawcard is the parade of little penguins that can be seen returning to their burrows every evening. Freycinet Connections (freycinetconnections.com.au) operates bus services between the campground and Bicheno.

CULTURE VULTURE

Wineglass Bay might be shaped like a lovely bulbous pinot noir glass, but its name actually traces back to the days when the bay would turn red with the blood of slaughtered whales at the whaling station.

EAT IT

On the way out of Coles Bay, stop at casual Freycinet Marine Farm (freycinetmarinefarm.com) for oysters by the dozen and bowls of steaming mussels. Tip for young families: If you want your kids to like oysters, order Kilpatrick. If you want them all to yourself, order natural.

AND ANOTHER THING

A ballot is drawn by Freycinet Visitor Centre in early August to allocate sites for the summer season (mid-Dec to mid-Feb) and also for Easter. At other times you can chance it. We camped here in September without a booking.

ALTERNATIVES

Also in the park, Friendly Beaches camping at Isaacs Point has sites tucked away in the coastal scrub. It's free and has pit-toilets but no drinking water, so make sure you take your own. It's open year-round.

Opposite Richardsons Beach with the Hazards mountain range in the background

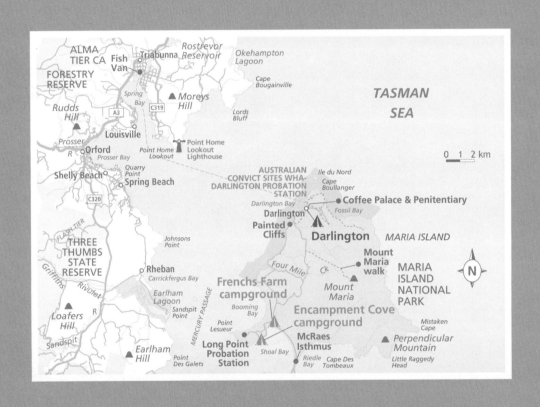

Laidback camping on an island replete with convict history and native wildlife.

Darlington
Maria Island National Park, Tas

ACTIVITIES

FACILITIES

I'm not exaggerating when I say wombats are as numerous as sheep on Maria Island. And just like sheep, they stand around eating grass without a care for us human interlopers. Similarly, Tasmania's native pademelons – small dark wallabies – hop about unencumbered, like they know they own the place. The resident Tasmanian devils are so at home, they have taken up residence under the floorboards on the verandah of the former Coffee Palace.

Maria (pronounced like Mariah Carey but no association) Island is a fascinating place, a car-free wonderland of native wildlife that coexists with the architecture, stories, infrastructure and history of a former penal colony. Daytrips and overnight stays (in the former penitentiary) are popular, but a camping trip to this laidback little island beats all.

To get here, book the ferry (*see* p. 254) and load up your gear at the ferry terminal in the small waterside town of Triabunna on the Tasmanian mainland, but note that you can't take your car (the only cars on the island are those of the park rangers). The ferry isn't cheap but it's a stylish modern boat and it's run efficiently. On the half-hour journey you can even kick off your adventure with a Tassie Moo Brew pale ale in a reclined position on the front deck. On arrival to the main island settlement of Darlington, established in 1832, luggage is delivered to the jetty from where campers can load it onto trolleys for transporting.

The campground is about 500 metres from the jetty, accessed by a road that cuts through a forest of towering pines. It's right beside a white arc of sand known as Darlington Bay, which you can walk to over a hillocky dune.

In the other direction, campers look across a grassy wombat-friendly field to the white, colonial-era buildings of the old penal settlement of Darlington Probation Station, which is recognised as a UNESCO World Heritage site – and alive with history.

The non-marked campsites are on a grassy space dotted with bushes that add a bit of privacy. Facilities include:

• Picnic tables
• A central sheltered eating area equipped with sinks and barbecues and a lovely big brick fireplace for cold-weather gatherings
• The amenities block has toilet facilities and coin-operated solar-panel hot showers (don't forget your $1 coins)
• Drinking water is available from signed taps
• Firewood is supplied

You need to bring all your own food and supplies but that just adds to the adventure.

Above The famous painted cliffs on Maria Island

CATEGORIES

Young Travellers, Family, Nature, Wi-Fi-Free, No Dogs, Boomers, Nomads

GO DO IT

WHO   Tasmania Parks & Wildlife Service;
       (03) 6257 1420; parks.tas.gov.au
WHERE Maria Island, Maria Island National Park,
       85km north-east of Hobart, Tas.
ACCESS Via a ferry from a jetty in the centre of Triabunna.

WHAT ELSE?

The Coffee Palace museum, a red-brick heritage building in what would have once classed as a town square, if a very basic one, has an exhibition with a voice-over telling stories of the island's past, including its post-penal days as a vineyard and cement manufacturing site. At one point Maria had enough residents to field a local football team.

There are no cars, except those of the park rangers, but the gravel roads are well maintained, which makes biking a great option. You can hire bikes from one of the businesses in the settlement houses or bring your own (free) on the ferry.

There are plenty of walks, my favourite being the 4.3-kilometre trail to the Painted Cliffs, a beautiful sandstone cliff-face, where water seepage has created lava lamp-like patterns on the rock. Depending on the tide, you can snorkel around in the rockpools underneath the cliffs and spy red sea anemone and bright green tendrils of sea grass.

CULTURE VULTURE

Darlington has a cluster of colonial-era buildings with interesting stories. The brick penitentiary was built by Joseph Merner who was transported for stealing two pairs of trousers. Another story tells of Seamus O'Brien, a wealthy settler who ended up in gaol having staged the Irish Uprising.

EAT IT

Load up on fish and chips at the Triabunna waterside Fish Van before having to supply your own food on the island.

FIRST PEOPLES KNOW-HOW

Wukaluwukiwayna has been home to the Puthikwilayti people for more than 40,000 years and the island contains a rich landscape containing important cultural materials and places precious to today's Indigenous community whose forebears were systematically and brutally murdered by the invading British colonisers.

WILDLIFE WATCH

Maria Island has become an ideal refuge for threatened species. The pademelons are native; but the forester kangaroos, Bennett's wallabies, Flinders Island wombats, Cape Barren geese and Tasmanian native hens are special guests thriving in their new home.

The island's 125 bird species – including 12 that are endemic to Tasmania – attract plenty of birdwatchers. Their binoculars are trained on the endangered forty-spotted pardalote, wedge-tailed eagle and swift parrot, northern migratory fly-ins such as Latham's snipe (aka Japanese Snipe), short-tailed shearwaters and little terns, which migrate huge distances from around the world.

Before or after your visit, promise to respect and protect the flora and fauna by signing the Maria Island Pledge online (eastcoasttasmania.com). It reads: 'When you trundle past me I pledge I will not chase you with my selfie stick, or get too close to your babies. I will not surround you, or try and pick you up. I will make sure I don't leave rubbish or food from my morning tea. I pledge to let you stay wild'.

STEP IT UP

Walks range from a short 1-kilometre exploration of the historic township, to longer day walks, including a 16-kilometre trek to Mt Maria. There are also walks to other campsites (*see* Alternatives).

AND ANOTHER THING

Encounter Maria Island (encountermaria.com.au) is the official ferry operator. Bookings are essential.

ALTERNATIVES

Two other campsites on the island require you to hike in. Encampment Cove, 12 kilometres south, a 4-hour walk from Darlington, is a base for exploring the convict ruins that once made up the Long Point Probation Station at nearby Point Lesueur. Frenchs Farm, 11 kilometres south, also a 4-hour walk, is a base for exploring McRaes Isthmus.

Ocean-side camping under a canopy of stringybarks in the iconic Tasmanian wilderness.

Fortescue Bay

Tasman National Park, Tas

MAP ON PAGE 256

ACTIVITIES

FACILITIES

Wild oceans, remote and windswept beaches, rugged bushland and towering trees – Tasmania's wilderness is like nowhere else on the planet.

Fortescue Bay Campground, in a sheltered bay in Tasman National Park, is a place that feels unchanged since forever. Look at a map and this tract of green land jutting into the Southern Ocean in the south-east of Tasmania, is almost as far south as it gets. Keep going and you'll reach Antarctica.

The 12 kilometre unsealed access road through the national park's coastal vegetation and tall forests is the perfect entrance – this is definitely camping for nature lovers. The circular bay has a dreamy beach with soft, white sands and a fringe of eucalypt trees looking out towards narrow headlands. It's ideal for swimming, snorkelling, sandcastles and sunbaking. The walks from the campground are equally immersed in the wild beauty (*see* p. 257).

Fortescue has two campgrounds, Banksia, and about 1 kilometre further in, Mill Creek. Facilities (at both campgrounds) include:

• Tank water
• Fireplaces
• Firewood
• Toilet block

The two campgrounds are suited to different needs. Mill Creek has 21 sites, half of them (sites 40–50) intended for larger vehicles – caravans and camper-trailers and anyone towing a boat (there's a boat ramp here too). The other half are tent sites (most with vehicle access, unlike Banksia). Generators are allowed here before 9pm.

We drove to Mill Creek first to check it out, but with a small vehicle and young family, we preferred Banksia, which is right on the beach. It has 26 unpowered sites, which are sprawled under teetering stringybark trees and demarcated with big logs. Sites 1–7 only are vehicle-access sites (note: vehicles are locked-in for duration of stay). For everyone else the carpark is separate so you'll need to walk your stuff 10–20 metres or so. On our off-peak September visit, we were able to nab site 9, which is right next to a carpark and close to the beach. Site 23 is another good pick, sidled up to a path leading to the beach.

Banksia also has a single hot shower (get tokens from the office) and a new timber day-use sheltered picnic area. It is well-appointed with a water-view deck, picnic tables and barbecues and contemporary storyboards with lovely graphics and information about the area. We regaled the kids with tales of wild and woolly shipwrecks along this coast and stories of disappearing ancient kelp forests and the near-extinct local fauna (*see* p. 257).

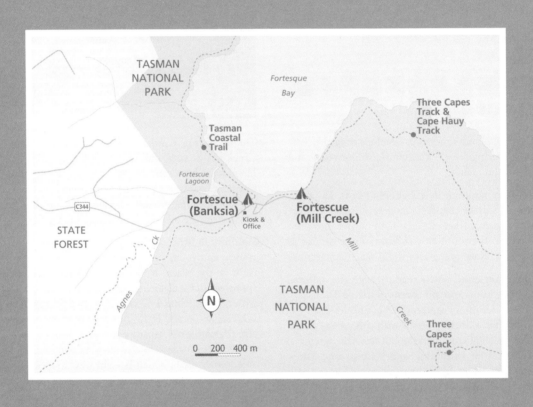

CATEGORIES

Young Travellers, Family, Nature, Wi-Fi-Free, No Dogs, Boomers, Nomads

GO DO IT

WHO   Tasmania Parks & Wildlife Service; (03) 6250 2433; parks.tas.gov.au

WHERE   Fortescue Bay in Tasman National Park, about 100km east of Hobart, Tas.

ACCESS From Eaglehawk Neck, continue along the A9 towards Port Arthur until you reach the junction with Fortescue Rd. Follow Fortescue Rd until you reach Fortescue Bay. This is a 12km drive along an unsealed road but is suitable for 2WD vehicles.

WHAT ELSE?

Fortescue Bay marks the end of the 48-kilometre Three Capes Track (threecapestrack.com.au), an iconic three-night journey through heathlands and forests and coastal scenery, staying in eco-cabins along the way. There's a bus service for walkers from the campground at 2pm and 4pm, and the kiosk opens with drinks and snacks, so you are bound to see some non-campers hanging around.

From the campground, the signed 4 hour return walk to Cape Hauy is a must to see the off-shore sea stacks known as The Lanterns. It traverses part of the last section of the Three Capes Track and has been named one of Tasmania's 60 Great Short Walks.

Heading north, the signed 5-kilometre walk along Tasman Coastal Trail to Canoe Bay reveals the rusted wreck of the *William Pitt*, a steel-hulled barge. It's great for swimming and snorkelling around. The trail continues the same distance again along a mainly coastal route to Bivouac Bay (10km return from campground).

CULTURE VULTURE

Port Arthur Historic Site (portarthur.org.au), 26 kilometres east of the campground, gives an insight into Tasmania's past as a penal colony. The once feared convict settlement is now a UNESCO World Heritage site and a popular tourist destination. Entry tickets give you two full days to explore historic buildings, ruins, walking trails and heritage gardens, and include a 40-minute introductory walking tour and a 25-minute harbour cruise. There's a Port Arthur Ghost Tour too.

WILDLIFE WATCH

According to a storyboard in the campground's sheltered picnic area, the old-growth blue gums (Tasmania's floral emblem) around Fortescue Bay's coastline are the feeding ground for the critically endangered swift parrot that arrives from mainland Australia every summer when the blue gums are flowering to breed in the tree hollows. With fewer than 1000 pairs remaining, they are one of Australia's most threatened species. Several other threatened bird species can be found here, including the wedge-tailed eagle and white-bellied sea eagle.

Another story tells of the loss of the giant underwater kelp forests that once flourished along this coast. They were a critical habitat for marine life to spawn, feed and find shelter, but since 2016 have disappeared.

AND ANOTHER THING

Bookings are not required during off-peak season. If the office is unmanned (like it was on our visit), there's a self-registration booth where you can pay fees in envelopes provided.

You'll need to be self-sufficient. Nubeena, a 45-minute drive away, is the nearest grocery store.

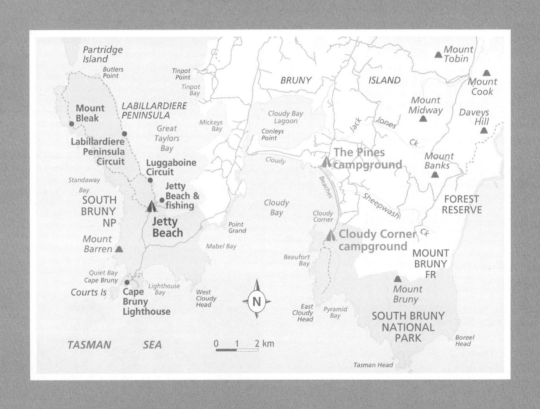

Partridge
Island

Butlers
Point

Tinpot
Point

Tinpot
Bay

BRUNY   ISLAND

▲ Mount
Tobin

▲ Mount
Cook

**Mount
Bleak**

*LABILLARDIERE
PENINSULA*

Cloudy Bay
Lagoon

Mount
Midway ▲

Daveys
Hill

**Labillardiere
Peninsula
Circuit**

*Great
Taylors
Bay*

*Mickeys
Bay*

Conleys
Point

Mount
Banks ▲

*Standaway
Bay*

**Luggaboine
Circuit**

Cloudy

**The Pines
campground** ▲

**SOUTH
BRUNY
NP**

**Jetty
Beach &
fishing**

Cloudy
Bay

Beaches

Sheepwash

**FOREST
RESERVE**

▲
**Jetty
Beach**

Point
Grand

Cloudy
Corner

Ck

**Cloudy Corner
campground** ▲

*Mount
Barren* ▲

Mabel Bay

**MOUNT
BRUNY
FR**

Quiet Bay
Cape Bruny

*Lighthouse
Bay*

*Beaufort
Bay*

▲ *Mount
Bruny*

Courts Is

**Cape
Bruny
Lighthouse**

*West
Cloudy
Head*

**SOUTH BRUNY
NATIONAL
PARK**

*Boreel
Head*

*East
Cloudy
Head*

*Pyramid
Bay*

TASMAN   SEA

0   1   2 km

Tasman Head

N

A blissful bayside campground with nature walks and solitude, on a spectacular foodie island.

Jetty Beach

South Bruny National Park, Bruny Island, Tas

ACTIVITIES

FACILITIES

Bruny Island is a famed contributor to Tasmania's incredible food scene. Within a 40-minute drive from Hobart, then a 20-minute ferry ride, you can be munching on the island's cornucopia of fresh natural produce and artisan goods without a care in the world. And once you've supped on fresh-shucked oysters, sipped on a Bruny Island craft beer and indulged your sweet tooth at the Chocolate Co. the rest of the island awaits.

Bruny Island is about 100 kilometres in length and covers 365 square kilometres; it's a mix of farms and grazing land and wild natural landscapes. It is made up of two distinct land masses – North Bruny and South Bruny, which are connected by a very narrow isthmus known as The Neck. North Bruny is home to the ferry terminal, rolling agricultural country and the food scene (*see* p. 261). The Neck is where short-tailed shearwaters and little penguins can be seen in their natural habitat. South Bruny is home to Bruny's main townships, Alonnah, Lunawanna and Adventure Bay, with beautiful beaches and sheltered bays that inspire swimming, kayaking and other water-based activities. Further south still, South Bruny National Park takes up most of the southern tip of the island. It has a timeless end-of-the-Earth quality, a palpable sensation – enhanced by the wild environment – that you're as far south as it's possible to go before hitting Antarctic waters. This is a land of shimmering bays, empty windswept beaches, rugged cliff-faces, lofty lookouts and coastal walks.

North-facing Jetty Beach is right in the heart of South Bruny National Park, on the sheltered shores of Great Taylors Bay. Its titular campground feels happily off-the-beaten track. This is definitely the place to come if you want to get away from it all. Its 20 unpowered and unmarked campsites (which you can't book, so it's first-come, first-served) are suited to tents, caravans and camper-trailers. The sites are unmarked so pick a spot under the neatly spaced towering gum trees. The ground is gravelly and hard, without much grass to speak of, but the campground makes up for this with direct access to Jetty Beach, a lovely curve of sand and cold, clear water that changes from pale blue to olive green, depending on the cloud cover. Facilities include:

- Two pit-toilets in little huts
- Non-treated tank water (which can run dry in summer so BYO drinking water)
- A sheltered picnic table
- Fire-rings

Families will love this place: kids will delight in frolicking and snorkelling in the gradually receding shallows, and running around on the expanse of sand shaded by bending eucalypt trees. Grown-ups will appreciate being able to launch kayaks and fishing boats directly from the beach. The stelliferous night sky is something to behold this far south.

CATEGORIES

Family, Nature, Wi-Fi-Free, No Dogs, Boomers, Nomads

GO DO IT

WHO   Tasmania Parks and Wildlife Service (Huonville Field Centre); (03) 6121 7026; parks.tas.gov.au

WHERE   Old Jetty Rd, South Bruny National Park, Bruny Island, on the south-east coast of Tas.

ACCESS Kettering is 33km south of Hobart, or a 40-minute drive, via Kingston on the A6 and then B68 roads. From Kettering take a vehicle and passenger ferry (sealinkbrunyisland.com.au) to Roberts Point on the island. Ferries depart regularly throughout the day and the crossing takes about 20 minutes. Bookings are not essential but it is a good idea to pre-purchase an open-dated ticket online to save time on arrival.
        Jetty Beach campground is just over an hour south of the ferry terminal. Follow the Bruny Island Main Rd south through Alonnah, and when you reach the T-junction in Lunawanna take a right onto the C629. After 17km, take another right into Jetty Rd.

WHAT ELSE?

Direct from Jetty Beach campground, Luggaboine Circuit is a 5 kilometre long easy-to-moderate walk (allow 90 minutes) traversing coastal heath, eucalypt forest and, for about half of it, stretches of mesmeric coastline.

Fishing is big here. Throw a line in to catch fish and chip shop favourites, including whiting, bream, trevally and flathead. If you don't have luck at the campground beach, head further around the shorelines to deeper sections.

The remains of the jetty at the western end of Jetty Beach are a nod to colonial-era days when supplies to the Cape Bruny Lighthouse were brought in to this sheltered bay by ship.

CULTURE VULTURE

About 4 kilometres south of the campground, atop one of the southern headlands, is heritage-listed Cape Bruny Lighthouse. It was first lit in 1838 and, as the only Southern Tasmania lighthouse open for tours, offers an insight into the dramatic history of this rugged coastline, which was ground zero to a litany of tragic shipwrecks and lost lives before the lighthouse was built. Be sure to climb the cast-iron spiral staircase to access the wind-pummelled balcony which overlooks heath-covered Courts Island and a coastline of wave-crashed rocks and cliffs.

Cape Bruny Lighthouse Tours (capebrunylighthouse.com) has daily lighthouse tours, including a special two-hour Lighthouse Sunset Tour. Book ahead.

EAT IT

Stock your camp hamper at the following Bruny culinary pit-stops:

• Plump Pacific Oysters from Get Shucked Oysters, in Great Bay, are harvested and shucked daily. All you need is lemon.
• Also in Great Bay is Bruny Island Cheese Co. and its partner Bruny Island Beer Co. that pair washed-rind cow's milk cheeses with golden Tassie ales.
• House of Whiskey in North Bruny stocks single-malt whiskeys from across Tasmania, including its own Trapper's Hut tipple.
• On South Bruny in Adventure Bay, Bruny Island Chocolate sells favourites such as honeycomb and fudge from a little roadside shop.
• Visitors to Bruny Island Berry Farm, also in Adventure Bay, can fresh-pick their own strawberries and buy other jams and sweet treats.

FIRST PEOPLES KNOW-HOW

Bruny Island is traditionally known as Lunawanna-alonnah. Its people are the Nuenonne band of the south-east tribe of Tasmanian Aboriginal people. Mangana was chief of the Nuenonne during the 1770s when explorers including Tobias Furneax and James Cook visited Bruny. One of the most well-known of the Nuenonne is Mangana's daughter, Truganini, a woman who is erroneously described as 'the last Tasmanian Aborigine' in accounts of the Black War, which saw the near-annihilation of Tasmania's First People. Truganini's remarkable story is told by Palawa Elder Rodney Dillon in Thomas Mayor's *Finding the Heart of the Nation* (published by Hardie Grant Travel 2019).

After surviving the devastation of her people in the 1820s – including the murder of her mother, Truganini was taken from Bruny in 1830 to guide self-styled missionary George Augustus Robinson on a journey to find other surviving First People, who would be sent into exile on Flinders Island. She managed to avoid incarceration herself by joining Robinson on a trip to Victoria, where she was implicated and later acquitted of the murder of two white men and sent back to Tasmania. She lived for another thirty-five years first in Oyster Cove and, for the last three years of her life, in Hobart. Her skeleton was put on display in the Tasmanian Museum and Art Gallery from 1879 until 1951. In fact, Truganini's dying wish for her ashes to be scattered in Bruny's D'Entrecasteaux Channel only came to pass in 1976,

just short of a century after she died. It formalised her place in history as an icon of a monumental tragedy.

WILDLIFE WATCH

South Bruny National Park, stretching across the southern tip of Bruny Island is your go-to for really tapping into this natural world. Its landscapes are habitats for endangered birds (including swift parrots and hooded plovers) and wildlife and conservation hot spots for rare and wondrous plants (such as Christmas bells and rare orchids). What's more, the fringing Southern Ocean and its rocky shoreline are the haunt of leopard seals, penguins and whales.

STEP IT UP

Also accessible from Jetty Beach campground is the demanding 18 kilometre Labillardiere Peninsula Circuit walk. It takes in the Bruny Island coastline, including the D'entrecasteaux Channel. You'll climb up Mt Bleak, traverse beaches and pass through heathland and eucalypt forests, spotting wildflowers, birdlife and (in summer) the occasional snake along the way. It's best to follow the route clockwise for better views. Allow six hours for the circuit.

AND ANOTHER THING

Be sure that your (pre-purchased online) national park and camping permits (parks.tas.gov.au) are properly displayed on your vehicle or you'll find a fine affixed to your windscreen.

ALTERNATIVES

At Cloudy Bay, 32 kilometres south, there's a (very) basic campground called The Pines. Far more exciting is nearby Cloudy Corner, a camping spot accessible via a 3-kilometre drive along the beach at low tide (4WD vehicles only).

Outside the national park, 55 kilometres north-east of Jetty Beach, The Neck Reserve campground is in a sheltered area behind sand dunes.

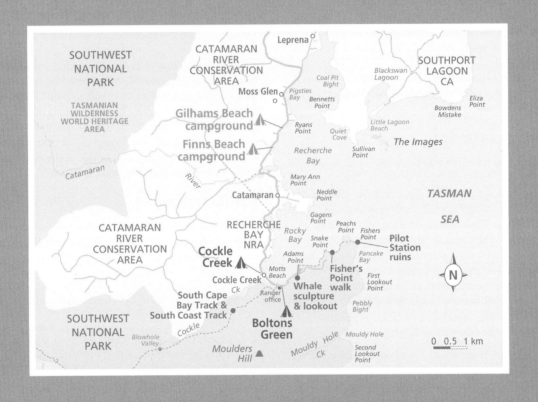

SOUTHWEST
NATIONAL
PARK

TASMANIAN
WILDERNESS
WORLD HERITAGE
AREA

Catamaran

River

CATAMARAN
RIVER
CONSERVATION
AREA

Leprena

Coal Pit
Bight

Blackswan
Lagoon

SOUTHPORT
LAGOON
CA

Moss Glen

Pigsties
Bay

Bennetts
Point

Little Lagoon
Beach

Eliza
Point

Bowdens
Mistake

Gilhams Beach
campground

Ryans
Point

Quiet
Cove

The Images

Finns Beach
campground

Recherche
Bay

Sullivan
Point

Catamaran

Mary Ann
Point

Neddle
Point

TASMAN

SEA

Gagens
Point

Peachs
Point

Fishers
Point

RECHERCHE
BAY
NRA

Rocky
Bay

Snake
Point

Pancake
Bay

Pilot
Station
ruins

Cockle
Creek

Adams
Point

Fisher's
Point
walk

N

Cockle Creek
Ck

Motts
Beach

First
Lookout
Point

South Cape
Bay Track &
South Coast Track

Ranger
office

Whale
sculpture
& lookout

Pebbly
Bight

CATAMARAN
RIVER
CONSERVATION
AREA

SOUTHWEST
NATIONAL
PARK

Boltons
Green

Mouldy Hole

Mouldy Hole

0 0.5 1 km

Blowhole
Valley

Cockle

Moulders
Hill

Mouldy Hole
Ck

Second
Lookout
Point

Beachfront camping in a protected bay with walks, whales and water activities when the weather is right.

Cockle Creek

Southwest National Park, Tas

ACTIVITIES

FACILITIES

If you have ever had an inkling to road trip as far south as is possible in Australia, nay the world, then you'll likely end up here at Cockle Creek, in Southwest National Park on Tasmania's south-east coast. It's not quite the end of the Earth, but it is the most southerly point you can get to in a car. There's even a sign stating 'the End of the Road' just so you don't keep driving into Recherche Bay and on towards Antarctica.

Navigational novelties aside, this is an exceptionally beautiful part of the world – the kind of place that feels like nature's own wellness escape for its pure bracing air, pristine native forest aromas, impeccable nature-scapes, crystal clear waters and serene isolation. That might sound like a travel brochure but it's all true. Southwest National Park is also part of the Tasmanian World Heritage Wilderness Area. Strap on hiking boots and head inland to some of the world's wildest untouched terrain (*see* p. 264), or pull on a beanie, shove your hands in your coat pockets and explore a coast known for its empty white sand beaches, shore-hugging forests, frigid waters and blackened wave-washed boulders.

The settlement here is tiny with just a few houses, a couple of national park's buildings and some characteristic beach huts or 'shacks' as they're referred to in Tasmania. There are no shops, service (petrol) stations or the like, so campers will need to be self-sufficient.

The camping area widely referred to as Cockle Creek, is technically two campgrounds that extend along the beachfront road. They are divided or connected (whichever way you want to look at it) by the bridge over the Cockle Creek inlet and are within about 500 metres of each other. Remarkably, they're both free. Recherche Bay Nature Recreation Area has campsites spaced along the road on the north side as you enter the area, with pit-toilets and fire-pits, but you'll need to BYO all your water. Dogs are allowed in this section.

Southwest National Park campsites (signed as, but not advertised as, Boltons Green) are beyond the bridge on the south side. They have pit-toilets, access to sheltered day-use picnic tables and tank water (a perk of paying the national park fees, which you'll need to do on this side). No dogs or fires are allowed. Some of these sites are larger and suited to vans. None of the sites at Cockle Creek have showers.

Both camping areas are similarly alluring, with informal grassy sites backed by bush and native trees and direct access across the dirt road to Motts Beach and the dreamily turquoise waters of Rocky Bay, which lies in the sheltered natural harbour of Recherche Bay. A walk along the beach (or the road) accesses the sandy shallows and clear twinkling water near the Cockle Creek inlet – the best spot for swimming. The water is warmer and temptingly tranquil and swimming under the bridge around the old pylons is lots of fun. On colder days, people are more likely to be throwing a fishing line off the bridge.

CATEGORIES

Young Travellers, Free, Dog-Lovers, Family, Nature, Wi-Fi-Free, Boomers, Nomads

GO DO IT

WHO   Recherche Bay Nature Recreation Area Ranger/
           Parks & Wildlife Tasmania Huonville
           Field Centre; (03) 6121 7031/(03) 6121 7026;
           parks.tas.gov.au
WHERE   Cockle Creek Rd, Cockle Creek, about
           120km south of Hobart, Tas.
ACCESS   From Hobart take the A6 via Huonville 84km,
           turn right onto C635 Hastings Cave Rd, continue
           straight onto Lune River Rd (C636) for 22km
           to Cockle Creek. The last 20km section is an
           unsealed and rough road but accessible in a 2WD.
           Caravans will need to take extra care, especially
           after wet weather.

WHAT ELSE?

From the carpark at the end of the camping area on Cockle Creek Rd, there's a short 5-minute walk to a promontory with a bronze sculpture of a young Southern-right whale, storyboard info about the area and excellent mountain views of La Perouse, The Coxcomb and The Hippo.

This is also the start of the easy 4 kilometre return Fisher's Point walk (allow two hours total) to see the ruins of Pilot Station, an old whaling station opened in 1836, that supported a local population of approximately 2000 people. The walk follows the coast so it's only accessible on a low- to mid-tide.

FIRST PEOPLES KNOW-HOW

Recherche Bay is the traditional land of Lyluequonny people. Local midden sites (which can be seen on the Fisher's Point Walk, *see* above) provide links to the people that lived on this land for more than 35,000 years.

WILDLIFE WATCH

Plenty of wallabies hang out around the campsites, and you might spot a brushtail possum by torchlight. Lyrebirds can be spotted on the South Cape Bay track. Southern-right whales were once hunted here but their numbers are now increasing. Spot them from June to October. Humpbacks can be seen from May to July and September to November.

STEP IT UP

On the right, just after the bridge is the start of the South Cape Bay track, a moderate 15.4 kilometre return walk (allow four hours return) inland heading south-west through bush and woodland to the cliffs of South Cape Bay. Experience the contrast between this weather-whipped place and the serenity of Cockle Creek. If the weather permits, take the steps down to the rocky beach for the trudge to Lion Rock.

This is also the eastern end (or beginning) of the popular South Coast Track, an 85 kilometre, week-long walk to Port Davey via Tasmania's southern coastline. It's one of Tassie's most challenging walks for (very) experienced hikers only. Mountains, muddy boots, buttongrass plains and rocky coastal headlands are some of the drawcards. Walkers can register at the Southwest National Park ranger's office at Cockle Creek, which is manned intermittently.

AND ANOTHER THING

There are no bookings for either the Recherche Bay Nature Recreation Area or Southwest National Park (Boltons Green) campgrounds of Cockle Creek.

BYO water, especially drinking water.

Note that different regulations apply depending on which side of the bridge you camp on.

You'll pass through Huonville, 39 kilometres south of Hobart and 85 kilometres north of Cockle Creek. It provides the last opportunity for supermarket supplies before Cockle Creek.

ALTERNATIVES

Gillhams and Finns Beach campgrounds, 5 kilometres north of the campground, off Cockle Creek Rd, are free waterfront campgrounds with basic facilities. BYO water.

Opposite View of Cockle Creek and Southwest National Park from Fishers Point

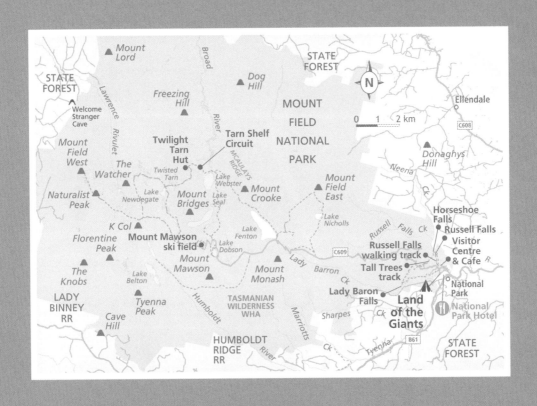

Riverside camping in a World Heritage area among creeks, rivers, waterfalls, platypus, echidna and the world's tallest trees.

Land of the Giants
Mount Field National Park, Tas

ACTIVITIES

FACILITIES

Who can resist a campground with such a fantastical name? Also known as Mount Field Campground, Land of the Giants is so-called because it is home to a magnificent forest of tall swamp gums, also called (and perhaps better known as) mountain ash or Eucalyptus regnans. These tall beauties native to Tasmania and Victoria are the tallest flowering plants in the world, and mature forests are said to lock in carbon like no other tree species. Their impossibly straight trunks, smooth and stark white especially at their lofty tip, are a sight to behold amid a rainforest understory of trickling creeks, huge ferns and fallen branches carpeted in soft, green lichen.

They're not the only attraction at Mount Field National Park, though. Just one hour's drive from Hobart, one of the state's oldest national parks – part of the Tasmanian Wilderness World Heritage Area – is also known for its trifecta of perfect waterfalls: Russell, Horseshoe and Lady Baron, which sit in the lower area of the park close to the visitor centre. They're a habitat for platypus and echidna. In the higher reaches, accessed via winding and unsealed Lake Dobson Road, the park's alpine region, with glacial lakes and a wet plateau of diverse plant life, is a destination for keen hikers, nature lovers and skiers.

The campground is in the forested main entry of the national park, a tranquil spot with plenty of shade and forest greenery. It's right on the Tyenna River, where you can swim on hot days, and it's handy to the Russell Falls walk. The Visitor Information Centre, cafe and day-use amenities are here too.

Fourteen powered campsites are grouped together near the entry to the campground. The 26 unpowered sites have a bit more space and sit closer to the river on a flat space covered with leaf litter and grass. Sometimes parts of the camping area might be cordoned off to allow for regeneration, which can make the remaining campsites a bit tight. It's first-come, first-served so largely luck of the draw, rather than booking ahead. The facilities are dated, but well-maintained and include:

- A central toilet and shower block
- Laundry with washing machines and clothes-dryers (coin-operated)
- A cooking area with electric barbecues, a washing-up sink and hot water (in a quaint timber shelter)

Timber tables and bench seats are plentiful throughout the campground (almost one per campsite) adding to the lovely picnic ground vibe.

Campers can get a jump on daytrippers with an early stroll to Russell Falls (see p. 268), its picturesque water cascading over a series of tiers. By night, be sure to creep along the Russell Falls track to see glow worms lighting up the inky night. You'll need to turn torches off for the full magical experience, but there are handrails to help with navigation.

CATEGORIES

Family, Nature, Wi-Fi-Free, No Dogs, Boomers, Nomads

GO DO IT

WHO   Tasmania Parks and Wildlife Service (Mount Field
           Visitor Centre); (03) 6288 1149; parks.tas.gov.au

WHERE   66 Lake Dobson Rd National Park, about 75km
           west of Hobart, Tas.

ACCESS   From Hobart via New Norfolk and Westerway take
           National Hwy 1 for 18km, merge left onto A10 for
           16km, continue straight on B61 for 19km, turn
           right onto B61 for 19km. At Westerway continue
           on the short, winding drive to the small township
           of National Park and the entrance to Mount Field
           National Park.

WHAT ELSE?

The visitor centre is open daily and has exceptionally friendly
staff who are a wealth of info on the local activities. Buy your
park and camping permits here, get walking maps and info
and check out the log-book where visitors have noted wildlife
sightings. Waterfalls Cafe has souvenirs, essentials, and take-
away food that can be enjoyed at day-use picnic tables along
the Tyenna River.

Russell Falls is particularly good after rain. From the
campground, it's an easy 1.5 kilometre return walk through
sweet-smelling musk and myrtle trees on a flat paved path.
You can return via the same path or take the loop walk back

on the track on the other side of the creek. Allow 25 minutes
return for both routes.

There's an option to continue from Russell Falls 200 metres
for some more waterspray at Horseshoe Falls (allow
5 minutes one-way), or follow signs 900 metres one-way
to the walk that connects with the Tall Trees track (allow
10 minutes one-way). This 1-kilometre circuit walk otherwise
starts along Lake Dobson Road on the right-hand side,
1.3 kilometres from the campground. Get a feel for these
forest giants or swamp gums. The biggest of them, topping
100 metres, were happily growing here before European
settlement. (Allow 30 minutes for the circuit.)

EAT IT

The lovely old National Park Hotel, built in 1920 is about
1 kilometre from the campground on Gordon River Road.
It serves excellent traditional pub fare: burgers, chicken
schnitzel, pie and mash, plus good old-fashioned Tasmanian
draught beer. A seat by the fire is the perfect end to a day's
exploring in the national park.

FIRST PEOPLES KNOW-HOW

The national park is in the traditional territory of the Big
River people, with the Pangerninghe clan located close by.
There are a number of Indigenous heritage sites within the
park, including several caves (not accessible to the public)
near the Florentine River that support evidence of First
People's occupation for more than 35,000 years.

WILDLIFE WATCH

Platypus can be spotted in among the rocky river banks of Tyenna River, Russell Creek and Lake Dobson and echidnas on the large grassy oval adjacent to the campground. Check the log-book at the visitor centre for recent sightings.

Wallabies and Tasmania's endemic pademelons can also be seen around the campground and rate highly on the cute scale but you'll need to hide food from them.

Other native species include the eastern quoll and the eastern barred bandicoot and 11 of Tasmania's 12 endemic birds.

The alpine tarns are home to mountain shrimps called Anaspides. They are 'living fossils' – tiny crustaceans that are almost identical to 250 million-year-old fossils.

STEP IT UP

Unsealed Lake Dobson Road extends 16 kilometres (allow 30 minutes one-way) from the visitor centre to Lake Dobson, first through rainforest and then into snowgum country. From the carpark you can access longer alpine walks, including Tarn Shelf Circuit – a moderate 12-kilometre hike for experienced bushwalkers. Highlights include Lake Newdegate, Twisted Tarn and the Twilight Tarn Hut, filled with skiing memorabilia (allow six hours).

Mt Mawson ski field is also here so if you're here in winter, you can downhill ski and snowboard. Check ahead with Southern Tasmanian Ski Association (mtmawson.info; (03) 6288 1166) to see if it's operating. In heavy snow, vehicles may require snow chains or the road might be closed. Check with the park ((03) 6288 1149). The road is not suitable for caravans.

AND ANOTHER THING

If you arrive late, there is a self-registration booth located at the entrance to the campground.

ALTERNATIVES

There are no other campgrounds in Mount Field National Park.

Five off-grid, rustic timber government huts, 15 kilometres from the visitor centre along Dobson Road, make for a good budget accommodation option. They sit in a pristine snowgum setting at an elevation of approximately 1000 metres, and have bushwalks from the doorstep. Each hut has bunks for six people, a wood heater, tables and chairs, cold water and a sink, but no electricity or gas services. There's a communal toilet block, but no showers. Book ahead: parks.tas.gov.au; (03) 6491 1179.

Opposite The giant base of a swamp gum

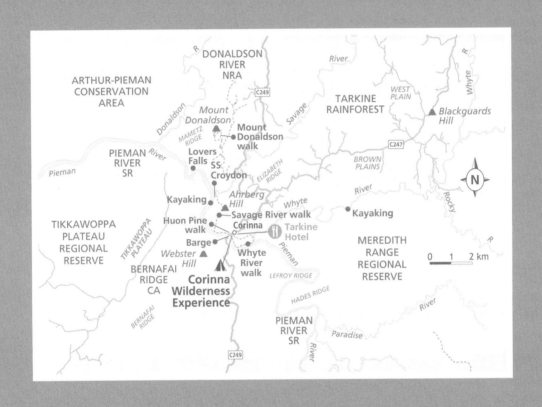

*Off-the-grid rainforest camping in historic Corinna,
a retreat and mining town surrounded by ancient
Tarkine wilderness.*

Corinna Wilderness Experience

Pieman River State Reserve, Tas

ACTIVITIES

FACILITIES

On the west coast of Tasmania, 20 kilometres as the crow flies from the wild and frothing Southern Ocean, the 19th-century mining town of Corinna still ticks along in the form of a wilderness retreat, with the rustic old Tarkine Hotel and characteristic mining cottages tricked up as accommodation options. The quaint little settlement takes up just 1.2 hectares, but it's what's on the doorstep that matters. Surrounding this slice of relatively recent history, is something much older – the 65 million-year-old Tarkine Rainforest, a 450,000-hectare wilderness of Middle Earth imaginings. It's where the girths of myrtle beech, leatherwood and Huon Pines are too wide to get your arms around, where you can sniff the pristine air for hints of native laurel and celery-top pine, and where a jump off the jetty into the serene Pieman River is as life-giving an exercise as any on the planet.

Adding to the ancient other-worldly vibe, Corinna is only accessible from the south via a boat barge over the Pieman River (highly recommended) or from the north on an unsealed 'silica road' (*see* p. 272) that is fine by 2WD but bone-rattling all the same. That Corinna is off the grid – with no phone coverage and no internet access – makes the immersive qualities of this wild and natural paradise all the more complete.

The campground is small with just ten campsites with seven suited to tents and swags and three suitable for campervans and caravans. Each site has a timber plank platform with access via a mossy boardwalk. They're close to the hotel amid a rainforest under a full canopy of trees and surrounded by soft tree ferns and eucalypts. Expect the full, wonderful cacophony of birdcalls. If you're on one of two sites sitting on the bank of the Pieman, the soft burble and gurgle of flowing water will send you to sleep.

You'll need to be self-sufficient – immediate facilities are limited to a small area in the campground where you can use wood to cook with. There is a public toilet block within the hotel area and coin-operated rainwater showers (bring $2 coins). A gas barbecue and eating area near the guest cottages can also be used.

Campers also have full access to all the Corinna nature-based activities, including walks and hikes straight from the campground, kayaking expeditions and river cruises on the historic *Arcadia II*, which was built in 1939 and has since been restored to ply the waters from Corinna to Pieman Heads. This is also a hot spot for birdwatchers and fishing and photography enthusiasts. Of course, a seat in the hotel bar (*see* p. 272), with the fire roaring and a glass of Tasmanian red at the ready, can also take up much of your time.

CATEGORIES

Family, Nature, Wi-Fi-Free, No Dogs, Boomers, Nomads

GO DO IT

WHO   Corinna Wilderness Experience; (03) 6446 1170; corinna.com.au

WHERE   1 Corinna Rd, Corinna, 91km north of Strahan, 150km south of Stanley, 125km south-west of Burnie and 350km north-west of Hobart, Tas.

ACCESS   Access from the south (Strahan and Hobart) is by crossing the Pieman River on the legendary 'Fatman' barge. The barge, the only cable-driven vehicular barge in Tasmania, allows vehicles to travel from north or south across the Pieman River, which is 130m wide and 20m deep. Taking this route really hams up the feeling that you're arriving in a remote wilderness. The barge operates between 9am and 7pm in the summer and 9am and 5pm outside daylight saving hours. The crossing takes about ten minutes.
Access from the north is via Smithton (Stanley) or Arthur River on the Western Explorer Hwy or Waratah (Burnie) on the B23. On these routes from the north, you will, for a few kilometres, take a section of the famous 'silica road', an all-weather surface using the tailings from the nearby silica mine. It will slow you down, but it's a sign that the wilderness is not far away.

WHAT ELSE?

Corinna is unique in Tasmania, in that it is the only remote mining town that has survived since its goldrush peak in the mid 1870s to the early 1880s. Back then, the population of eager prospectors and associated trade topped 2500 people and the river was busy with sailing ships and steamers.

The Tarkine Hotel has a restaurant (see Eat it) and the reception has basic snacks and supplies, but note that no petrol is available.

Hire a kayak from reception for a self-guided paddle along the Pieman and Whyte rivers and other tributaries.

Guests can fish from the riverbanks or from boats and kayaks in the Pieman River and its tributaries. Large sea-running ocean trout are the catch of the day.

There are walks aplenty from Corinna. The 3 kilometre one-way Savage River walk treks past Huon Pine, moss-covered logs, colourful fungi and huge ferns to the sunken SS Croydon at the mouth of the Savage River. Allow 3 hours return or organise to kayak back to Corinna.

The Whyte River walk is similarly beautiful with boardwalks through a green kaleidoscope of temperate rainforest. Allow an hour.

The shorter Huon Pine walk is an easy stroll with intriguing storyboards detailing the local flora and fauna. Allow 15 minutes.

A cruise on the Pieman River is an essential Tarkine wilderness immersion. The historic Arcadia II journeys along the river to the wreck of the SS Croydon at the mouth of the Savage River and to Lovers Falls near the mouth of the Donaldson, with commentary on local history and the ancient rainforest thrown in. There's also the Sweetwater vessel cruise, which is shorter and smaller, so it has the advantage of being able to moor at the boardwalk to Lovers Falls and at the shipwreck at Savage River. From here you can alight and walk back to Corinna via the stunning Savage River walk (see above).

EAT IT

The Tarkine Hotel is a cosy hub for visitors to Corinna, with moody views out over the Pieman River and logs crackling in the fire. Settle in here for a Tassie pinot noir or craft beer, before pulling up a seat at Tannin restaurant, which serves heartening meals like soup and crusty bread for lunch and Strahan Atlantic salmon for dinner. Packed lunches from the restaurant are available for daytrips. Restaurant meals are only available in summer so prepare to bring your own food at other times.

FIRST PEOPLES KNOW-HOW

The Tarkine is named after the Tarkiner people who have inhabited the region for at least 30,000 years.

WILDLIFE WATCH

Rare quolls, Tasmanian devils, wedge-tailed eagles, eastern pygmy possums, platypus and giant freshwater lobsters are all resident here. You'll certainly see Bennett's wallabies grazing on the grass at dusk and you have a chance to see white-breasted sea eagles and little hopping blue wrens.

STEP IT UP

The easy to moderate Mt Donaldson walk is a gradual ascent that rewards with sweeping wilderness views of the Pieman River, the Tarkine and the Southern Ocean. Allow 4 hours return. It's accessed via the carpark just after the Savage River bridge, a 10-minute-drive north from the campground along the Western Explorer (C249).

AND ANOTHER THING

Corinna's campground flies under the radar in terms of promotion and marketing, with little-to-no mention of it on the retreat's website and with no online booking facility. It's best to call or email ahead: (03) 6446 1170; corinna.com.au

ALTERNATIVES

If you miss out on a campsite, Corinna has plenty of accommodation alternatives: the original roadman's cottage, the old Tarkine Hotel which is now a guest house and 16 new wilderness retreats all named after a pioneer from the area. They are in the original style but with mod-cons, such as ensuites and cutesy verandahs that back onto the Tarkine. See: corinna.com.au/accommodation

Basic beachside camping is available at Trial Harbour Campground, 66 kilometres south (allow 90 minutes), and at Granville Harbour, 31 kilometres south (allow one hour).

Middle Corinna seen from the campsite *Bottom* This is a kayaker's dream

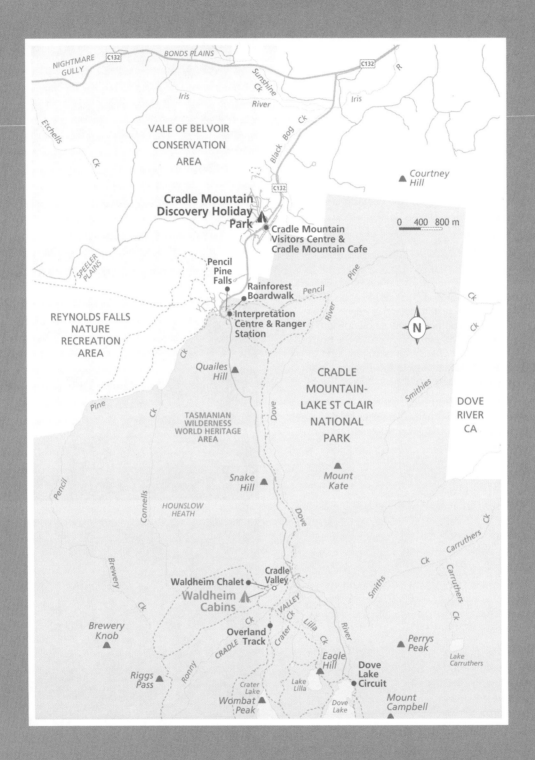

Alpine camping on the doorstep of mossy forests, glacial lakes and iconic Cradle Mountain.

Cradle Mountain Discovery Holiday Park

Cradle Mountain-Lake St Clair National Park, Tas

ACTIVITIES

FACILITIES

Cradle Mountain–Lake St Clair National Park is not your stereotypical Australian landscape but it is some of its most iconic. When walking around pristine, icy-cold Dove Lake with mist-covered Cradle Mountain in the distance and stands of leafy deciduous trees throwing shadows across the trail, you'd be forgiven for thinking you were trekking somewhere in the mountains of Europe. Which must be what Gustav Weindorfer loved about it. The Austrian, who emigrated to Australia in 1899, was obsessed with the rugged mountains, alpine heaths, ancient moss-covered rainforests and glacial lakes. Having campaigned for it over many years, he and his Australian-born wife Kate Cowle were largely responsible for it being preserved as a nature reserve, then a national park in 1947. Their legacy lives on in their home (*see* p. 277) and for visitors who come here to glimpse exquisite endemic flora (King Billy pine and fagus trees) and fauna (*see* p. 277) and breathe the rarefied mountain air. The park is part of the Tasmanian Wilderness World Heritage Area and home of the Overland Track, Australia's bucket-list multi-day bushwalk.

There is no camping in the national park itself, but Cradle Mountain Discovery Holiday Park, an atypical commercial caravan park, sits across the road from the visitor centre at the park entry and reaps the rewards of a wilderness on its doorstep. The caravan park's design and natural aesthetic is such that it feels much like it is part of the park. The

reception looks like a ski lodge, the campsites are enclosed by towering gum trees, wildlife roams freely and the cabins and accommodation are fashioned from timber and stone. The looming presence of Cradle Mountain seals the deal.

The caravan park's 56 campsites are suited to tents, caravans, camper-trailers and bigger vehicles. The 27 unpowered sites are open for summer getaways between December and February (it snows readily here at other times). The 29 powered sites are open year-round, but from March to November you'll need a caravan or motorhome, rather than a tent (it's too cold).

The campsites are spaced alongside the park's numerous cabins and cottages on a 500-metre stretch of land. The gravel-based roadside clearings are nicely protected by bush and trees. True to the caravan park experience, facilities include:

- An activity room
- Barbecue area
- Kiosk and store (with basic grocery items)
- Laundry
- Camp kitchen
- Drinking water (rainwater)
- Shower block (dam water)
- Wi-fi

In keeping with the mountain atmosphere, the big camp kitchen has rock walls that lend it a ski lodge ambience, with two huge fireplaces you can stand around with a glass of wine. Timber tables and chairs are perfect for swapping travel tales with fellow guests.

The caravan park has limited rain water (for drinking) and dam water (for showering) so BYO drinking water and fill up tank water in caravans and larger vehicles where possible.

CATEGORIES

Family, Nature, No Dogs, Boomers, Nomads

GO DO IT

WHO   Cradle Mountain Discovery Holiday Park; 1800 068 574/(03) 6492 1395; discoveryholidayparks.com.au

WHERE   Cradle Mountain Rd, Cradle Mountain, 77km south-west of Devonport; 140km west of Launceston; 320km north-west of Hobart, Tas.

ACCESS   The caravan park is located at the northern end of Cradle Mountain–Lake St Clair National Park. From Launceston via Sheffield, take the C136 29km, turn left on C132 (which becomes Cradle Mountain Rd) for 25km to the park entrance. From Devonport, take B19 for 7km, turn left onto C132 for 65km, then left onto Cradle Mountain Rd for 4km to the park entrance. Coming from the south, there is no direct road link joining the two ends of Cradle Mountain–Lake St Clair National Park.

Please ensure you register be

WHAT ELSE?

Across the road from the caravan park, Cradle Mountain Visitor Centre (open daily 8.30am–4.30pm, longer at peak times) sells parks passes and has information about walks and activities, including canoe tours, guided walks, horseback trail rides and helicopter flights. It is also the departure point for shuttle buses into the national park (private vehicles are not permitted in the park during shuttle bus operating times). Cradle Mountain Café is here too (and they're responsible for the 24-hour fuel bowser). The Interpretation Centre and Ranger Station, just inside the national park entrance, has informative displays, an art gallery, day-use picnic shelters and electric barbecues.

Accessible direct from the caravan park, Pencil Pine Falls and Rainforest Boardwalk is an easy 1.1 kilometre circuit (allow 20 minutes) that will give you a little taste of the national park. Walk from the Interpretation Centre and Ranger Station through mossy pencil pine forests and myrtle trees, along a burbling creek to pretty Pencil Pine Falls.

There are plenty of longer walks accessed via the shuttle bus. If you only do one, make it the 6 kilometre moderate circuit walk around Dove Lake. It starts from the Dove Lake carpark and skirts the scenic clear-water edge, past the 1940s boat shed, and through the myrtle, sassafras and King Billy Pine in the Ballroom Forest, with the craggy Cradle Mountain silhouette looming in background. Allow two to three hours. The (free with a parks pass) Dove Lake shuttle bus leaves from the visitor centre (*see* above).

CULTURE VULTURE

For an insight into the park's history and the lives of its biggest fans, aforementioned Gustav and Kate Weindorfer, check out Waldheim Chalet (about 5km north of the visitor centre). The couple built the rustic chalet or 'forest home' as it translates, in 1912 as a bolthole for friends and guests to appreciate the surrounding beauty. The original building was razed by fire in 1976 but the replica is said to be an accurate reconstruction of the chalet as it was when Gustav died in 1932.

WILDLIFE WATCH

The national park is home to many of Tasmania's endemic species. At the caravan park you'll meet Bennett's wallabies, pademelons, possums and wombats. In the park itself, look out for Tasmanian devils, quolls, platypus, short-beaked echidna and black currawong.

STEP IT UP

The famed Overland Track (80km one-way) is a strenuous six-day hike from the Dove Lake carpark through a kaleidoscope of blissful Alpine landscapes to Lake St Clair in the south of the park. It requires payments, permits and planning ahead. The Overland Track check-in counter is inside the visitor centre.

AND ANOTHER THING

Bookings are expected but are often available at short-notice.

Mountain weather can change in an instant. Pack appropriate cold weather clothing and do your homework on conditions before setting out on a walk.

ALTERNATIVES

There is no camping in the national park, but check out Cradle Mountain Waldheim Cabins, 5 kilometres north of the visitor centre, for a wilderness experience. The eight cabins (with four, six and eight berths) are snuggled into the forest. They have electric heating, single bunk beds and basic cooking facilities. You'll need to BYO bedding and toiletries. The cabins share two amenities blocks with showers and flushing toilets. Park walks start from your doorstep.

Opposite A quiet spot to take in views of iconic Cradle Mountain and Dove Lake

Index

About the author

Award-winning writer, journalist and author Penny Watson has travelled the world, written feature articles for countless magazines and newspapers, and researched a number of travel books including *London Pocket Precincts* and *Slow Travel*, both released in 2019. She has camped across NSW as a kid, across the world as a travel writer, and across Australia as a parent. This book is a direct response to these privileged experiences and her ensuing love of and passion for Australia's wild and wondrous natural beauty. Penny is a member of both the British Guild of Travel Writers, and the Australian Society of Travel Writers. She currently resides in Melbourne with her family, Pippy, Digby and Etienne.

Acknowledgements

Big thanks as ever to the Hardie Grant team for publishing my fifth solo book – I am always so proud of being part of this progressive and thoughtful business. Thanks especially to editors Alice Barker and Megan Cuthbert for being the constant keen eye, steady keel and support at the end of an email. Also, to publisher Melissa Kayser who first floated the idea of a camping book over coffee in Richmond. I have received so many camping tips from both strangers and friends, the thanks of which I hope you'll find hidden in the words on these pages. So too to all the friends and family I camped with during the making of this book – my note-taking and camera-toting often came at the expense of mucking in. On that note, enduring gratitude also to my partner Pipster who single-handedly pitched so many of the tents we slept in, and then some. I finished much of this book while in lockdown 1.0 and 2.0 in Melbourne in my makeshift home office – thanks to my loving and beautiful children Digby and Etienne who homeschooled alongside me to the finish line. What a strange and incredible time.

Photography credits

All images copyright Penny Watson, except the following:

Stocksy front and back cover; Tourism Australia ix, xvii (top), 26, 132, 153, 155; Sean Scott Photography xiv (top), 135, 136, 245; Chris Duffield/Erika Osawa xvi (top), 107, 157, 159, 273; Shutterstock xvii (bottom), 22, 51 (top left and bottom right), 77, 265; iStock iii, xvi (bottom), 23, 25, 223, 251; Dirk Hartog Island xix; Destination New South Wales xxii, 18, 38; John Spencer 5, 10, 39; Alamy 11, 200, 263; John Yurasek 37; E Sheargold 45 (top left and right); Murray van der Veer 45 (bottom left); Visit Victoria 64, 73 (bottom right), 85, 89, 102 (bottom); Parks Victoria 68, 69, 79, 80-1, 83, 87, 101; Apertunity 149, 151; Tourism Northern Territory 177, 178, 181, 182; World Expeditions / Great Walks of Australia 179; Tropical North Queensland 201, 219; Tourism and Events Queensland 214, 215, 221, 222, 231, 232, 233, 237, 239, 241; Tourism Tasmania/Andrew Wilson 259; Tourism Tasmania/Rob Burnett 260, 268; Lusy Productions 275; Tourism Tasmania/Chris Crerar 276.

Published in 2020 by Hardie Grant Explore, a division of
Hardie Grant Publishing

Hardie Grant Explore (Melbourne)
Wurundjeri Country
Building 1, 658 Church Street
Richmond, Victoria 3121

Hardie Grant Explore (Sydney)
Gadigal Country
Level 7, 45 Jones Street
Ultimo, NSW 2007

www.hardiegrant.com/au/explore

The maps in this publication incorporate data © Commonwealth of
Australia (Geoscience Australia), 2006. Geoscience Australia has not
evaluated the data as altered and incorporated within this publication,
and therefore gives no warranty regarding accuracy, completeness,
currency or suitability for any particular purpose.

© Imprint and currency – VAR Product and PSMA Data
"Copyright based on data provided under licence from PSMA Australia
Limited (www.psma.com.au)".
Hydrography Data (Nov 2012)
Transport Data (Feb 2020)

Maps contain parks and reserves data which is owned by and copyright
of the relevant state and territory government authorities.

© Australian Capital Territory. Data is supplied under Creative
Commons Attribution 4.0 International (CCBY v4.0), © Office of
Environment and Heritage (OEH) (NSW) 2018. Data is supplied
under Creative Commons 4.0 International (CC BY 4.0), Department
of Environment, Land, Water and Planning © State Government of
Victoria. Data is supplied under Creative Commons Attribution 4.0
International (CC BY 4.0), Department for Environment and Water
2017 © State of South Australia. Data is supplied under Creative
Commons 4.0 International (CC BY 4.0), Department of Biodiversity,
Conservation and Attractions. © Government of Western Australia.
Data is supplied under Creative Commons Attribution 3.0 Australia
(CC BY 3.0 AU), Department of Environment and Natural Resources
© Northern Territory Government. Data is supplied under Creative
Commons Attribution 4.0 International Public License (CC BY 4.0),
© State of Queensland (Department of Environment and Science)
2018. Data is supplied under Creative Commons Attribution 3.0
Australia (CC BY 3.0 AU), © State of Tasmania. Data is supplied
under Creative Commons Attribution 3.0 Australia (CC BY 3.0 AU)

A catalogue record for this
book is available from the
National Library of Australia

Hardie Grant acknowledges the Traditional Owners of the country on
which we work, the Wurundjeri people of the Kulin nation and the
Gadigal people of the Eora nation, and recognises their continuing
connection to the land, waters and culture. We pay our respects to their
Elders past and present.

Ultimate Campsites: Australia
ISBN 9781741176384

10 9 8 7 6 5

Publisher
Melissa Kayser

Project editor
Megan Cuthbert

Editor
Alice Barker

Proofreader
Rosanna Dutson

Cartographer
Claire Johnston, Emily Maffei

Design
Andy Warren

Typesetting
Megan Ellis

Index
Max McMaster

Colour reproduction by Megan Ellis and Splitting Image Colour Studio

Printed and bound in China by LEO Paper Products LTD.

The paper this book is printed on is from
FSC®-certified forests and other sources. FSC®
promotes environmentally responsible, socially
beneficial and economically viable management
of the world's forests.

Disclaimer: While every care is taken to ensure the accuracy of
the data within this product, the owners of the data (including the
state, territory and Commonwealth governments of Australia) do not
make any representations or warranties about its accuracy, reliability,
completeness or suitability for any particular purpose and, to the extent
permitted by law, the owners of the data disclaim all responsibility
and all liability (including without limitation, liability in negligence)
for all expenses, losses, damages (including indirect or consequential
damages) and costs which might be incurred as a result of the data
being inaccurate or incomplete in any way and for any reason.

Publisher's Disclaimers: The publisher cannot accept responsibility
for any errors or omissions. The representation on the maps of any
road or track is not necessarily evidence of public right of way.
The publisher cannot be held responsible for any injury, loss or
damage incurred during travel. It is vital to research any proposed
trip thoroughly and seek the advice of relevant state and travel
organisations before you leave.

Publisher's Note: Every effort has been made to ensure that the
information in this book is accurate at the time of going to press.
The publisher welcomes information and suggestions for correction
or improvement.